Elizabeth Gilbert Davis Martin

The Duchess of Berry and the Court of Louis XVIII.

Elizabeth Gilbert Davis Martin

The Duchess of Berry and the Court of Louis XVIII.

ISBN/EAN: 9783337419189

Printed in Europe, USA, Canada, Australia, Japan

Cover: Foto ©ninafisch / pixelio.de

More available books at **www.hansebooks.com**

THE
DUCHESS OF BERRY

AND THE

COURT OF LOUIS XVIII

BY

DE SAINT-AMAND

TRANSLATED BY

ELIZABETH GILBERT MARTIN

WITH PORTRAIT

NEW YORK
CHARLES SCRIBNER'S SONS
1892

CONTENTS

CHAPTER		PAGE
I.	CHILDHOOD	1
II.	THE MARRIAGE BY PROXY	13
III.	THE DEPARTURE FROM NAPLES	21
IV.	THE LAZARETTO OF MARSEILLES	29
V.	ENTERING MARSEILLES	42
VI.	FROM MARSEILLES TO FONTAINEBLEAU	48
VII.	FONTAINEBLEAU	59
VIII.	THE ENTRY INTO PARIS	68
IX.	THE MARRIAGE	77
X.	THE EARLY DAYS OF MARRIAGE	83
XI.	THE TUILERIES	89
XII.	THE ÉLYSÉE	96
XIII.	THE FIRST SORROW	102
XIV.	1818	111
XV.	1819	121
XVI.	COUNT DECAZES	132
XVII.	THE DUKE OF BERRY	139
XVIII.	LOUVEL	146

CHAPTER		PAGE
XIX.	The Murder of the Duke of Berry	155
XX.	The Day after the Murder	171
XXI.	The Obsequies of the Duke of Berry	185
XXII.	The Widow	192
XXIII.	The Birth of the Duke of Bordeaux	205
XXIV.	The Rejoicings	219
XXV.	Chambord	229
XXVI.	The Baptism of the Duke of Bordeaux	239
XXVII.	The Countess of Cayla	256
XXVIII.	The End of the Reign	266
XXIX.	The Death of Louis XVIII	283

The Duchess of Berry

AND THE

Court of Louis XVIII

THE DUCHESS OF BERRY AND THE COURT OF LOUIS XVIII

I

CHILDHOOD

MARIE CAROLINE FERDINANDE LOUISE DE BOURBON, the future Duchess of Berry, was born November 5, 1798. Her parents were Francis, Duke of Calabria, hereditary Prince of the Two Sicilies (son of King Ferdinand IV. and Queen Marie Caroline), and the Archduchess Marie Clémentine, daughter of the Emperor Leopold II. The Bourbons were no longer reigning in France at the time of her birth, although they continued to do so in Spain and the Two Sicilies. Two direct descendants of Louis XIV., Charles IV. and Ferdinand IV., occupied respectively the thrones of Madrid and of Naples. Both of them were grandsons of Philip V. of Spain, that French Prince who, when he ascended the throne of Charles V., had caused his grandfather, the Sun-King, to say: "There are no more Pyrenees."

In 1725, Philip V. had endowed his second son, Don Carlos, with the kingdom of the Two Sicilies. He reigned at Naples until, in consequence of the death of his elder brother, Ferdinand VI., who had succeeded Philip V., he inherited the throne of Spain, and assumed the title of Charles III. Before departing for his new dominions, he invested his young son, Ferdinand, with the crown of the Two Sicilies, October 6, 1759. As he transferred to him the sword which Philip V. had received from Louis XIV., he said: "Preserve it for the defence of religion and thy people."

The new King, who was only eight years old, took the name of Ferdinand IV. On April 7, 1768, he married a daughter of the great Empress Maria Theresa, and a sister of Marie Antoinette: the Archduchess Marie Caroline.

Between 1772 and 1793 Marie Caroline had no fewer than eighteen children, of whom only six survived. One of these was Francis, Duke of Calabria, hereditary Prince of the Two Sicilies, born August 19, 1777. On September 19, 1790, this Prince married his cousin-german, the Archduchess Marie Clémentine, daughter of the Emperor Leopold II., niece of Marie Antoinette, Queen of France, and of Marie Caroline, Queen of Naples. The Duchess of Berry sprang from this marriage which united the Bourbons to the Hapsburghs. Under the title, "An Epitome of the Events of my Life from my Birth until my Marriage," she wrote a journal which she presented to General Dernoncourt, who gave it to the celebrated novelist, Alexandre Dumas. Our own acquaintance with this precious manuscript is due to the courtesy of our friend, Alexandre Dumas *fils*.

At the time when the Princess came into the world, Naples and Sicily were in a profoundly disturbed condition. A bitter strife was raging between the partisans and the adversaries of the French Revolution. Deeply irritated against the men and things of 1793, agonized by the executions of her sister and her brother-in-law, and feeling a religious devotion, almost amounting to fanaticism, for the ancient principles, Marie Caroline, whose hates and loves were alike prodigious in their violence, fought relentlessly against the liberal movement. Upheld by the English Admiral Nelson, and swayed by the influence of the too-famous Lady Hamilton, the admiral's mistress and the wife of the English ambassador to Naples, she struggled against the new ideas with a stubbornness that bordered on frenzy. At the close of 1798, however, she was obliged to flee before the Revolution, with the King and the royal family. She sought shelter on an English vessel, the *Vanguard*, which carried her from Naples to Palermo. A frightful storm broke out during the voyage, and the Queen lost her youngest son, a boy of seven years. "We are all going to rejoin him at once," cried she, in a paroxysm of fear and grief. The ship which contained the future Duchess of Berry, then not quite two months old, had one of its masts broken and was tossed about on a troubled sea for five days before entering the harbor of Palermo.

The Neapolitan republic was proclaimed, but was of brief duration. Cardinal Fabrice Ruffo, that warlike prelate who boasted of employing the keys of Saint Peter and the sword of Saint Paul by turns, re-conquered Naples for the King in June, 1799, and entered the capital in triumph. A bloody reaction at once set in. The most distinguished personages were sent to the scaffold, and "one hardly calumniates this frightful epoch," says Baron Louis de Viel-Castel, "by comparing it to the Terror of 1793."

Marie Clémentine, wife of the Prince-royal and mother of the future Duchess of Berry, had a kind and generous soul. She shuddered at the horrors that were taking place. Among the victims sentenced to death was a pregnant woman, Luigia Sanfelice, who inspired her with profound pity. This was in August, 1800. The Princess had just borne a son who had received the name of Ferdinand, and, in virtue of a very ancient custom existing in various royal families, she was thereby entitled to ask three favors from the sovereign. In order the better to assure the success of her application, she united all three into one, — a petition for the pardon of the wretched Sanfelice. King Ferdinand was inflexible, and the victim was beheaded directly after her confinement. This horrible tragedy filled Marie Clémentine with consternation, and from that time she pined away. Her son died the same year. She herself was attacked by a cold which developed into lung disease, of which she died, November 16, 1801. Marie Caroline, who was tender and affectionate in her family, though cruel where politics were concerned, wrote as follows to Lady Hamilton, on December 6: —

"Of course you have heard of the frightful misfortune I have had in losing my dear, good daughter-in-law. This destroys the only comfort I had left, — that of perfect domestic union and harmony. She died like a saint, the dear and good Princess, and her husband is in the depths of despair. My poor children do nothing but weep for their sister-in-law, who was a tender sister to them, and who, after my death (which cannot be far off, considering my pains and troubles), would have been like their mother."

The Duchess of Berry was then only four years old. In her journal she devotes these touching lines to the mother so soon removed from her by God: —

"I was then too young to be able to remember her; but I have found ineffaceable souvenirs of her in the hearts of all who were so happy as to be near her and admire her virtues. May Heaven grant to her prayers the favor I beg of laboring to merit her virtues, her enlightened piety, her beneficence; in a word, all that deepens my regret for not having known her! How I would have cherished her! So I judge from the sentiments I experience for her whom Heaven has given me as a second and affectionate mother, in the person of S. A. R. the Infanta Marie Isabelle of Spain, whose kindness to me is unfailing."

This Infanta was the daughter of Charles IV., King of Spain. She became the second wife of the father of the Duchess of Berry, July 6, 1802.

The Duchess of Berry had just entered her eighth year when, on January 23, 1806, her family were for the second time obliged to fly from Naples and take refuge in Sicily. Napoleon had written, in a violent bulletin: —

"I send General Saint-Cyr to punish the treasons of the Queen of Naples, and to cast from the throne that guilty woman who has so often and with so much effrontery profaned every law, human and divine. The Bourbons of Naples have ceased to reign, thanks to the latest perfidy of the Queen. Let her be off to London, then, to complete the number of brigands!"

The throne of Naples was occupied by Joseph Bonaparte until 1808, and by Murat from 1808 until 1815, Ferdinand, meanwhile, reigning only in Sicily, under the protectorate, say rather the tyranny, of the English. Thus, from her very infancy, the Duchess of Berry had known all the trials and vicissitudes of politics.

"Born in an epoch of troubles and revolutions," says the eloquent historian, M. Alfred Nettement, "her first impressions were grave and serious. Her ears were accustomed early to the noises of war, the ominous pealing of bells, the thunder of cannons, and the clamor of the populace, as well as to the roaring of tempestuous seas. Thus her childhood had served an apprenticeship which her youth was to find advantageous. Later, when she had to cross the ocean and the Mediterranean, when she was obliged to brave every danger, endure all fatigues, and lead the life of battle-fields, that vigorous soul which had been tempered in her childhood came anew to her aid, and in danger she recognized the familiar companion of her earliest years."

From her infancy the Duchess of Berry had given promise of quick intelligence and a sympathetic character. The German biographer of. Queen Marie Caroline, Helfert, says concerning the little Princess: —

"Many hopes were entertained of her; her constitution was good, she was full of gaiety, and had a broad mind and generous heart."

Her education was conducted with great care, and she was very early taught to love the arts. Among those who instructed her, she praises especially in her journal her governess, the Countess of La Tour, and a prelate called Olivieri: —

"I habitually received," she says, "the tenderest care from all my family. The Queen lavished continual attentions on me, for which I shall be eternally grateful."

The Duchess of Berry was ten years old when she

first saw a man who was to be fatal to her,— the Duke of Orleans, Louis Philippe. This was towards the middle of 1808. The young Princess was with her grandmother, Queen Marie Caroline, when she saw King Ferdinand enter suddenly, looking perplexed and agitated. "Here," said he, holding an open letter in his hand, "is an exile belonging to a great family who is hounded by misfortune, for he has just lost his only surviving brother at Malta. He has landed at Messina. Would it displease you if I were to invite him to my court?"

"What is his name?" asked the Queen.

"The Duke of Orleans," replied the King.

At these words the little Princess experienced a keen emotion; it was as if she had foreseen the future. But this painful impression soon passed away. The Duke of Orleans had written to the King:—

"Sire, the greater the faults of my father were, the more am I bound to prove that I do not share his aberrations; they have done too much harm to my family."

The exiled Prince received a courteous welcome and magnificent hospitality at the court of Palermo. There he made a conquest of one of the King's daughters, Marie Amélie, born April 26, 1782, whom he married at Palermo, November 25, 1809. The future Duchess of Berry and the future Queen of France were on mutually friendly terms. They lived near each other until July 27, 1814, when

Marie Amélie left Palermo to rejoin her husband at the court of King Louis XVIII.

At Palermo, the *palazzo* Orleans was a centre of liberal opposition, as the Palais Royal was afterwards to be at Paris. In his remarkable and conscientious *Vie de Marie-Amélie*, M. Trognon relates that Queen Marie Caroline said to her daughter, apropos of the Duke of Orleans: —

"Since I was stupid enough to take him for my son-in-law, I must put up with him as your husband and the father of your child" (the Duke of Chartres, afterwards Duke of Orleans, born at Palermo, September 3, 1810). "But he ought to be convinced that legitimate authority always succeeds in the end, and that it is necessary to remain attached to it."

Exasperated by the yoke of the English, Marie Caroline now detested them as much as she had loved them at the beginning of her political career. They inspired her with such horror that she ended by preferring Napoleon, and in her distress she sought the aid of her former persecutor and warned him of the approaching defection of Murat. Lord Bentinck, who had occupied Palermo with twelve thousand English soldiers of all arms, acted like a veritable proconsul in Sicily. He required the departure of Marie Caroline, and on June 15, 1813, the unhappy Queen left like an outlaw, never to return. The future Duchess of Berry loved her grandmother tenderly, and it was with profound grief that she saw her depart. She was then fourteen, but in spite of her youth she understood how cruel were the humiliations and the exile inflicted on the energetic and unfortunate sovereign.

Some years later, in Paris under the Restoration, the Duchess of Berry was paying a visit to her aunt, Marie Amélie, at the Palais Royal. Perceiving Lord Bentinck, she started violently and went away at once, without a word. The next day, in church, her aunt having inquired the reason of her brusque departure, she replied: —

"I could not look on coolly while such a cordial welcome was given to a man whom I consider your mother's murderer."

Queen Marie Caroline's last days were profoundly sad. After a perilous journey of more than seven months she reached Vienna, where she had asked an asylum from the Emperor Francis, who had been her son-in-law. One of her daughters, Princess Marie Thérèse (born June 6, 1772; married September 19, 1790; died April 13, 1807), was the second wife of this sovereign, and the mother of the Empress Marie Louise (hence the Duchess of Berry was the cousin of the King of Rome). The Congress of Vienna was sitting, and Marie Caroline did not receive the welcome she expected from her former son-in-law. At this time the Austrian court was still in favor of Murat, and the daughter of the great Empress Maria Theresa vainly claimed the restitution of the Kingdom of Naples. In her affliction, she wrote to her daughter, the Duchess of Genevois, afterwards Queen of Sardinia: —

"Nothing on earth moves me any more; my fate was settled and decided the day that I was chased like a play-actress and thrust out of Sicily. . . . My life is ended in this world. . . . I am no longer interesting except to a few old women who never stir out of their own doors, but who come to see the last of the great Maria Theresa's children. The Prater is in its lovely green and full of flowers; but nothing seems beautiful to me any longer."

A few days later — during the night of September 7-8, 1814 — the old Queen died of a sudden attack of apoplexy in the little chateau of Hetzendorf, beside Schönbrunn, where her great-grandson, the former King of Rome, was living. Marie Caroline had been a woman whose faults and whose qualities were alike extraordinary. Napoleon, who once used such violent and insulting language respecting her, ended by citing her as a model worth imitating in his correspondence with King Joseph. "That woman," he wrote to his brother, "knew how to think and act like a queen, while preserving her rights and her dignity."

The Duchess of Berry lamented her grandmother deeply. She says in her journal: "The Queen's death, in 1814, affected me keenly. In her I lost a support, a mother, and I still regret not having been able to attend upon her."

Eight months after the death of Queen Marie Caroline, her husband recovered the Kingdom of Naples. This restoration, far from being sullied by such excesses as those of 1799, was arranged by compromise, and Murat's generals were treated with the same benevolence by King Ferdinand as those of Napoleon were by Louis XVIII. Fortune smiled at the same time on the Bourbons of Naples and the Bourbons of France.

II

THE MARRIAGE BY PROXY

THE Duchess of Berry had been a lovable and pretty child. She became a graceful and sympathetic young girl. Without being beautiful she was nevertheless very pleasing. The Countess of Agoult (Daniel Stern) portrays her thus: "She was not regularly handsome, her features were not at all remarkable, her glance was wavering, her lips thick and almost always open. She carried herself badly, and the best-disposed observer could not call her bearing noble. But this blonde Neapolitan had her own charm, a marvellous splendor of coloring, silky fair hair, the loveliest arms in the world, and feet which, in spite of being pigeon-toed, were nice to look at, so small and well-made were they." In mind she was still more charming than in body. Engaging and benevolent, kindly to every one, pious, but not aggressively so, proud of her origin, yet as polite, as amiable, to a poor man as to a great lord, easily amused, and always disposed to see the good side of things, a southern nature, enlightened, and vivified by the brilliant sun of Italy, she enjoyed mere living, and looked towards the future with confident and joyous eyes. From a political point of view, her infancy had been a sort of prologue to her destiny. She who was to be the victim of revolutions at every period of her life, had been condemned from her cradle to a series of portentous misfortunes. But, far from being affected by them, she had always felt persuaded that a brilliant destiny was reserved for her. Her romantic imagination was excited by the recital of the glories and the misfortunes of the house of Bourbon. As valiant as her ancestor, Henri IV., she was to live in an epoch as troublous as that of the Béarnais, and, like him, to preserve a truly prodigious ardor, boldness, and gaiety in the midst of the most terrible crises and the greatest dangers. Her grandfather, King Ferdinand, who greatly preferred the society of the lazzaroni to that of the best born personages of his kingdom, and who amused himself by selling the produce of his fishing expeditions on the docks, had accustomed her to familiarity with the *bourgeois*, the peasants, and the common people. The etiquette of the Sicilian court did not resemble the grave and gloomy solemnity of that of Spain, and there was nothing severe or sombre about the palaces of Naples and Palermo.

Nearly the whole existence of the young Princess had been passed in the picturesque and charming island of Sicily, which rises from the sea like a basket of perfumes and flowers. After the beginning of 1806 she did not return to Naples, but always resided either in Palermo or its environs.

She extremely liked the Sicilian capital, that half-Arabian, half-Italian city which has so much originality and so much charm. She loved the *Palazzo Reale*, which was begun by Robert Guiscard and which was at first a fortress. She loved the Palatine chapel which, with its Arabian arches, its granite columns, its walls covered with mosaics on a gold background, is perhaps the most beautiful chapel in the world. She loved the cathedral, consecrated to Saint Rosalie, the patroness of the Palermitans, who annually celebrate her feast with great piety and splendor.

The young Princess was at Palermo when she learned that the Duke of Berry had asked for her hand. She wrote in her journal on this subject:—

"It was in January, 1816, that my father first acquainted me with the projects of marriage formed by the royal family of France, and proposed to the King, my august grandfather, who was left absolute master of his determinations. The same liberty was accorded to me by that tender father. I made no use of it except to conform myself with pleasure and confidence to whatever my dear parents should desire. Count de Blacas came from Naples to Palermo in February. His presence, and the conversation, which related to the subject of my marriage and my journey, caused me an embarrassment and timidity I had never experienced before."

The young Neapolitan spoke French as well as Italian, and from her infancy had been accustomed to consider France, the cradle of her ancestors, as a second fatherland. She was greatly pleased with the marriage proposed to her, and it was not without pleasurable emotions that she received from the Duke of Berry this really charming letter: —

"PARIS, 18 February, 1816.

"MADAME, MY SISTER AND COUSIN, — I have long desired to obtain the consent of the King your grandfather, and the Prince your father, to make a request on which hangs the happiness of my life; but, before obtaining their approval, I come to Your Royal Highness to entreat that you will deign to confide the happiness of your life to me by consenting to our union. I dare flatter myself that age, experience, and long adversity have disciplined me sufficiently to render me worthy to be your husband, guide, and friend. On leaving parents so worthy of your love, you will find here a family which will remind you of patriarchal times. What can I tell you about the King, my father, my brother, and above all, about that angel, Madame, the Duchess of Angoulême, that you have not heard already, unless it be that their virtues and goodness are above all possible praise? The most intimate union prevails amongst us, and is never disturbed; all my relatives impatiently desire that Your Royal Highness should crown my wishes and consent to augment the number of the children of our family. Deign, Madame, to yield to my prayers and to hasten the moment when I can lay at your feet the homage of the respectful and tender sentiments with which I am,

"Madame, my Sister and Cousin, of Your Royal Highness the very affectionate brother and cousin,   "CHARLES FERDINAND."

After obtaining the approval of the Princess at Palermo, Count de Blacas returned to Naples and laid before the King a formal proposal which was accepted. We read as follows in the journal of the Duchess of Berry: —

"I started for Naples, April 2, 1816, on the frigate *Sirena*, commanded by dear Barone. The squadron comprised thirteen different vessels of war, all under the orders of Ignazio Statti. We had stormy weather on the 3d, which caused us to make good time, but from which we suffered greatly. The 4th we sighted the islands of Ischia and Capri; but the calm which set in prevented us from passing them and from entering the Bay of Naples until early in the morning of the 6th. The weather was superb and gratified my curiosity to see the city of Naples and its environs plainly. I was greatly pleased with the enchanting spectacle that met my view. I was much more so to see my uncle Leopold, who came on board the frigate by eight o'clock in the morning. We landed with him and went straight to the palace to find His Majesty, who was still somewhat indisposed. We saw people all day long. The 7th the weather was very bad, and prevented us from going out until afternoon, when we visited the Portici palace and garden."

The Princess, who had but a vague recollection of the curiosities of Naples and its environs, beheld these marvels anew with extreme pleasure. She loved the arts and knew how to appreciate all that is beautiful. Here are some extracts from her journal: —

"The 9th we took a walk after dinner in the Villa Reale public garden.

"The 11th I received the Easter sacraments with my dear parents. Afterwards we heard Mass in the royal chapel. After dinner we visited seven churches, the crowd accompanying us everywhere. On our return we listened to the sermon on the Passion by Père Calé, preacher to the King. The 12th we were present at the morning and evening offices in the royal chapel. The morning of the 13th, Count de Blacas brought my father the portrait of Mgr. the Duke of Berry, to let us see it before presenting it in due form. After dinner we walked to the royal residence of Capo di Monte. The 14th, Easter Sunday, there was a drawing-room at the palace, and after dinner a walk to Pausilippo."

On the following day, April 15, 1816, the marriage contract was signed. The third article of it was thus expressed: —

"His Majesty the King of the Two Sicilies gives as dowry to the Most Serene Princess his granddaughter the sum of one hundred and twenty thousand Neapolitan ducats, or five hundred thousand francs, payable in eighteen months, which sum the said Princess may use and dispose of according to the laws and customs of France. The said sum of one hundred and twenty thousand Neapolitan ducats, or five hundred thousand francs, is independent of another sum, likewise of one hundred and twenty thousand Neapolitan ducats, or two hundred thousand florins, which comes to her from the dowry of her mother, Princess Marie Clémentine of Austria, of whom she is the sole and only heir, which sum, as well as the interest due from S. M. the Emperor of Austria, not forming part of the dowry of the Most Serene spouse, she can use and dispose of as her private property. . . .

"Article 5. — In addition to the said dowry, S. M. the King of the Two Sicilies makes a present to the Most Serene Princess Caroline Ferdinande Louise, of rings and jewels worth five hundred thousand Neapolitan ducats."

Let us return to the journal of the Princess: —

"On the 16th, Count de Blacas came before his dinner to present the portrait of Mgr. the Duke of Berry with all the usual formalities. I was sensibly touched by the nobility of his discourse and the sentiments he knew so well how to express. Not being able to reply to him, I intend to show him my gratitude and my sensibility on the first occasion I have to see him. From this moment France becomes dearer to me, and I promise myself to divide my affections between my own family and that which I have the happiness to enter.

"The 19th we started in the morning to visit Pompeii, which I had seen in my childhood. I had not the least recollection of it, so that all I saw was new to me and interested me infinitely. . . . Count de Blacas was one of the party. We left Pompeii at the close of day. The crowd that was there often obliged us to halt. We met as many in passing the Torre dell' Annunziata and the Torre del Greco. Everywhere we heard acclamations and cries of 'Long live the King!' which caused us the greatest pleasure.

"The 22d we visited Pozzuoli, the temple of Serapis, and we walked in the environs, so rich in mythological and historical souvenirs.

"The 24th I went to confession and communion before making my full toilet to be married in the royal chapel. The entire court, the King's ministers and those of the different Powers, the generals, etc., were invited. The Cardinal-Archbishop gave me the nuptial benediction. My uncle Leopold represented the Duke of Berry, in virtue of a legal instrument, which was publicly read by the Marquis of Circello, Minister of the King. There was a drawing-room afterwards, and in the evening the Fondo theatre, where an allegorical ballet, interspersed with songs, and called *Les Noces de Thétis et de Pélée*, was performed. Everything terminated with a transparency representing the King of France, the Duke of Berry, and me."

III

THE DEPARTURE FROM NAPLES

THE moment of departure was approaching. The Duchess of Berry already felt herself a Frenchwoman, and experienced an attachment for the Prince whom she did not yet know. A wife before having seen her husband, she wrote him the following affectionate and touching letter on the very day of the marriage by proxy: —

"NAPLES, April 24, 1816.

"I have just taken at the altar, Monseigneur, a solemn engagement to be your faithful and tender spouse. This dear title imposes duties on me which I most willingly commence to fulfil from this moment, by assuring you of the sentiments my heart has already vowed to you for life; its sole occupation shall be to seek means of pleasing you, conciliating your friendship, and meriting your confidence. Yes, you will have all my affections, all that is mine; you will be my guide and my friend; you will teach me how to please your august family; you will (I doubt not) lessen the keen regret I shall feel in leaving my own. It is on you, in a word, that I cast all the care of my conduct in order that it may be guided to all that may procure your happiness. That shall be my habitual study. I hope I may be successful in it, and prove to you how highly I value the privilege of being your companion! In these sentiments I am, for life,

"Your affectionate spouse,

"CAROLINE."

On his side, the Duke of Berry was already in love with his young wife, and wrote to her, the same day, from Paris: —

"Your amiable letter has given me a pleasure which I cannot express to you, Madame and dear wife, since to-day we have mutually plighted our faith. From this day we are united by the sacred bonds of marriage, bonds which I shall ever seek to render easy to you. You deign to thank me for having chosen you as the companion of my life! How many thanks do I not owe Your Royal Highness for having acceded so promptly to the wishes of your excellent parents! I feel how much it must cost you to leave them, and to come, almost alone, into a foreign country, though one which will soon be no longer foreign, in order to unite yourself with a man you do not know. I have composed your household of ladies whose virtue and kindliness I am acquainted with, and the King has approved my choice. Your lady-of-honor, the Duchess of Reggio, is in despair at not being able to go to meet you. Madame de La

Ferronnays, your lady of the bedchamber, will be the first to have the happiness of paying her court to you; she is a model of virtue and the sweetest amiability. I recommend her especially to you; she will present your ladies-in-waiting. The Duke of Levis, your gentleman-in-waiting, is a man as distinguished for his qualities as for his talents. The Count of Mesnard, your first equerry, is a loyal chevalier who did not return to France until I did. In a word, I hope that when you know them you will find them worthy of the honor of being in your service. How impatiently I await the news of your arrival in France! How happy I shall be, my dearest wife, when I am able to call you by that sweet name! All that I hear of your qualities, your goodness, your intelligence, and your grace, charms me and kindles my desire to see and embrace you as I love you. "Charles Ferdinand."

All the royalists shared the Duke of Berry's joy. Even before the contract was signed, the French government had announced an event of so much importance to the dynasty, by calling on the Chambers to make suitable pecuniary arrangements for it. This announcement was greeted by the Chamber of Deputies with transports of enthusiasm. In a lyrical outburst M. de Marcellus exclaimed: "Oh, august race of our kings, be thou blessed! Illustrious lily stalk, glow with renewed lustre! May flowers innumerable embellish thee!" The Ministry had demanded for the Duke of Berry: 1. An annual endowment of one million, which for the first five years should be reduced to five hundred thousand francs in consideration of the heavy burdens France was bearing. 2. One million for the festivities and other expenses of the marriage. The Chamber of Deputies granted still more. M. de Castelbajac having made his report, it resolved that the endowment should be one million from the start, and that the sum asked for the marriage expenses should be increased to fifteen hundred thousand francs. The Chamber of Peers was enthusiastic in its approbation; but a letter from the Duke of Richelieu, president of the council, while thanking the Chambers for their votes, assured them, in the name of the Duke of Berry, that he had resolved to apply what had been added to his endowment towards the aid of the departments which had suffered by the foreign invasion.

The marriage by proxy had been celebrated at Naples, April 24, 1816. The Duchess of Berry remained there twenty days longer before embarking for France. Nearly all this time was taken up in excursions and festivities, "brilliant festivities," says Chateaubriand, "which seem to be eternally preparing on the shores of this bay, where all that meets the eye — sky, sea, plains, palaces, ruins — reminds of present pleasures or past joys." April 25, the young Princess went to Caserta, the Versailles of the Neapolitan Bourbons. She admired the royal palace, the gardens with their clipped hedges, statues, fountains, and cascades. We read in her journal: —

"The palace is the grandest and most magnificent that could be imagined. Four immense courts surrounding the main building show how vast were the ideas of its builder, King Charles III. After passing through part of the palace and praying in the chapel, which is modelled on that of Fontainebleau, we dined, and then drove out to see the lake, which is in the midst of beautiful thickets. From there we went to my father's little castle, and then to receive benediction in a little church he had established so as to render it easy for the country people to perform their religious duties; the chaplain made a discourse inviting those present to give thanks to God for having granted the return of the King and the royal family, and the *Te Deum* was chanted. The people, who assembled from all parts of the neighborhood, often prevented my parents from going forward. Every one showed the utmost pleasure at seeing us, and addressed us in the most touching language."

May 11, the Princess went to visit La Favorita, one of the royal pleasure-houses, which has a beautiful view of the Sorrento peninsula. The 12th she was present at a comedy played by amateurs at the residence of her uncle, the Prince of Salerno. The 14th she sailed for France.

Let us recall the persons who at this time composed her family: —

Grandfather: The King of the Two Sicilies, Ferdinand I., born January 12, 1751.

Father: Francis, Prince-royal, Prince of Calabria, born August 19, 1777 (he ascended the throne January 3, 1825, and died November 8, 1830).

Stepmother: Marie Isabelle, sister of the King of Spain, Ferdinand VII., born July 6, 1789.

Brothers: 1. Ferdinand Charles, Duke of Nolo, born January 12, 1810 (the future King Ferdinand II.).

2. Charles Ferdinand, Prince of Capua, born October 10, 1811.

3. Leopold Benjamin, Count of Syracuse, born May 22, 1813.

Sisters: 1. Louise Charlotte, born October 3, 1804 (in 1819 she married the Infant of Spain, Francis of Paula, by whom she had King Francis of Assisi, husband of Isabella, Queen of Spain)..

2. Marie Christine, born April 27, 1806 (who in 1829 married Ferdinand VII., King of Spain, and became the mother of Queen Isabella).

3. Marie Antoinette, born December 19, 1814.

Uncle: Leopold John, Prince of Salerno, born July 2, 1790; married July 28, 1816, to Marie Clémentine, Archduchess of Austria, born March 1, 1789, daughter of Francis I., Emperor of Austria, and sister of the Empress Marie Louise.

Aunts: Marie Christine Amélie Thérèse (the future Queen of Sardinia), born April 26, 1782; married November 25, 1809, to Louis Philippe, Duke of Orleans.

All the relatives of the Duchess of Berry displayed much affection for her, and their good wishes accompanied her on her departure.

The Duke of Narbonne-Pelet, French ambassador to Naples, wrote, May 14, 1816, to the Duke of Richelieu, Minister of Foreign Affairs:—

"S. A. R. Madame the Duchess of Berry embarked this morning in very good health and excellent weather on board the Neapolitan frigate *Sirène*, which sailed for Marseilles in company with a ship of the line and a corvette. It had been intended to sail on the 11th, but a hard gale which was blowing for two or three days delayed it until to-day. The French schooner *Momus* accompanies the squadron, and will probably reach Marseilles some hours earlier."

The Duchess of Berry, on her part, wrote this in her journal:—

"I embarked at nine o'clock on the morning of the 14th. The King, my father, and my uncle, had the kindness to accompany me. An indisposition which had lasted some days prevented the hereditary Princess from going on board the frigate *Sirène*, the same which brought us here. When we reached it, the crew saluted us with a cry of 'Long live the King,' which they repeated nine times. The *Ferdinand*, carrying eighty cannons, and the corvette *Fama*, which accompanied us, fired a salute of twenty-one guns. We sailed just after nine o'clock with a light wind from the southwest. At half-past ten, the

King, my father, and my uncle, left me, and also the French ambassadors. My suite comprised the Prince of San Nicandro, the Countess of La Tour and her daughter, the Count La Tour, and my attendants."

The young Princess had a fortunate passage across that sea which, as Chateaubriand remarks, had witnessed the passage of her ancestress, Marguerite of Provence, the wife of Saint Louis, returning from the Holy Land, where she had shared the misfortunes of her husband and her king. May 21, 1816, after a seven-days voyage, the Duchess of Berry arrived off Marseilles.

IV

THE LAZARETTO OF MARSEILLES

THE *Moniteur* of March 25, 1816, had published the names of the persons who were to make up the household of the Duchess of Berry. They were as follows: First almoner, Abbé de Bombelle; lady of honor, the Duchess of Reggio; lady of the bedchamber, the Countess of La Ferronnays; ladies-in-waiting, the Viscountess of Gontaut, the Viscountess of Bouillé, the Countess of Hautefort, Countess Charles de Béthisy, the Countess of Lauriston, the Countess of Gourgues; gentleman-in-waiting, the Duke of Lévis; first equerry, the Count of Mesnard; equerry commandant, Marquis Anjorrant.

One of the ladies-in-waiting, the Viscountess (afterwards Duchess) of Gontaut, writes as follows in her unpublished Memoirs: —

"I was summoned one day to the Tuileries by Monsieur. He kindly informed me that the marriage of M. the Duke of Berry with the Princess Caroline of Naples had just been arranged, and that he was anxious to let me know I had been appointed one of the ladies-in-waiting to the Princess, and even commissioned to go and receive her at Marseilles. I felt my very heart moved with profound gratitude to the royal family who had deigned to choose me among the throng of applicants surrounding them, all converted, as people were at the time, to sentiments of love and devotion for the court."

Madame de Gontaut went to bid farewell to the King and the Princess before her departure. She adds: "The Duchess of Angoulême condescended to explain to me in detail the composition of the household of Madame the Duchess of Berry, which she had provided should be established on the same scale as her own: six ladies-in-waiting, of whom two should be on duty every week. She told me that the Countess of Bouillé had just been appointed and was to go with me. I did not know her. 'She is a pretty American, married to the best of men,' said she; 'perhaps she will amuse you. But she of whom I especially wish to speak to you is the Maréchale Oudinot, Duchess of Reggio, one of the ladies-in-waiting. She is charming in face, conduct, and tact; in fine, she is gentle, kindly, and attractive; I am sure she will please you; her appointment is an excellent one which will gain universal approbation. I don't doubt that the Duchess of Berry will know how to appreciate her. She will start after you do, with another lady-in-waiting, Madame de La Ferronnays, whom you have known this long while. Their mission is the same as yours, — to go to Marseilles and wait there for the Princess. The

Countess of Hautefort and the Countess of Béthisy, the Countess of Lauriston [afterwards *la Maréchale*], and the Countess of Gourgues, will be stationed at intervals along the road and follow the Princess to Fontainebleau. There she will be received by the King.'"

Madame de Gontaut started for Marseilles in the same carriage with Madame de Bouillé. "As we approached the South," she tells us, "enthusiasm increased and cries of 'Long live the Duchess of Berry!' were heard on all sides. Madame de Bouillé was enchanted, and showed herself as much as possible to the public, saying with naïve complacency, 'Let us make them happy.'

"What a host of reflections occurred to me when the King's servants who were with us said that the carriage we occupied was that in which Napoleon had returned from Waterloo to Paris! I was even told, by way of entertaining me, that I could find the mysterious hiding-places in which the Emperor carried his despatches, treasures, etc. This research amused me during the monotony of the journey. But, seeing one of the principal springs, I had the unfortunate notion of pressing it, and on the instant a board sprang up and carried me with it. I found myself lying on a hard, narrow, immovable, quilted mattress, and I rolled about all night on this poverty-stricken bed of the great Emperor, unable for several hours to find the secret spring which could deliver me from this perilous position, and not daring to call a halt to the column of travellers who were with us.

"The Duke of Havré, representing the King, and accompanied by various officers of the royal household, body-guards, etc., had started twelve hours before us; in every city he was received with the boisterous honors due to his mission. Discharges of artillery, bells, and speeches greeted his arrival and departure; everywhere receptions, honors, and fatigue.

"Baron de Damas, who was in command at Marseilles, received us with cordiality and politeness; so did his mother, who assisted him very graciously in doing the honors of the city. Our joy at attaining the goal of our journey was very soon disturbed. A despatch sent to Baron de Damas informed him that a sort of plague which had broken out in one of the towns in the Neapolitan dominions had delayed the arrival of the Princess. As he was reading it a doleful expression came over his face, caused, doubtless, by the number of our colony; I heard him say to his mother in an undertone: 'How are we to amuse them?' I could not help laughing. Something had to be done, and the best way was to turn the thing into a jest, which set us all at our ease. The noble and conciliatory manners of former days of which the Duke of Havré was a model, and the gracious ways of the Duchess of Reggio, consoled our hostess: the difficulties vanished. As we were received courteously and kindly by everybody in the city and neighborhood, this dreaded time passed very quickly."

The sanitary committee had resolved that the Princess and her Neapolitan suite should be quarantined for ten days before entering Marseilles, and this decision had been made known to them at Naples before they sailed.

May 21, 1816, the frigate with the Duchess of Berry on board arrived off Marseilles and was saluted by a hundred discharges of artillery from the fort. In an instant the roadstead was covered with small craft adorned with flowers and white flags, but they were not allowed to cross the line prescribed by the quarantine regulations.

"We tried to make out the Princess from a distance," says Madame de Gontaut in her unpublished Memoirs. "She saw us; we knew that by her kindly gestures. We followed her with eyes and hearts until she entered the lazaretto. When we came back to the prefecture, we looked for Madame de La Ferronnays, whom we had not been able to find; to our astonishment, we learned that as soon as Madame's arrival had been signalled, she had started all alone in order to shut herself up in the quarantine hospital. The Duke of Havré and the Duchess of Reggio were ignorant of this and seemed surprised, but expressed no opinion on the subject, nor did I ask any questions.

"After Madame's arrival at the lazaretto she sent us word to come there; we saw her through a grating in a little parlor where we presented ourselves every day. We thought Madame gracious, agreeable, good, kindly, and gay; in a word, she charmed us. The remarkable gentleness of the Duchess of Reggio pleased her at once. Madame de Bouillé surprised her. Madame had learned from the Duke of Havré the sacrifice I had made in leaving my children to come to her, and she was always talking to me about it. Wishing to know what interested each of those who were about to be in attendance on her, she induced us to talk about ourselves, and, with a true princely memory, forgot nothing, which we thought very amiable. We noticed that Madame de La Ferronnays was in company with Madame de La Tour and all those who had come from Naples, and thence concluded, though without being certain of it, that being established at the quarantine hospital, she must needs remain there as long as Madame."

In thus enclosing herself in the lazaretto, the lady-in-waiting had outstepped her instructions, and thereby displeased the King. On this head Madame de Gontaut says: —

"Madame de La Ferronnays's intention was to seek a natural occasion to acquaint the Princess with the noble sentiments, the wit, and the good heart of Monseigneur, and thus teach her to love him in advance. Her zeal led her astray; she did not consider how improper this proceeding would seem to the Duchess of Reggio and Monseigneur; whom she ought to have consulted. It was not a rash or impulsive action; afterwards, being timid in character, she did nothing to repair what Marshal Oudinot, Duke of Reggio, took for an insult and complained of to the King."

The Duchess of Berry received the following letter from her husband on reaching the hospital: —

"Paris, May 10, 1816.

"I profit, Madame, by the departure of the Duchess of Reggio, to tell you how deeply your second letter has touched me; that letter which you wrote immediately after the ceremony by which you confided your destiny to me. I have your happiness in charge, and it shall be the sweet and constant occupation of my life. I have seen with regret the delay on your departure from Naples; the quarantine you will necessarily submit to, although shortened as much as possible, compels me to conclude that I shall not have the happiness of seeing you until early next month. How sorry I am not to be able to go to Naples to meet you! But we must conform to the wishes of our parents, and, as the first of subjects, we owe them the example of obedience. All France awaits you with the keenest impatience, and I more than any one else. I recommend to you the Duchess of Reggio, who, in spite of her delicate health, was bent on going. She thinks herself very happy to be able to begin her duties near you.

"Adieu, Madame; I am impatient to receive a

letter from Your Royal Highness dated in France. The wind, which is blowing violently, makes me tremble.

"Charles Ferdinand."

So long as the Duchess of Berry was in the lazaretto of Marseilles, the city was hung in the daytime with flags, festoons, and flowers, and in the evenings the illuminations which blazed until midnight continued to show the Princess what enthusiasm was kindled by her presence. Amusements were contrived which should make the delay imposed by the quarantine regulations seem shorter to her. In the evening of May 23 she had a sail in a superb yawl placed at her disposal by Admiral Missiessy. This yawl was speedily surrounded by a multitude of small boats crowded with people anxious to see how the young Princess looked. The shore, from the lazaretto to the end of the esplanade of La Tourette, was thronged with innumerable and clamorously enthusiastic spectators.

On arriving at the entrance of the harbor, the Duchess of Berry's yawl made its way with difficulty through the crowd of boats awaiting her at this point. The health officers thereupon concluded that if they carefully surrounded the yawl and prevented it from holding communication with any other vessel, there would be nothing hazardous in allowing it to enter the port. This was done amid shouts from the crews of every boat, and an immense crowd that had rapidly assembled on the wharves. The Princess stood up in the stern of the yawl, where every one could see her, and affectionately saluted the enthusiastic people. The yawl came close to the Cannebière wharf and then turned slowly, to regain first the entrance of the harbor, and then the quarantine hospital. During this sail, the Duchess of Berry wore a robe of rose-colored levantine, cut heart-shaped and trimmed with tulle. A little striped cashmere shawl was thrown negligently around her shoulders; a large white straw hat trimmed with a wreath of lilies covered her beautiful hair, and was tied with a ribbon of the same color. Leaning against the gallery which separated her from the rowers, the Princess looked at the crowd with emotion. "Ah!" said she, "perhaps it is not very easy for me to shed tears, but to-day I must let them flow."

In the evening of May 25, a concert was given in front of the lazaretto by the orchestra of the Grand Theatre. The next day she wrote as follows to her husband: —

"From the Lazaretto of Marseilles, May 26, 1816.

"Your kind letters, Monseigneur, have already accustomed me to your interest in me. I owe it to Your Royal Highness to inform you with the confidence which you inspire, of all that I am doing here, and first of all concerning my health, which is very good. I rise rather late, because I like to sleep in the morning; hence I do not hear Mass until between nine and ten o'clock. The good Duke of Havré takes the trouble to come a great distance to be present at it, and so do the prefect, M. de Villeneuve-Bargemont, M. de Montgrand, the mayor, and the health officers whenever their public duties permit. So they see me at the very *respectful* distance imposed by the quarantine regulations. Then I go back to my own apartments until dinner time, after which I profit by the excellent society of Madame de La Ferronnays; it is doubtless to her attachment to Monseigneur that I owe such a touching proof of her devotion in coming to shut herself up here with me. I appreciate it greatly, as also the Duchess of Reggio's request to do the same. I had the pleasure of seeing her in the parlor with Madames de Gontaut, de Bouillé, de Lévis, de Mesnard, and all those presented to me by the Duke of Havré; that is my occupation after dinner, before a promenade, or a fishing-excursion, pleasures which the health officers have twice procured for me."

In the same letter the Princess speaks thus of the excursion of May 23:—

"Last Thursday I had a delightful sail in a yawl which the commandant of the marine sent for from Toulon; they let us enter the harbor, and as it seems that the good people of Marseilles were very pleased to have me find a way of showing myself, I have asked to have the excursion repeated to-day, if the weather permits. They have had musical performances for me several times; in a word, Monseigneur, nothing has been omitted which could give me pleasure."

The young Princess thus terminated her pleasant epistle: —

"I am very grateful, I assure you, and I should like to show it as I feel it; but I cannot overcome my timidity all of a sudden. My age and the few opportunities I have had of going out ought to excuse me to those who know these reasons; others will perhaps judge me less indulgently. That will not trouble me except on account of Your Royal Highness, to whom I should like to give all kinds of satisfaction. They are to show me Toulon, and I shall enjoy this pleasure all the more because it will not entail a delay, but only occupy the days of grace accorded me by the health commissioners; the arrangement was made by the excellent Duke of Havré. I am not writing to-day to the King our uncle nor to your father, lest I should weary them; but kindly interpret my sentiments of respect and attachment for them, as well as my friendship to the Duke and Duchess of Angoulême. I am longing to make the acquaintance of a family already so dear to me. You will show me how to please them, Monseigneur; you will tell me very frankly all I ought to do to accomplish that, and above all how to merit your affection. "CAROLINE."

On the same day on which the Princess wrote this letter to her husband from the lazaretto of Marseilles, the Prince wrote to her from Paris: —

"I cannot express to you, Madame, how happy I

am to hear of your arrival at Marseilles. I would gladly have shortened the tiresome quarantine of Your Royal Highness, and fear you will find the time very long. You have already gained the hearts of those who have only caught a glimpse of you. You are already so much loved in France! People greatly desire to see you! When I go out nowadays, they no longer cry, 'Long live the Duke of Berry!' but what pleases me a great deal more, 'Long live the Duchess of Berry! Long live the Princess Caroline!'

"I should like, Madame, to forestall all the wishes of Your Royal Highness, and to know what would please you. Here you will have a charming residence which the whole family occupies itself in arranging. You like to ride; I will find very steady horses for you. I know that you are afraid of nothing; but, for my part, I am afraid for you. Speaking of courage, you were in great danger at sea, near that villainous island of Elba, whence all our woes proceeded last year. That made me tremble; but I liked to hear that you had not felt the slightest fear. The blood of Henri IV. and Louis XIV. was not untrue to itself."

The Duke of Berry terminated his affectionate letter by these lines full of tenderness: —

"Adieu, Madame and dearest friend, my good and amiable wife; while awaiting June 15, which is still so far off, I repeat that I love you, and that I will do all that lies in me to make you happy.

"Charles Ferdinand."

While the Duke of Berry was wholly wrapt in his ideas of conjugal love and domestic happiness, the gay, smiling, and high-spirited young Princess was thrilling with joy and hope. The hospital, an abode ordinarily so gloomy, took on for her all the illusions and dreams of a southern imagination. Marseilles seemed like a splendid scene, whose distance even increased its enchantment. She made her formal entry into the city on May 30.

V

ENTERING MARSEILLES

MARSEILLES is in holiday attire from daybreak on May 30, 1816. Never has the Phocean city presented a more grandiose appearance. The sky, whose azure rivals that of the sea, is illumined by a splendid sun whose golden reflections make the waves sparkle like diamonds. The gardens of numberless *bastides*, as the pleasure houses which surround the city with a belt of foliage are called, are filled with orange, citron, and myrtle trees. It is a festival of springtime, light, and flowers. When the people of Southern France set out to be enthusiastic, their enthusiasm becomes a sort of madness. They are intoxicated with noise, shouting, and racket of all sorts. Do you see the windows adorned with women, flags, and garlands, the National Guards and troops of the line drawn up in double rows on the wharves and in the streets, the flat roofs crowded with innumerable spectators? Do you hear the bells ringing, the cannon roaring, the vivas splitting the air? Do you see the magnificent roadstead where whole fleets ride at anchor, the hill where rises the poetic chapel of Notre Dame de la Garde, patroness of sailors, the mountains on the horizon which frame in the magical picture? What a display, what a spectacle! Truly it is fairy-like, enchanting, dazzling.

It is nine o'clock in the morning. The Duchess of Berry, coming out of the lazaretto, embarks on a boat belonging to the royal marine commanded by M. de Damas, captain of a ship of the line, for the Place de l'Hôtel de Ville, where she is to land. On entering the port, she is saluted by thirty-six guns from the forts and the King's vessels. Every craft in the harbor is hung with flags. As she lands, one hundred and fifty National Guards and as many of the Royal Guard form a double line. The troops present arms. The flags are lowered, the officers bow, and the drums beat a salute. A detachment of Sicilian troops escort the Princess to the Hôtel de Ville, where the ceremony of delivery is to take place.

The same ceremonial is observed as had been followed on May 6, 1770, for the Dauphiness, Marie Antoinette, in the larger island in the Rhine, near Strasbourg, and on March 16, 1810, for the Empress Marie Louise at Braunau. Conformably to diplomatic usage, the Hôtel de Ville has been declared neutral ground by special act. The apartments on the right of the principal hall have been arranged for the reception of the Princess, her Neapolitan household, and the Prince of San Nicandro, ambassador of her grandfather, the King of the Two Sicilies. On this side the Neapolitan colors are raised. The apartments on the left remain the property of the King of France. Here are stationed the Duke of Havré, ambassador of Louis XVIII.; the Duchess of Reggio, lady of honor to the Duchess of Berry; the Countess of La Ferronnays, lady of the bedchamber; the Countess of Bouillé and the Viscountess of Gontaut, ladies-in-waiting; the Duke of Lévis, gentleman-in-waiting; and the Count of Mesnard, first equerry. The Sicilian body-guards draw up in line in the great hall, beneath their national standard. The French body-guards do the same, on the opposite side. In the middle of the hall stands a table covered with green velvet fringed with gold. Here the delivery is to be effected according to the protocol of royal marriages.

The Princess comes forward through the great hall and sits down at the middle of the table, on the Neapolitan side, with the Prince of San Nicandro on her right, and behind her the Countess of La Tour, her lady of honor, as well as the Prince of Ruffo-Scilla and General de La Tour, both of whom were witnesses of the marriage by proxy at Naples. On the other side of the table the French household remain standing. After the reading of the official documents, and an exchange of speeches, thirty-six discharges of artillery announce that the delivery has been effected. The Prince of San Nicandro has just presented the Princess to the Duke of Havré, representative of Louis XVIII. She has said farewell to the members of her Neapolitan household, who fling themselves on their knees, weeping as they kiss her hands. Then she crosses over to the other side of the table. She is a Frenchwoman now. Her new lady of honor, the Duchess of Reggio, comes forward. The Princess embraces her. Then the Duchess presents the Countess of La Ferronnays, the Countess of Bouillé, the Viscountess of Gontaut, the Duke of Lévis, the Count of Mesnard; and the Countess of La Ferronnays, in her capacity as lady of the bedchamber, offers her the trousseau and the corbeille, presented by the King. Afterwards she enters a chamber, where, according to usage, she lays aside her Neapolitan garments for others exclusively French. This change of dress is symbolical of the change of country. It is a farewell to the past, a greeting to the future. On one hand regret, on the other hope. One might apply to the Princess, who thus begins a new existence, Victor Hugo's famous line: —

"Depart with a tear, enter with a smile."

Resplendent in her French toilet, the Duchess of Berry goes down into the Place de l'Hôtel de Ville, where she receives the compliments of General Baron de Damas, commander of the 8th Military division, and of the Prefect of the Bouches on Rhône department. She re-embarks afterward in order to make a formal entry at Monsieur's quay, in front of the Cannebière. This time she does not take a boat belonging to the royal marine, but a gilded longboat belonging to the Marseilles merchant service, which is manned by twenty-four oarsmen dressed in white satin, with blue and gold scarfs. Sheltered by the royal standard bearing the arms of France and Navarre, and seated beneath a crimson velvet canopy surmounted by a crown of colossal proportions, the young Princess advances through a forest of masts draped with greenery and pennants. One might think her the Queen of the Mediterranean. She lands on Monsieur's quay. The mayor pays his homage. The troops are in battle array. Again a salvo of thirty-six guns is fired, and all the church-bells ring. The Princess goes by way of the Cannebière and the Cours to the church of Saint Martin, where the clergy offer her holy water and conduct her processionally into the sanctuary, where she hears Mass and a *Te Deum*. Then she goes to her palace, where thirty young girls salute her and offer flowers. She dines alone in grand state. After dinner she goes to the theatre, where her presence calls forth great applause. The whole city is illuminated.

Enjoy your triumph, Madame. Look well at these festive shores where a magnificent reception greets you, where everybody swears devotion and fidelity, where you make your appearance like a queen, almost like a divinity. You will return to them again in less than sixteen years. You will return, but in what different attire!

A proscript, when it becomes a question how you

shall vindicate the rights of a son despoiled of his inheritance, you will say to yourself: "I must begin on the shores of Provence. Can Marseilles, which gave me such a brilliant reception, fail to recognize me?" But this time you will find no triumphal arches; your road will not be strewn with flowers. You will be obliged to hide in an obscure house in the suburbs, awaiting with feverish impatience through a cruelly long night the pretended movement in your favor. In the morning you will learn that this movement has wretchedly miscarried. And in your distress you will say: —

"Alas! where are they who made me such splendid promises, and shouted so for me? I am sad, I am alone, I am deserted, and I shall soon have no place to lay my head."

And then you will begin that campaign so full of danger, so full of anguish, which will end by the treachery of a Judas and the captivity of Blaye. How the bells, how the trumpets, how the shouts resound to-day! Why think of the future? Young and brilliant Princess, be happy while you may.

VI

FROM MARSEILLES TO FONTAINEBLEAU

BEFORE leaving Marseilles finally, the Duchess of Berry was to make a short excursion to Toulon. Starting from Marseilles, in the morning of May 31, 1816, she returned in the evening of the following day. Compliments followed her as far as the limits of the department of the Var, and triumphal arches of foliage spanned the road at intervals. On reaching Toulon during the day, the young Princess found all the streets hung with flags and all the houses decked with garlands. The people took the horses from her carriage and drew it themselves. In the evening there were fireworks. The next morning at eight o'clock she reviewed the National Guard, and then took a boat to the *Royal Louis*, a man-of-war, where Admiral Missiessy gave her a breakfast and afterwards entertained her with a mimic naval combat. On returning to Marseilles the Princess wrote this letter to her husband, June 2: —

"What a pleasure for me, Monseigneur, to receive your most amiable letters, written five days ago, but written far too rapidly! Permit me to make a tiny reproach to Your Royal Highness. You will excuse me, because you assure me that you wish to give me all sorts of pleasure, and yet you delay that I have in reading you by the study I am obliged to give your writing. Don't go to thinking me hard to please and a scold after this.

"Last evening I came back from Toulon, where every instant was employed in receiving homage and festivities by land and sea. The whole city was decorated with emblems and allegorical inscriptions. Impossible to describe the enthusiasm of these good Provençaux; they spoil me; they move my heart by their repeated expressions of love for the King and all his family. At the same time, they have the tact to huzza also for my Neapolitan relatives. Is not that charming? All the authorities are excellent according to common report; it is certainly they who encourage these good sentiments. I have had the pleasure of seeing that excellent Rousse of Toulon, the only person who caused Louis XVII. to be recognized, and who by an entire and disinterested devotion, continues to be useful to his country and his King.

"I was taken through the arsenals. The land arsenal, which was not in existence four months ago, is now in a condition to arm more than thirty thousand men. This is owing to the indefatigable activity of the colonel in charge, whose name is Laferrière. This little journey has interested me in every way. Nowhere, I think, could one get a

juster idea of the resources and capabilities of France than by visiting this fine harbor. If it produces this effect on me, who understand nothing about it, what must it produce on better instructed persons? In thirteen days, Monseigneur, I shall see you, and be able to judge for myself all that is told me of the goodness of your heart and mind, and to repeat to you that I am for life your faithful and affectionate
"CAROLINE."

The journey of the Princess was a continual ovation all the way from Marseilles to Fontainebleau, where it had been settled that the first interview of the married pair should take place in the forest on June 15. The *Moniteur* of April 29, 1816, had published the following note: —

"S. A. R. the Duchess of Berry will be received on her journey through France with the same honors accorded to the Countess of Provence and the Countess of Artois. Each prefect will accompany her to the limits of his department, where he will be relieved by the prefect of the next one. At the entrance of each city she will be received by the mayors and deputies. The guards and troops of the line will be under arms. If the Princess takes up her residence at the archbishopric or bishopric, she will be received by the archbishop or bishop as she alights from the carriage, and, if she enters a church, she will be received there by the clergy with the archbishop or bishop at their head. During the stay of the Princess in each city, the master of ceremonies will present the clergy and the authorities to her."

This ceremonial was observed in all its details. The first city in which the Princess made a halt was the old parliamentary town of Aix. She was present at the curious annual procession founded by King René, in 1448. The Duchess of Gontaut gives the following description of it: —

"This festival was intended to represent the triumph of the Christian religion over idolatry, by means of allegorical personages and heathen gods, who are driven back to hell by the presence of the Saviour. At the head of the procession we saw Mercury; the Goddess of Night; Pluto, surrounded by a multitude of demons; Diana, Love, Venus, Mars, walking one after another; then the lepers, the commanders of the city, horse-guards, dancers, tambourine players, etc. After the mythological divinities were Scriptural personages: The Queen of Sheba coming to see Solomon; Moses carrying the Tables of the Law, and trying to bring back to the worship of the true God the mocking Jews, who were dancing round a pasteboard golden calf. Following the Jews came the apostles, with the perfidious Judas in advance, holding in his hand a purse containing the thirty pieces of silver earned by his treason; the other apostles were beating him over the head with sticks of wood in punishment for his infamous behavior. The Abbé of Youth, the

King of the Basoche, and the Prince of Love preceded the canopy covering the Blessed Sacrament, which was followed by an immensity of priests in different costumes. Death closed the cortège. All the church bells of the city were ringing while the procession lasted."

Leaving Aix, the Princess went to Orange, where she admired the ancient theatre and the arch of Marius, two magnificent vestiges of Roman grandeur. Thence she passed in triumph through the department of the Drôme. Meanwhile, her husband wrote her as follows from Paris, June 4: —

"I received yesterday, Madame and dearest friend, your kind and amiable letter of the 27th. Everybody says all that is good about you; but I can appreciate your worth better from your letters, which I find charming. You ask me to give you advice, and I will tell you everything that I think you may find useful. You complain of your timidity; it is becoming to your youth, and you know how to combine it with kindness and nobility. You are surrounded by the love of the people of the South of France, who are very good. You are a presage of happiness to France, and the terror of the seditious.

"CHARLES FERDINAND."

The Princess wrote to her husband the next day: —

"MONTÉLIMART, June 5, 1816.

"Monseigneur's letter of May 31 was brought to me before I was able to finish my reply to that of

the 26th. I thank you deeply for the second as well as the first. You gave me a great pleasure by sending that of my parents. People still continue to show me France in gala dress. In every place I pass through the acclamations are continual, and likewise the compliments of the authorities. I feel this deeply; but I will whisper to Monseigneur, from whom I have nothing to hide, and to him only, that I also feel the weight of these honors, and am never intoxicated by them. I am longing to enjoy a quiet family life. Meanwhile, I assure Your Royal Highness of my affection; it will last as long as my life.
"CAROLINE."

After Montélimart the Princess visited Vienne in Dauphiny, where she saw Pontius Pilate's tower on the bank of the Rhone, and the superb Gothic church of Saint Maurice, with its gigantic nave, its stairways of a thousand balusters, and its ceiling sown with golden stars. She reached Lyons June 8, at half-past three in the afternoon. A triumphal arch had been erected in her honor on the Place de la Charité. One hundred ladies and thirty young girls paid her their compliments. The next day, after Mass, she went to the Hôtel de Ville, and thence to Saint Peter's House, where the Chamber of Commerce presented their homage in the shape of a handsome basket containing stuffs from the manufactures of Lyons. In accepting this offering, the Princess removed the shawl she was wearing and put on one of those presented to her, saying that she would wear it to the theatre the same evening. During the day she wrote this letter to her husband: —

"LYONS, June 9, 1816.

"Your letter of June 4, Monseigneur, was handed to me on the evening of my arrival at Lyons. I don't want to keep on repeating that I thank you; once for all, count on my tender gratitude, and be sure that nothing escapes my susceptibility; you have touched it keenly.

"You say you are content with me, Monseigneur. That is doubtless to reassure me; for I know that I lack much, very much of being what I would like to be in order to please you and to correspond with the too flattering idea that has been given you of Caroline. Believe in her good heart and her desire to respond to your confidence by giving you all her own. That is all I can answer for; your care, your kindness, will do the rest.

"I am very grateful for all that has been done to embellish my habitation, and for me. How can I show my gratitude to everybody? You will help me, Monseigneur; it is only with you that I already try to need no interpreter, for I tell you very frankly that you are dear to your

"CAROLINE."

In the evening there was a state dinner at the archbishop's palace, and a gala representation at the Grand Theatre. They played *La Partie de*

Chasse de Henri IV., and a piece composed for the occasion called *La Nymphe de Parthénope*. At the close of this piece, Flora, followed by her nymphs, passes in front of the stage, taking lilies from her basket and throwing them to the spectators. All the nymphs carried clusters of the same flower, and likewise threw them into the hall. At the same moment a shower of lilies fell from the ceiling, and a dove came to place a crown on the Duchess of Berry's head. All the spectators rose at once, waving their lily stalks and crying: "Long live the King! Long live the Princess!"

The Duke of Berry wrote to his wife the same day: —

"Paris, June 9, 1816.

"It is, Madame and dear friend, by one of the most devoted adherents of our house that I write you to-day, — the good Prince of Castelcicala. I have no need of recommending him to you; he knows me well, having seen me so long in England. How gladly I would take his place! I shall see you in six days, then! I am always fearing that you will not find me handsome, for the Parisian painters are not like those of Palermo; they flatter. What pleasure it will give me to press your hand! Press mine also if you do not find me too displeasing. The constraint we shall be under for two days annoys me much. My Caroline, I am going to make your happiness and your pleasures my occupation. I know you like going to the play, and I have boxes in all the theatres. I have a country seat which you have heard of, where we shall often go together. I hunt often, and you shall come too, in an open carriage; you like music, and I am very fond of it also. In a word, Madame, I will try to make you happy, and I hope to succeed. If I am to believe those who have seen you, you possess good-nature, gentleness, intelligence, and gaiety; what better could one ask? However, we shall find out each other's faults; *tender indulgence* shall be our motto.

"Charles Ferdinand."

After having left Lyons, where she found two of her ladies-in-waiting, the Countess of Hautefort and the Countess Charles de Béthisy, the Princess went towards Moulins, where she arrived June 11. Evidences of sympathy and enthusiasm were seen everywhere along the route. The authorities, the people, the army, the National Guards, rivalled each other in their zeal to welcome the amiable young Princess, who seemed like a rainbow after the storm. Smiling and gracious, looking at everything through the prism of illusion and hope, she fancied that the nation was forever reconciled with its King, that the white flag had no rival to fear, and that the race of Saint Louis was once and forever established on the throne of France. How was it possible to doubt so many protestations of devotion and fidelity? There was such an accent of loyalty in every speech, such an expression of confidence, affection, and joy on every countenance! The young Princess felt that for her to suspect the future would be a sacrilege. She hoped, and she believed.

Just as the Duchess of Berry was about to enter the department of Seine-et-Marne, where her first interview with her husband was to take place, Louis XVIII. published the following decree, dated at Fontainebleau, June 13, 1816: —

"LOUIS, etc. The department of Seine-et-Marne is full of monuments of religion and of monarchy. Melun has seen Clotilde, the daughter of its counts, placed by Providence on the throne of Clovis in order to give Christian kings to France. It was for Melun that Saint Louis left Vincennes. Fontainebleau recalls the glorious times of Francis I. and of Louis XIV. Meaux has been the see of a bishop whose genius and virtues have raised him to an equality with the Fathers of the Church. Nearly every city, town, and simple village of this department has been the scene of some memorable event in the ancient wars of which Paris was the centre and the object. In these latter times we have been touched by the afflictions suffered by the inhabitants of Seine-et-Marne, the patience with which they have endured them, and the marks of affection given us by so many faithful subjects abiding in their region. We wish to attest this by associating them in the rewards we have decreed to the National Guards of several departments, and we have chosen this period when we are going amongst them to receive our beloved daughter, the Duchess of Berry."

The Princess arrived at Nemours in the daytime, June 14. Her carriage was overflowing with flowers that had been presented on her journey. She was complimented and received by the Dukes of La Châtre, Maillé, and Damas, who led her to the Hôtel de Ville, where she was to pass the night, and presented two of her ladies-in-waiting, the Countess of Lauriston and the Countess of Gourgues. The next day, June 15, she left Nemours, and passed through the forest toward the crossroads of La Croix de Saint Hérem.

VII

FONTAINEBLEAU

THE Duke of Berry was impatiently awaiting his young wife at Fontainebleau. He had written her from there, June 12, 1816: —

"Your letter from Lyons, which was handed to me by the King, gave me inexpressible pleasure. I am charmed at your scolding me about my handwriting; you are quite right; but when I write to you, my heart carries me away, and you have no idea of the trouble it gives me to be legible. Three days longer! I am burning to see you. To-day I feel a great happiness; I have your portrait. At the very least, it cannot disfigure you; and even if it flatters you a little, one could be very agreeable without being so charming as this portrait."

And again, June 14: —

"The Prince of Castelcicala has given me your letter from Moulins, which is still kinder than the others. To-morrow I shall see my wife at last, my wife whose happiness is to be my work."

After having cited this correspondence of the married pair who had not yet seen each other, Chateaubriand says: —

"Alas! the Prince caused the unhappiness of her whose felicity he aimed at. But who is to blame for it? How this young couple loved France! What sincere gratitude (for it was well hidden in these letters) for the homage paid them! Do these letters contain a single word which the simplest, the noblest, the tenderest soul could disavow? Who, in reading them, would not be glad to have those who wrote them as brother and sister, as son and daughter? There was a touching resemblance in the destinies of the Duke and Duchess of Berry; sprung from the same race, both Bourbons, both having seen the fall of their ancestral thrones, both having regained their rank, they had known scarcely anything but exile and misfortune before their marriage. Beaten by the same tempest, they had united to give each other mutual support. After so many misfortunes they sought some moments of happiness; their letters prove how cruel it was to tear it from them."

The entire royal family were assembled at Fontainebleau, awaiting the Princess who was the object of so many hopes. June 14, there was a grand dinner at the chateau in the Hall of Fêtes. The beauty of this hall, which was built by Henri II., added much to the splendor of the banquet. Sixty persons were admitted to the honor of dining at the royal table. During the repast the chapel band played *Vive Henri IV.* and *Charmante Gabrielle.* At six o'clock an immense crowd was allowed to enter the hall and pass around the table.

The road from Fontainebleau to Nemours was thronged the next day from early dawn. The peasants in their holiday attire went to meet the Princess and offer her bouquets. Musicians playing national airs wandered along the highway. The National Guards of the neighboring villages were under arms.

The Princess had just passed through the town of Nemours. "Madame the Duchess of Berry is in the forest of Fontainebleau," said the Duchess of Reggio, her maid of honor. This simple remark produced an extraordinary effect upon the Princess. Listen to Chateaubriand on the subject: —

"The first marriage pomps beneath the trees were charming. One would say that the descendants of the long-haired [1] kings have maintained a secret predilection for forests; it has pleased them to choose solitudes for their palaces and to have the enchantments of their courts overshadowed by great oaks. How many souvenirs must not Fontainebleau, where twenty-nine kings have lived since Robert, have offered to the young Princess! Saint Louis, the august chief of his race, had caused a hospital to be built there for the poor, among whom, as he said, he sought Jesus Christ. Other centuries added the works of Charles the Victorious, and of Francis the restorer of learning, to those of the Saint. Henri IV. dated his letters from his *delicious deserts* of

---

[1] The Merovingian kings were thus styled.

Fontainebleau. . Louis XIII. embellished them still further. Then came the unfortunate Louis XVI., who covered the rocks with a mourning-veil of pines; and thirty years later a Pope was imprisoned amidst these thickets where Louis XIV. had loved La Valliére, — and all these things, which for the rest of the world are history, were merely family traditions to the house of France."

It was at Moret, near Fontainebleau, that on September 4, 1725, Louis XV. saw his wife, Marie Leczinska, for the first time. It was at the crossroads of La Croix de Saint Hérem, in the forest of Fontainebleau, that the Duchess of Berry was about to meet her husband. Less than twelve years before — November 25, 1804 — it was at the same place that Napoleon saw for the first time Pope Pius VII., who had come to France to crown him. Louis XVIII. had the same grand chamberlain as the Emperor, Prince Talleyrand, who was at the Cross of Saint Hérem, June 15, 1816, as he had been November 25, 1804. How many changes had occurred in less than a dozen years, while he, the spectator of so many vicissitudes, had always fulfilled the same functions! Such irremovability was more than strange and must have surprised even him who was its object!

The crossroads of La Croix de Saint Hérem, where the Duke and Duchess of Berry were about to meet, is in the depths of the forest, about a league from Fontainebleau. Two superb tents had been set up there, one of which was intended for the royal family, and the other for the suite of the Duchess of Berry. The first had been carpeted, and contained an armchair for the King, covered with sky-blue velvet, embroidered in gold, and twelve campstools for the princes and princesses of his family.

Two carriages containing the members of her household preceded the open barouche in which sat the young Princess with the Duchess of Reggio, her lady of honor, and the Countess of La Ferronnays, her lady of the bedchamber. The Duchess of Reggio said to her: "I must inform Your Royal Highness that we are about to arrive at the Cross of Saint Hérem. There you will find the royal family." The carriage stopped in another instant. "The King is coming forward to meet Your Royal Highness," added the lady of honor. On alighting from the carriage, the Princess was to be received according to the same etiquette as had been observed on the arrival of Queen Marie Leczinska. She was to cross, all alone, half of a carpet spread on the grass, while the King, leading the royal family, crossed the other half. But the lively Duchess found the solemn slowness of such a ceremonial tiresome. Recollecting the neutrality of the Marseilles Hôtel de Ville, she asked in an undertone if the carpet was neutral. Then, springing forward with one bound toward the King, she threw herself at his knees, kissed his hands, and said something which he seemed to approve. Louis XVIII. raised her, pressed her to his heart, and presented her to the Duchess of Angoulême. The Duke of Berry advanced. "Nephew," said the King, "it is my daughter that I give you, whom I already love like a father. Make her happy." Then he joined their hands. The Duchess of Gontaut, a witness of this touching scene, says: "The two spouses looked at each other. What a moment, when each sought to divine what their whole life was to be! . . . She seemed to please him. . . . I heard him say in a low tone to Madame de La Ferronnays: 'I shall love her. . . .' The moment when Monsieur held out his arms to his young daughter-in-law, and she implored his protection and he promised it, was strikingly affecting. Monseigneur, seeing that the Princess was frightened, spoke to her in a gracious tone that reassured her. He seemed to please her. She said to me that she found him better looking than his portrait which had been sent to her at Naples."

The young Princess produced the most favorable impression. Her kindly and prepossessing face, large blue eyes, and curling fair hair made her very charming. She wore a diadem of fine pearls surmounted by a wreath of roses. The weather had been misty all the morning, but at the moment of the interview the sun came out brilliantly. The uniforms, the feathers, and the ladies' dresses glittered. The whole open space was crowded with generals and officers of the King's household. The troops on duty were the body-guards, the Hundred

Switzers, and two hundred grenadiers of the infantry guard. The princes seemed to have attained the summit of felicity. Never had such satisfaction been visible on the face of Louis XVIII. The interview, which took place at half past two, lasted ten minutes. Then the King returned to Fontainebleau, taking the Duke and Duchess of Berry with him in his carriage, as well as the Duke and Duchess of Angoulême. They entered the chateau through the court of the *Cheval Blanc,* where three regiments of the royal guard were drawn up in battle array: the lancers, the hussars, and the first infantry regiment. The principal door of the perron of the stairs called the *Fer-à-Cheval* was adorned with flowers so arranged as to form a portico, the plinths and the inner side of the arch being symmetrically diversified and shaded, and the words, "Long live the King!" traced in china-asters. The royal guard celebrated the arrival of a Bourbon princess on the same spot where Napoleon uttered his pathetic and memorable farewell to the imperial guard.

What changes two years had brought about! The spectators were thoughtful.

During the whole evening the courts of the chateau were filled with countless crowds. At six o'clock the King sat down at table, and the public were admitted to the honor of seeing him dine. The Duchess of Berry, who was on the monarch's left, beside her husband, was the centre of observation. After dinner Louis XVIII. showed himself at one of the windows of the Hall of the Guards which gives on to the oval court, that court of marvellous architecture whose entrance gate is the baptistery of Louis XIII. After making signs of good will to the crowd who were crying, "Long live the King!" he took the Duchess of Berry by the hand and presented her to the people. She responded by a graceful salute to the demonstrations of joy made on beholding her. In the evening there was dancing on the public squares and the town was illuminated.

The favorite city of Francis I. enchanted the Duchess of Berry. Nowhere in France, and perhaps nowhere else in the world, is there a residence so picturesque and charming, so full of poetry and souvenirs, as Fontainebleau. The forest is a great wonder of nature, and the palace a great miracle of art. A nameless spell proceeds from this magnificent abode which penetrates the soul. There one sees the power of man triumph, and still more that of God. No spot could have been better adapted to dazzle the young Princess and impress her imagination. As she crossed the threshold of the legendary palace, it seemed as though all the glorious centuries of France rose to life and bade her welcome. Primaticcio's frescoes in the luminous Hall of Fêtes were suitable to the splendors of a joyful marriage. The art-lover was enchanted. The Italian woman enjoyed the palace so dear to Catherine and Maria de' Medici. She admitted that what had been told her concerning the pomp and splendor of the court of

France was not an exaggeration. Sincerely moved by the joy apparent on all faces, by the paternal welcome of the King, the affection displayed by her husband, and the respectful sympathy shown by all classes of society, she thought it would be easy to become the idol of the French nation. She slept at the palace of Fontainebleau on Saturday, June 15. Her husband did not pass the night there, custom forbidding a married pair to sleep under the same roof until after the celebration of the religious marriage. On Sunday morning, June 16, she departed with the entire royal family to make, on the same day, her formal entry into Paris.

VIII

THE ENTRY INTO PARIS

FOR several weeks the marriage of the Duke of Berry had been the universal topic of conversation at Paris. June 5, 1816, M. Charles de Rémusat wrote to his mother: —

"We are all thinking about the marriage. Everybody goes to see the corbeille, the robes, and the trousseau. We expect to be very gay at the wedding, and to sing and dance a good deal; I hope we may."

And the former mistress of the Empress Josephine's household replied, June 11, from Toulouse, where her husband was prefect: —

"I hope Providence will protect us, but we have great need of it; for these poor French no longer know what they are doing. I see nobody but the Duke of Berry who really does what he should do. He is getting married; he will give us sons and daughters; he will enliven us; I await all your accounts most impatiently. I am sure that the King and our Princess will be charming in this family festivity, and that the joy of the Parisians will be very sincere. Probably it will be the first genuine sentiment they have felt in a long while."

The *Moniteur* of June 4 described the visit of the princes to the *Hôtel des Menus-Plaisirs* to examine the trousseau and wedding presents of the bride. A pedestal covered with red velvet drapery stood on a platform of white marble. A lily stalk, surmounted by a wheatsheaf embroidered in gold, sprang from each corner of it. On its four faces were the arms of the two houses of Bourbon and the interlaced monograms of the spouses. On top of it was a clump of greensward whence issued a colossal lily with golden leaves and silver flowers. This was called the corbeille. On all sides of it were baskets laden with garlands of flowers and cashmere shawls. The wedding dress, embroidered in silver and adorned with diamonds, a white cut velvet mantle similarly adorned, a tulle robe embroidered with pearls, and another with steel, were especially admired. All the fashionable women of Paris were in ecstasies over those wonderful toilettes.

The King, hearing that the city wished to make a grand display of fireworks on the occasion of the marriage, expressed a desire that the funds intended for this purpose should be expended in a more useful manner, and one calculated to produce durable results. It was decided, in consequence, that on the day of the Prince's marriage, fourteen poor orphans, born in Paris, should be married and endowed by the city with fifty louis each. On Saturday, June 15, in Saint John's Hall at the Hôtel de Ville, the signatures were affixed to the fifteen marriage contracts.

Count de Chabrol, prefect of the Seine, addressed the intending couples as follows: —

"Young spouses, the touching ceremony which brings you hither, causes your hearts to thrill with joy and gratitude. Your marriage is to be celebrated under the happiest auspices, because it associates you in a way with the august ceremony of the marriage of a Prince and Princess who are the hope and ornament of France. Some day it will be sweet for you to remember, in the bosom of a happy household, that you owe your happiness to the fortunate and ever-memorable epoch of an august union by which all the wishes of France are crowned. You will bring up your children to love our good King, and feel for him those sentiments of devotion and respect which are due to his sacred person. . . . His Majesty deigns to permit you to be present as he passes by to go to Notre Dame for the marriage ceremony of the Duke and Duchess of Berry. You will have the happiness of beholding his cherished features. In his presence you will feel your young hearts inflamed with a new love for his august person, and you will go back to your homes repeating that cry of gratitude and love so dear to all Frenchmen: Long live the King!"

The Odéon, Gaîté, Ambigu, Variétes, and Porte Saint Martin theatres gave plays composed for the occasion in the evening of June 15. The *Chemin de Fontainebleau*, by MM. Georges Duval and Rochefort, produced at the Odéon, seems to have been very successful. Speaking of this charming trifle, the *Moniteur* of June 17, said: —

"Much laughter was caused by the character of a newsmonger of a gamekeeper who could predict no misfortunes except for Tonquin and Cochin China. The vaudeville that terminates this little piece is ingenious and very effective. The couplets successively designate the monarch who reunites the wisdom and virtues of the best of his royal ancestors, the Prince who has given us the model of chivalrous freedom and French gallantry, the Antigone of our days, the heroic deliverer of the South, and finally the happy couple to whom Heaven will grant the favor of augmenting the number of the inheritors of Henri IV. A transparency lights up at the refrain of each couplet and displays the features of the person to whom homage has just been paid. These pictures were received with unanimous applause. It is true that every spectator thought himself on the Fontainebleau road, and it was the same idea which caused one of our journals to remark that the piece of MM. Georges Duval and Rochefort would cause the public to take the road to the Odéon very often."

The Duchess of Berry was to make her formal entry into Paris on Sunday, June 16, 1816. It was the feast of Corpus Christi. It was raining so hard the previous evening that fears were entertained lest the solemnities of the following day should be spoiled. We have at hand a letter addressed to his wife by the Baron of Frémilly, peer of France, which has been communicated to us by his great-grandson, our friend the Marquis of Pimodan. It describes well the feeling of the moment: —

"SATURDAY EVENING, June 15.

"All Paris is in tears and fears [*dans les larmes et dans les alarmes*]. It rains! And the processions, the cortège, the illuminations, and the marvels of the royal faubourg! Do you know what the royal faubourg is? The Faubourg Saint-Antoine, which not knowing how else to wash off its original sin, has unbaptized itself. Madame de Damas, who has just come from there, was overjoyed by eight thousand workmen who have assessed themselves twenty sous a head in order to make porticos, garlands, cupids, doves, and a thousand other things which they are so secret about, that these good people spend all day in their workrooms and watch all night, in order that their whole fabric, of which there is not as yet a vestige to be seen, shall spring up at a whistle, and the King, who pays them the compliment of entering by their gate, shall have the first sight of it."

By eight o'clock in the morning of June 16, the Parisian National Guard was under arms. The inhabitants of all the streets through which the procession of the Blessed Sacrament was to pass, had adorned their houses with tapestries, hangings, branches, religious emblems, and devout pictures. Magnificent repositories had been arranged. That which had been prepared at the Luxembourg palace for the procession of Saint Sulpice overlooked the rue de Tournon and produced the most beautiful effect. At ten o'clock the processions began to move from all parts of the capital. At two, the twelve legions of the National Guard repaired to the posts assigned them. The troops formed a double line from the Barrier of the Throne as far as the Carrousel. The weather, which had been threatening in the morning, and rainy toward noon, became splendid at three o'clock. A good omen! cried the flatterers of the new Duchess. At four o'clock the cannon of Vincennes announced the coming of the royal family, and the procession which was to precede it formed at the Barrier of the Throne. In front marched the staff-officers of the place; then a detachment of National Guards from the adjacent departments, a regiment of dragoons, the Berry hussars, the staff-officers of the royal guard, commanded by the Marshal Duke of Reggio, the mounted National Guard, the first carriages of the cortège, the body-guards, the barouche of the King, who had the Duchess of Angoulême on his left, and the Duke and Duchess of Berry opposite; Monsieur, Count of Artois and the Duke of Angoulême rode beside the carriage doors. The mounted grenadiers of the guard, some detachments of gendarmes, and the court carriages closed the march.

A halt was made at the Barrier of the Throne, where the prefect of the Seine made a speech.

A numerous group of young girls, chosen from the twelve arrondissements of Paris, afterwards offered flowers to the new Duchess, and six of them sang one of Cherubini's cantatas. Then the cortège moved on, advancing with majestic slowness under a double arch of white flags adorned with royalist emblems, and greeted by the acclamations of an innumerable crowd filling the whole space which separates the end of the Faubourg Saint-Antoine from the palace of the Tuileries. As the King and his family were crossing the Faubourg Saint-Antoine, and just opposite the rue Saint Bernard, where the church of Saint Marguerite is situated, they met the Abbé Dubois, curé of that parish, accompanied by his clergy. The royal carriage having stopped, the curé presented holy water and incense. Then, having called the King's attention to the fact that all the houses of this faubourg of the common people were draped, he said: "Sire, these are not the tapestries of the Louvre, but they express the purest, sincerest love of the inhabitants of this quarter for Your Majesty and all the royal family."

Louis XVIII. replied: "Their homage is all the more affecting to me, and the people of the Faubourg Saint-Antoine could not have a better interpreter than you." The procession passed on to the boulevard of the Temple. In front of the Apollo café a rope had been stretched across the boulevard. At the moment of the King's passage, an acrobat, dressed as a warrior, sprang onto this rope, and dropped a crown on his head. The Gaîté, Ambigu, and Porte Saint Martin theatres had erected scaffoldings on which were groups of musicians playing *Vive Henri IV.* The further they advanced along the boulevards, the more fully they found them decorated with white flags and royalist emblems. The young Duchess was completely dazzled and surprised. The cortège entered the Tuileries at about half-past six through the Louvre gate. Louis XVIII. conducted the Duchess of Berry to the Pavilion of Marsan, where she was to spend the night, the Duke meanwhile repairing to the Elysée, the spouses not being allowed to dwell under the same roof before the religious marriage.

The next day M. Charles de Rémusat wrote his mother the following account of the entry of the Princess: "We were at the wedding, my dear mother; we were at the wedding, and you were not! Our Princess came to us yesterday. I will not recount to you all that you can read in the journals. The King was received with admirable enthusiasm at Fontainebleau and all along the road. The Grand Chamberlain (M. de Talleyrand) was in the carriage with him, and took the place of first gentleman; he took everything; which occasions a good deal of talk, I don't know why; it is etiquette. As for him, they say he was as charming as possible, laughing, amusing the King, telling a thousand stories, perfectly at ease, with nothing ministerial about him, and especially nothing to suggest a minister in disgrace. When the Princess threw herself at the King's feet, the King said to her: 'You are very good-looking!' Then he said to the Duke of Berry: 'Here is the wife God gives you.' He wrote to the Minister of Police: ' The Duke of Berry is in love with the Princess, and we are all of us his rivals.'— Yesterday, in the procession, he looked like a bridegroom; his face was serene; he was content, — more content, on my word, than his nephew. The Duchess looks very young; she is very white and very thin; whom do you think she is fearfully like, though on a small scale? Eh! on my honor, the eldest daughter of the Emperor of Austria! Those who have seen her in Provence and at Lyons say she squints, which would be unpleasant. But, so far, we have not noticed it at Paris. They say she is still younger in character than in age, and very intelligent and simple. The Duke of Berry sleeps to-night at our Elysée. To-morrow the marriage will take place before the altar and elsewhere."

To sum up, the formal entry of the young Duchess had passed off very well. The coincidence between the *Fête Dieu* and the royal fête had been fortunate. While the cannons were thundering in token of joy, and the bells were pealing their merriest, the chasubles of the priests, the young girls' white frocks, and the military uniforms presented a picturesque appearance. It was the double apotheosis of the altar and the throne. Incense had been burned to God and to the King.

IX

THE MARRIAGE

ON Sunday, June 17, 1816, Paris was *en fête* from early dawn. The marriage of the Duke and Duchess of Berry was to be celebrated that day at Notre Dame. In the morning, an article signed by M. Charles Nodier appeared in the *Debats*, in which it was said: —

"Yes, the Bourbons are still more our relatives than our masters, or rather, they reign over the French by an hereditary right which they have never used except to make us happy; and when they marry off their children, none but those who have abjured the name of Frenchmen or who have not the honor to bear it, can be indifferent to the cause of public joy. The rest share in their happiness as if it were a family festivity."

The sun rose in a cloudless sky. The weather was magnificent. At eight in the morning the battalions of the Parisian National Guard, the royal guard, and the departmental legions entered the open space in front of the metropolitan church, and then formed into double lines, reaching from Notre Dame Place as far as the Tuileries. In front of the cathedral there is a portico of sixteen columns surmounted by an amphitheatre which contained musicians and spectators. The interior of the church was brilliant. The lateral fasciæ of the nave were decorated with the interlaced monograms and escutcheons of the Duke and Duchess of Berry and those of France and Navarre, supported by angels boldly outlined above the pointed arches. Gilded escutcheons bearing the names of the good cities of the realm, adorned with captured spears, and surmounted by mural crowns and heralds' rods, were attached to the immense columns. The choir was superbly decorated. Around its circumference, on panels of Languedoc marble, fourteen medallions represented a series of allegorical subjects pertaining to the events of Louis XVIII.'s reign. On the capitals of the small columns supporting the galleries above the choir, were magnificent trophies, before each of which hung blue oriflammes adorned with pictures of various holy personages, among them the patron saints of the two spouses. In the choir were six angels in bronze on white marble pedestals; Louis XVIII.'s coat of arms was emblazoned on the base of the statues of Louis XIII. and Louis XIV.; a Christ nine feet high in silver-gilt rose from the steps of the altar. Savonnerie carpets covered the pavements of the choir and nave, and a profusion of lamp-stands, girandoles, and rock crystal chandeliers bearing numberless candles were distributed throughout the whole edifice.

The procession left the Tuileries at half-past eleven. One noticed in it the staff of the First Military Division, the staff of the National Guard, some detachments of the military household, and the royal guard. There were thirty-six carriages; twenty-four from the King's stables, and twelve from those of Monsieur. All the houses on the line of march were draped. At noon discharges of cannon, peals of bells, and the cheers of the crowd announced the arrival of the procession in front of Notre Dame. Abbé Jalabert, at the head of the metropolitan chapter, addressed Louis XVIII. at the entrance of the church. The King replied: "I am much affected by the sentiments of the chapter of Paris. It is to consecrate the happiness of my people that I have wished that a union so dear to my heart should be celebrated in the metropolitan church, under the invocation of the Mother of God, the august patroness of this church, and the protectress of France and my family."

The King then advanced processionally, under a canopy, as far as the choir. He wore a uniform heavily embroidered in gold; the Duke of Angoulême, that of a lord-high-admiral; Monsieur, the silver-embroidered uniform of a colonel-general of the National Guard; the Prince of Condé, the white uniform of a colonel-general of French infantry; and the Duke of Berry, the grand court-costume, a coat of cloth-of-gold, lace cravat, silk stockings, and mantle. The toilette of the Duchess was adorned with the finest of the crown jewels.

The royal family took their places in the choir. The King's chaplain-in-ordinary, Abbé de Villeneuve, said Mass. The Duke and Duchess of Berry went forward to the oblation after the celebrant had offered the paten to the sovereign to be kissed. A candle in which were fastened some gold pieces, whose number and value were prescribed by ancient usage, had been presented in the name of the two spouses. The Grand Almoner of France gave the nuptial benediction. The canopy was upheld by Mgr. de Latil, Bishop of Amiclée, Monsieur's first almoner, and by Abbé de Bombelles, first almoner to the Duchess of Berry. The four witnesses were Marshal Victor, Duke of Belluna, representing the army; Count Barthélemy, the Chamber of Peers; M. Bellart, the Chamber of Deputies; M. de Sèze, the Court of Cassation. The Grand Almoner delivered a discourse in which he celebrated the royal family, — "that family not alone grand beyond comparison, the most illustrious in the universe, but also the kindest and most paternal that ever was." He exclaimed enthusiastically: "Yes, Lord, this is truly the special work of Thy mercy, and an admiring silence alone befits our gratitude." After exhorting the bride to join the prudence of Rebecca to the amiability of Rachel, the goodness of Esther to the fidelity of Sara, he thus terminated his discourse: "Be thou blessed, O Princess, daughter of our Kings! A Frenchwoman by the blood flowing in your veins, and the sentiments it has transmitted, which to-day return to their source to be still further strengthened and perfected, it is in the name of all France, in the name of this brave and religious Prince, and of that heroic Princess in whose company you will find such virtuous examples, that we address to you the prophetic desires faithfully accomplished by the holy family: *Soror nostra es, crescas in mille millia.* You are of our nation, by your origin you belong to us, you are our sister; increase in a thousand ways; multiply the scions of a stem so dear to us; be fruitful in saints and heroes! May the princes to be born of you ever follow in the steps of their ancestors, triumph by courage and virtue over all their enemies, and forever assure the welfare of peoples and the glory of religion!"

The ceremony was over. Salvos of artillery announced the King's return to the palace at half-past three.

In the evening there was a royal game of cards in the Tuileries at seven o'clock, and a state dinner at night in the private theatre at nine. More than six hundred persons were in the gallery, where thirty card-tables were set. Louis XVIII. played with the Duchess of Angoulême, the Duchess of Berry, and several other ladies. M. d'Avaray had also the honor of being one of the King's party. The royal repast was afterwards served according to the ancient ceremonial. Only the royal princes and princesses sat down at the King's table; the princes of the blood were not admitted. The Duke of Bourbon, who as Grand Master of France should have presided at the feast, was replaced by the Grand Chamberlain, Prince Talleyrand.

The King was served by the Duke of Escars, first *maître d'hôtel*. When he desired to drink, his cup-bearer announced it in a loud voice. Behind his armchair stood the Grand Almoner, the Grand Chamberlain, and other persons entitled to do so by their places at court. Everybody remained standing, except the duchesses, who were supplied with stools. Towards the end of the repast the King's musicians executed several pieces and cantatas composed for the occasion, and the diplomatic body passed before the King, who addressed some remarks to nearly all the representatives of the Powers, especially to the Duke of Wellington.

At ten o'clock the King left the table. People thought he was fatigued. Not at all. At half-past ten he called for a carriage. He proposed to accompany the wedded pair to the Elysée palace and then return to the Tuileries by the Champs-Elysées, to see the illuminations, which were splendid. The principal architectural lines of the Tuileries were defined by bands of light. The Temple of Hymen in the garden was much admired. Transparencies representing the arms of France upborne by genii with garlands of olive and lily crowned the pediments of the façade. Forty-four columns covered with lanterns and linked together by bands of flame gave to this radiant monument the aspect of a temple built by fairies.

X

THE EARLY DAYS OF MARRIAGE

THE impression produced by the young Princess was excellent. From the day of her entrance into Paris, her white robe, the clustering white feathers of her head-dress, her skin, fair as her robe, her infantine and pleasing face, the mingled grace and dignity of her bearing, had excited admiration. Baron de Frémilly wrote concerning her: "Taken all together, she is very agreeable, and seems all the more so because we had been told that she was ugly, which she certainly is not." People thought her wonderfully well dressed at the ceremony at Notre Dame, and full of modesty and charm. Baron de Frémilly wrote again: "As to the little Duchess, all Paris is as much in love with her as her husband is, which is no small thing to say. She has health, gaiety, wit, grace, and candor."

The first days of marriage were spent amidst continual festivities. The court was full of jollity, and every good courtier was bound to seem enchanted.

June 18. — The newly wedded pair, who had installed themselves at the Elysée the day before, breakfasted at the Tuileries with the King, the Count of Artois, and the Duke and Duchess of Angoulême. The diplomatic bodies were presented when Mass was over, and the Duchess of Berry afterwards received fifty young girls dressed in white, who offered her, on behalf of the Twelfth Arrondissement (the Faubourg Saint-Marceau), a large basket of flowers in the midst of which were two turtle-doves softly bedded in roses, pansies, and immortelles. At three o'clock the husband and wife returned to the Elysée, to go from there to Saint Cloud. The carelessness of the coachman caused an accident which, happily, had no ill consequences. In passing through the gate of the rue de l'Echelle, the carriage struck violently against a post, and the wheel broke, but neither the Duke nor the Duchess received any injury. They dined at Saint Cloud with the royal family, the table being laid for forty persons. The principal officers of the Crown, Marshal Macdonald, the captains of the guards, the chief nobility, and several ladies and gentlemen of the court were admitted to the King's table. The Duke and Duchess drove around the park in an open carriage, saw the great waterworks in play, and returned in the evening to the Elysée.

June 19. — M. Charles de Rémusat wrote to his mother: "Our marriage is concluded, and when once this evening's ball and to-morrow's review are over, no one will think any more about it. Everybody is greatly pleased. The festivities have been less boisterous than gay. The people displayed a good will and subdued joy which were in very good taste, and a hundred times preferable to convulsive enthusiasm." The ball at the Tuileries was magnificent. It took place in the private theatre, which was lighted up by eighteen large chandeliers. All the columns were hung with garlands. A circle of richly dressed ladies filled the first seats of the three tiers of boxes. The Duke of Angoulême opened the ball with the Duchess of Berry.

June 20. — A review on the Champ-de-Mars. Benediction and distribution of flags to the royal guard. The King, in the uniform of a colonel-general of the guard, left the palace of the Tuileries at 12.30, having the Duchesses of Angoulême and Berry with him in his open carriage. Monsieur the Count of Artois and his two sons accompanied the carriage on horseback. On arriving at the Champ-de-Mars, Louis XVIII. was greeted by Marshal Macdonald, Duke of Tarento, major-general of the guard. He passed the troops in review and then sat down on his throne. The colonels advanced one by one. Marshal Clarke, Duke of Feltre and Minister of War, presented the flags to the sovereign, who, aided by his brother, inclined the head of the staff first to the Duchess of Angoulême and then to the Duchess of Berry. The two Princesses successively attached the tassels to the flags and standards, which were then given back by Louis XVIII. to the colonels, who, escorted by picked companies from all the regiments, repaired to the altar that had been erected in the Champ-de-Mars. The Grand Almoner of France there blessed the flags and standards amidst salvos of artillery from the royal guards, pronouncing afterwards an address in which he said: —

"Gentlemen, it is not enough for the royal guard to be the first to set the whole army an example of all warlike virtues; they ought also to be the model of the virtues of religion. A soldier of the royal guard should be a Christian soldier, not less solicitous to serve God than to serve his King; as exact in fulfilling the essential obligations of religion as in obedience to the orders of his chiefs; seeking to save his soul as well as to perform his military duties, he should be convinced that piety in camps, far from being a defect liable to weaken souls, reassures them, on the contrary, and makes them strong."

When the review was over, the King caused Marshal Macdonald to approach, and said to him: —

"Marshal, tell my royal guard how pleased I am with the order, perfect discipline, and excellent spirit I have observed in all the regiments. Add that I feel certain they will defend unto death the flags they have just received from their father and their King. Tell them, moreover, that like the knights of old, they should remember the hands that fastened on their tassels."

In returning from the Champ-de-Mars the crowd halted on the Place Louis XV. to witness a balloon ascension. Mademoiselle Garnerin went up in a basket of flowers which served her as a car. While the balloon was rising, the young aëronaut saluted the palace of the Tuileries by waving a white flag emblazoned with lilies, and by scattering among the multitude couplets and verses celebrating the marriage of the Duke and Duchess of Berry.

On the same day (June 20), the municipality of Paris came to the Elysée to congratulate the married pair, and, in conformity with an ancient custom, to offer them the gifts of the city, consisting of perfumed torches of white wax, and dried fruits. "Monseigneur, Madame," said the prefect of the Seine, "the municipality of Paris, in presenting its respectful felicitations to Your Royal Highnesses, comes to offer you the same presents which our fathers offered to your ancestors. This modest homage, consecrated by the ancient usage of the monarchy, attests the simplicity and moderation of our august masters. We have preserved its character with religious respect, assured that the offering which comes from the heart is the only one that would be worthy of you and that could be accepted."

June 21. — Gala representation at the Opera: *Les Dieux rivaux, ou la Fête de Cythère*, an operatic ballet in one act, a singular mixture of mythology and royalism.

June 22. — The Duke of Berry gave the royal family a fête and a dinner at Bagatelle. During the day there was hunting in the Bois de Boulogne.

June 23. — Theatricals at the court. The opera troupe played the *Caravane*.

While these festivities were in progress, the more or less sincere enthusiasm of the official world was displayed in speeches and addresses which renewed, almost word for word, the wishes, the homage, and the predictions promising the advent of the golden age in France, which had been used six years before at the marriage of Napoleon and Marie Louise. Nevertheless, there were many dark clouds in this apparently serene sky. The government was carrying out a revengeful system. Throughout the kingdom the assize and provost courts and the councils of war were pronouncing sentences of death. The pardons granted on account of the marriage of the Duke of Berry extended to none of those condemned for political offences. As has been remarked by a royalist historian, M. Alfred Nettement, the public mind remained disunited and uneasy, passions were inflamed, parties irreconcilable, and the festivities, like fire-works set off in darkness, only lighted up the shadows of the situation for a moment, without causing them to disappear.

XI

THE TUILERIES

THE Duchess of Berry was not sorry not to live in the Tuileries palace, a gloomy abode in spite of its éclat, where many intrigues, jealousies, and rivalries were concealed under an appearance of inflexible discipline and absolute tranquillity. The royal family, so united according to official reports, was in reality divided against itself. Two opposite systems confronted each other, and Louis XVIII. was the constant object of criticisms, all the keener because they were obliged to remain secret. Between the King and his brother there existed a latent rivalry, dating back to the old régime, and daily becoming too prominent for any shrewd observer to fail to notice it. If the Duchess of Berry had lived much longer with them, she would have found it difficult to satisfy both her uncle and her father-in-law.

Louis XVIII. had long been tormented with a gouty tendency which frequently endangered his life. The ambitious fancied that in rallying to the party of which the heir to the throne was the secret head, they were playing a skilful game and opening the ways to fortune in the near future. Kept informed of all that was going on by his favorite, Count Decazes, Minister of Police, the King was not ignorant of the offensive speeches the royalists made about him, nor of the joy they manifested whenever disquieting rumors got about concerning the state of his health. He was profoundly embittered by all this, and had as little confidence in his own family as in the set around him.

Such a situation imposed extreme reserve on the attitude and language of the courtiers. Their antecedents were too widely diverse to permit their talking politics together. All conversation of that sort would necessarily have contained wounding allusions. Even praise was dangerous. To laud Louis XVIII., the King of to-day, was implicitly to condemn Monsieur, the King of to-morrow. Criticism was more difficult still. For some time it had been good form to insult *Buonaparte*. But this fashion could not last. What family, in fact, had been unrepresented in the ranks of the imperial army? how many great lords and ladies had held no place in the Emperor's household or those of the Empresses? Napoleon was no longer insulted at court; a pretence of forgetfulness was made, but at every instant some importunate souvenir of him sprang to life.

In bringing men of the most widely diverse parties around him, Louis XVIII. had required them to respect each other. Any allusion to former disputes would have been severely repressed. Political quarrels, so heated elsewhere, were extinguished on the threshold of the Tuileries, where reigned those ancient traditions of politeness, so long the boast of French society. When they met in small parties away from the palace, the *émigrés* and ultras gave way to their customary wranglings, but their behavior at the Tuileries was always irreproachable. Though a man might cordially hate M. Decazes, yet he was respectful to him, because M. Decazes was the minister of the King.

As an epoch of transition and amalgamation between the most widely diverse elements, the Restoration is assuredly one of the most singular periods in history. Two rival worlds encounter each other here: the last glimmer of the old régime and the dawn of the parliamentary system; the fusion between French ideas and English manners; the conflict between religious minds and the Voltairians, between the partisans of throne and altar and the revolutionists; between the white flag and the tricolor. From the social, political, and literary point of view, never had there been such a brilliant shower of sparks produced by the concussion of beliefs, opinions, principles, and ideas. But such debates were impossible at court, where the soldiers of Condé's army lived in perfect harmony with the volunteer republicans of 1792. The promotion of the marshals of France, which took place on the occasion of the Duke of Berry's marriage, contained four titularies: two *émigrés*, — the Duke of

Coigny and the Count Vioménil, and two soldiers of the Revolution and the Empire, — Bournonville and Clarke, each of whom had been Minister of War, one during the Terror, and the other during the last days of Napoleon's reign.

Among those of the old régime who presented themselves at court a mingled feeling of satisfaction and of bitterness prevailed. They were glad to have recovered their houses and castles, their titles and honors. Past catastrophes gave a special savor to the moral and material well-being they enjoyed after so many trials. It pleased them to have been proved in the right against both republicans and imperialists. They said to themselves: I saw how it would be. My predictions are fulfilled. The usurper is at Saint Helena. The regicides are in exile. The old aristocracy has risen to life again although its enemies believed it dead. The Faubourg Saint-Germain sets the fashion. Bonaparte's quondam generals are very proud of being chamberlains or chief equerries of the King. The marshals think more of the blue ribbon of the order of the Holy Ghost than of the red ribbon of the Legion of Honor. The former officers of the imperial guard aspire after the cross of Saint Louis.

But the joy of the royalists was not unmixed. They found their triumph incomplete. It was quite another sort of Restoration that they had imagined. Louis XVIII. was not a king according to their own hearts. They would have accused him of Bonapartism and Jacobinism if they had dared. They thought him ungrateful toward the *émigrés* and the Vendéans. While the five children of Cathelineau, the commander-in-chief of the Vendéan army, vegetated in poverty, Robespierre's sister received an annual pension of six thousand francs. The government did not even pay the expenses of the last campaign in Vendée, that of 1815, which had, nevertheless, been undertaken only by the King's command, and they had to be met by the officers. And yet at the same time, the arrears due for the expenses of the Republic and the Empire, and even those of the Hundred Days, were paid without examination. To the *émigrés* a government which did not restore national property to its former owners was simply a continuation of the Revolution. The most discontented of all were perhaps Louis XVIII.'s companions in exile, the courtiers of Mittau and Hartwell, who, having been present in time of trial thought they had a right to form part of the triumph. These could not console themselves for the preferment of a Pasquier, a Mounier, a Portalis, a Siméon, a Decazes. The favors heaped by the King upon Napoleon's favorites seemed to them an insult to monarchy, a blow aimed at royalty by the King himself. They could hardly conceal their exasperation under an enforced politeness. When, on September 5, 1816, Louis XVIII. issued his celebrated decree dissolving the Chamber of Deputies, described as the undiscoverable chamber, the fury of the ultras knew no bounds. They were obliged to put an almost superhuman pressure on themselves to prevent its exploding in the palace itself.

It was said that no one but Queen Hortense, his former friend, could have inspired M. Decazes with a measure so fatal to royalty. A story was told of one noble lady whose indignation was so great that she ordered her chambermaid to take the bust of Louis XVIII. from the salon to the garret, using the most slighting expressions concerning him as she did so. As soon as he learned that the famous decree which excited such anger had been signed, Chateaubriand added the following postscript to his just finished work, *La Monarchie selon la Charte:* " Good Frenchmen must not lose courage, but crowd to the elections; only, let them beware of a trap very difficult for us to avoid. People will talk to them of the King and his will. French hearts will be moved, tears will start; when they hear the King's name they will take off their hats and accept the ballot offered by a hostile hand, and deposit it in the urn. Suspect the snare; save the King in any case!"

While the ultras maintained that Louis XVIII., a prisoner in his own palace, was delivered up to the tyranny of his ministers, the sovereign considered himself perfectly free at the Tuileries, and derided the fury of the extreme monarchists. After the elections, Chateaubriand wrote in a rage: "Bonaparte made use of revolutionists while despising them; now, people want to use and honor them.

The royalists are in consternation at this. Could they have believed that apostles of legitimacy would be sought among such agents? Could they possibly understand such an inversion of ideas? The Jacobins have issued from their dens, uttering howls of joy that have been heard by their brethren throughout Europe; they have presented themselves at the elections full of surprise at having been called thither, and astonished to see themselves caressed as the real upholders of monarchy."

The Duchess of Berry took good care not to mingle in these quarrels, and whenever she repaired to the Tuileries, bringing joy and gaiety with her, she avoided speaking of politics, not only with the King and the princes, but with the ministers and courtiers.

XII

THE ÉLYSÉE

THE residence of the Duke and Duchess of Berry was the Elysée. This pleasant palace, so well situated, elegant, and agreeable, was called the Elysée-Bourbon at the time, in memory of the Duchess of Bourbon, who had owned it toward the close of the eighteenth century. It was suggestive of many reflections upon the vicissitudes of human affairs. Built by the Count of Evreux in 1718, inhabited several days by Madame de Pompadour, sold in 1773 to Beaujon the financier, bought by the Duchess of Bourbon in 1780, it became national property during the Revolution, and was let to some contractors for public fêtes, who transformed it into ballrooms and gambling saloons, and called it the Elysée. Murat acquired possession of it in 1803, and relinquished it to Napoleon in 1808. It was then occupied by the Empress Josephine for some time after the divorce, and Napoleon spent part of the Hundred Days there. It was from there he started, at first for Waterloo, afterwards to Saint Helena. It was from there also that the Duke of Berry departed before falling under the poniard of an assassin. But no fatal presentiment clouded the Prince's mind in 1816. All things wore a smiling aspect for him, and he enjoyed his happiness in peace.

Born at Versailles, January 24, 1778, the Duke of Berry was thirty-eight years old at the time of his marriage. But his gait, his manners, and his tastes were those of a young man. Chateaubriand has drawn this portrait of him, like, though possibly a trifle flattered: —

"His head, like that of the chief of the Capets, was large, with tangled hair, a broad forehead, a ruddy face, staring blue eyes, and thick red lips. His neck was short, and his shoulders rather high, like those of all great military families. The breast wherein his heart beat without suspicion or fear afforded plenty of room for the poniard. Mgr. the Duke of Berry was of medium stature, like Louis XIV. He looked brave, and the expression of his face was candid and clever. His gait was active, his action prompt, his glance steady, intelligent, and kindly, and his smile charming. He expressed himself with elegance in ordinary conversation, with clearness when discussing public affairs, and with eloquence when moved by passion. One saw in him the prince, the soldier, the man who had suffered, and felt drawn toward him by the mingled bluntness and good grace pervading his whole person."

The Duke of Berry appreciated his happiness all the more because his youth had been so full of trials and difficulties. Exiled from France in 1789, at the age of eleven, he did not see his native land again until 1814. He was barely sixteen when he enlisted as a volunteer in Condé's army, and he won every advancement in rank at the sword's point. He was bent on being present in the least skirmish as well as in battles, and when reminded that he might be wounded, exclaimed: "So much the better; that will do honor to the family." He wrote to a woman: "War is about to begin. The princes will be in it. For the honor of the corps, it is to be hoped that some of us may be killed." Among his comrades in arms he gained a great reputation for frankness and loyalty, boldness and courage. He preferred camp life to any other. When he was not fighting he was travelling all over Europe, where he knew the principal languages. In 1800 he visited Naples and Rome, took up the study of painting and music, and learned to play several instruments. He sang well and drew fairly, especially military subjects; he understood pictures thoroughly. He was a gentleman, a soldier, and an artist.

Great resemblances in character existed between the married pair; they had the same frankness, enthusiasm, and gaiety, the same love for the arts, and the same thirst for pleasure. The Duke became attached at once to his young companion. Neither pretty nor ugly, she had the charm and sprightliness of youth, fair curly hair, a keen glance, a fine expression, a slender figure, and a graceful walk. Her nature was impulsive, her conversation amusing and sometimes girlish, her mind free from prejudices, her devotion pleasing and in nowise austere, her animation southern, and, so to say, sunbeaten. She never gave the slightest occasion for calumny or detraction throughout her married life. A faithful wife, she and her husband lived most happily together. Both the court and the city rendered her justice. All was innocent in her passion for pleasure. People liked and respected her.

How well M. de Pontmartin has described this woman, Italian by birth, education, and instinct, who became a Frenchwoman at seventeen; "this flower of Ischia and Castellamare, transplanted to the shores of the Seine, under the gray sky of Paris, in that palace of the Tuileries which the revolutions had peopled with so many phantoms before converting it also into a spectre"! How well the eminent critic sums up in a few words the rôle of the bride in that court dominated by the note of gravity, overshadowed by clouds of sadness, where the ceremonial of the old régime reappeared, bristling with the constraints of etiquette. "She represents the future, youth, joy, smiles, radiance and the dawn in the royal family which welcomes her as daughter by adoption and the harbinger of its approaching destinies; just as the Duchess of Angoulême personifies the past, majesty, sanctity, tradition, the immortal melancholy of a soul which seems to live on the steps of a throne, but which exists only by and through the souvenirs of the Temple and the visions of heaven. The contrast is striking. Charming women, elegant patricians, group themselves around Marie Caroline who might, without flattery, be called a charmingly plain woman. Her blunt and good-natured husband lends himself all the more readily to her taste for pleasure because he shares it, and possibly grants much in order to be excused something. They dance and amuse themselves, they promenade, frequent the theatres, protect artists, visit studios, buy pictures, run the risks of the Opera ball, and the young Princess is never happier than when she can remember that she is young, and forget that she is a princess."

The little court of the Elysée bore no resemblance to the solemn and severe court of the Tuileries. The heavy yoke of etiquette weighed but lightly on the new-married pair, who enjoyed the simplicity of an almost *bourgeois* existence. They often went out together on foot and unattended, through the gate opening on the Champs-Elysées, and going down the avenue mingled with the promenaders, who recognized and saluted them with respectful sympathy. People met them in the shops, where they did a good deal of buying, and paid very dear for all they bought. Their alms amounted to more than a hundred thousand crowns a year, and they often went in person to visit the poor whom they assisted. The military bluntness of the Duke combined great simplicity and real goodness, and was not unpleasing, especially to people in humble circumstances, who always like to have princes on familiar terms with them. As to the Duchess, she was grace and attractiveness itself in her relations with persons of all social ranks whatever. The pair took part in all the agreeable incidents of Parisian life, in festivities and first representations; they went to the minor theatres, they visited the studios of the principal artists, who recognized a connoisseur in the Duke at a glance. The Duchess painted, and the Duke spent hours in painting beside her. This life so tranquil and well occupied by the arts and beneficence made them both popular. The young wife conciliated everybody. She pleased the King, Monsieur, and the austere Duchess of Angoulême. In a time of pamphlets and violent animosities she was respected by all parties without exception. She lived on good terms with the ultras and also with M. Decazes. Making no distinctions between the *émigrés* and the quondam Bonapartists so far as her own amiability was concerned, she meddled with none of the court intrigues. The fury of the Faubourg Saint-Germain at the time of the dissolution of the "undiscoverable chamber" left her indifferent. Domestic happiness sufficed her for all things. This woman, destined to endure so many trials and to pass through so many vicissitudes and catastrophes, did not even suspect the snares of every kind which already surrounded her, and, satisfied with the present, she looked forward to the future with all the confident illusions of youth.

XIII

THE FIRST SORROW

HAPPY as she was at the beginning of her married life, the Duchess of Berry soon beheld her joy troubled by a first sorrow, the forerunner of the deceptions and griefs fate held in store for her. In the *Quotidienne* we read: —

"To-day is the 17th of June, the anniversary of the marriage of the Duke and Duchess of Berry. We recall the joy testified by all France to the King and the royal family on that occasion. Since Heaven has blessed the union by deigning to promise a new scion from this august stem, the satisfaction of France is greater still, and it awaits with confidence the happy moment which shall crown it. Gentle, good, lively, and truly French, the young Princess wins the respect, affection, and gratitude of all who have the honor to approach her. The attachment felt for her by her illustrious spouse, the sentiments entertained by the King, so good a judge of merit, the paternal love whose proofs are lavished on her by Monsieur, the applause which greets her wherever she appears, all prove how worthy she is to be cherished; and if she were not so modest she would be proud of her success. May the pious and faithful subjects of the King obtain from Providence a new successor to the throne of the Bourbons, — those Bourbons who in all times have been distinguished by their affability, goodness, and beneficence."

Royalist France was in expectation. The *Moniteur* of July 11, 1817, said: —

"Every arrangement has been made for informing the King so that His Majesty may at once repair to the Elysée-Bourbon, as well as Their Royal Highnesses and others whose rank or duty may invite their presence. The happy event so impatiently awaited will be announced by a salvo of artillery. Twenty-four guns will be fired if a prince is born, and twelve if it be a princess."

Madame de Rémusat had written to her husband on July 7: "The Duchess of Berry is near her time, and we are all expecting the birth from one minute to another. It would be good if it came to-morrow, for the anniversary of the second entry of the King. They have had the politeness to exhibit Gérard's fine and much-expected picture, *la Rentrée d'Henri IV. dans Paris*, for that day. The allusion is in good taste." Again, on July 10: "Here all ears are cocked to hear the cannon which are to announce the delivery of Madame the Duchess of Berry. She has been suffering a little for two days, and we are expecting the little prince. The King's carriage is harnessed up night and day, and the court and the ministers have been warned to be in readiness; for it seems they desire that the delivery should take place in presence of a numerous assemblage. Madame de Montsoreau has been appointed governess. The King looked very well indeed last Wednesday. It was splendid weather. All Paris was out on the boulevard, crying, 'Long live the King!' I remarked that nobody cheered on the terrace of the Hôtel de Gontaut, where we had so many great ladies. The King did not seem at all affected by it."

On Sunday, July 13, 1817, at twenty-five minutes past eleven in the morning, at the Elysée-Bourbon palace, the Duchess of Berry brought a daughter into the world, whose certificate of birth designated her as the "very high and powerful Princess Louise Isabelle of Artois, Mademoiselle, granddaughter of France." Those present at her birth were the King, Monsieur, the Duchess of Angoulême, the Duke of Angoulême, the Duke of Berry, Mademoiselle of Orleans, the Duke of Orleans, the Duchess of Bourbon, the dowager Duchess of Orleans, the Prince of Condé, the Duke of Uzés, the Duke of Richelieu, the Count of Pradel, the Marquis of Brézé, the Duke of Luynes, Chancellor Dambray, and the Count of Sémonville. In the evening the theatres, in token of joy, gave pieces composed for the occasion, full of enthusiasm and monarchical protestations.

Madame de Rémusat wrote to her husband the next day: "I must stop everything else to tell you that Madame the Duchess of Berry was brought to bed yesterday morning with a daughter. The whole royal family were not only present at the delivery, but remained in the chamber itself, and the chancellor, the ministers, and high personages of the court were very near at hand. When it was over, the King went into the salon where his ministers were, and said to them: 'Gentlemen, they (*elles*) are both doing well.' Twelve guns were fired.

"Everybody began to count; then they said: 'It is a daughter,' and picked up the thread of their discourse. The little Princess will be called Mademoiselle; she was held at the baptismal font by the King and his aunt, the Duchess of Orleans. Last night the houses were illuminated."

Unfortunately, the very high and powerful Princess, as she was called in the birth certificate, died almost immediately. The *Moniteur* of July 16 said: —

"PARIS, July 15.

"The happy deliverance of Madame the Duchess of Berry gladdened all hearts; every one shared in the joy of the royal family. Imagination, looking into the future, took pleasure in embellishing the life of the august infant whom Heaven had given to France; some day she would have all the graces and virtues of her mother. This earliest pledge of fecundity opened our hearts to newer hopes; nor are these hopes torn from us; we do not doubt their realization. But was it necessary that sorrow and mourning should so soon replace delight? Mademoiselle is no more. . . . She lived only two days.

Last evening we were apprised of the loss we had just suffered. The Princess died between eight and nine o'clock. The royal family are plunged in sadness. We have shared their joy; we weep with them. Nothing can equal the grief of Mgr. the Duke of Berry. If anything can lessen the pain caused by this cruel event, it is the certainty that the health of the Duchess of Berry occasions not the least uneasiness."

Madame de Rémusat wrote, July 15: "Here is a misfortune, my friend; the poor little Princess died yesterday morning; she was choked by something, I don't know what, and in a convulsion. They say the King is greatly afflicted, and he has reason to be; for although this loss may be easily repaired, yet it will have a bad popular effect which one would be glad to get over. . . . I don't like, either, this rain which begins with the moon and falls on the cut rye. I am rather blue this morning."

At nine o'clock, July 16, the King went to the Elysée and spent an hour with the Duke of Berry.

"The sorrow of the Prince," said the *Moniteur*, "was somewhat lessened by the monarch's paternal consolations; they solaced their hearts by blending their tears. Let them not ignore the public affliction. It is the guarantee of the love and gratitude we bear the royal family. May these sentiments contribute to calm the sorrow of the august spouses, and may a prospering Heaven cause long years of happiness to succeed these days of sadness!"

Madame de Rémusat wrote the same day to her husband, then prefect of Lille: —

"Paris, Wednesday Evening, July 16, 1817.

"The King has put a good face on the death of the Princess. Monsieur is profoundly afflicted, and the Duke of Berry is perfect to his young wife, who weeps bitterly. The Duke of Orleans has offered condolences to Monsieur, who answered him in an obliging tone: 'If we needed princes, we should know where to find them.' Popular gossip was unpleasant and was kept up for eight hours; afterwards, nobody thought anything more about it. Rumor says Madame the Duchess of Berry can have no more children; I hope she will soon give the lie to that; the Orleans are talked about a little more. All this will quiet down. The rye is coming up again; they say it is doing well and that it fell too quickly. It would have been bad if the rain had lasted; but the weather is fine to-day and the barometers are rising."

At the same moment the mortal remains of the little Princess were being transported to Saint Denis. She had been put in a coffin covered with white satin, on which was a red plaque bearing this inscription: "Here is the body of the very high and very powerful Princess Louise Isabelle of Artois, Mademoiselle, granddaughter of France, daughter of the very high and very powerful Prince Charles Ferdinand of Artois, Duke of Berry, and of the very high and very powerful Princess Caroline Ferdinande Louise, Princess of the Two Sicilies, died at Paris, in the Elysée-Bourbon palace, July 14, 1817, aged one day."

The coffin was exposed during the day, July 16, in a hall of the Elysée, on a platform decorated with white draperies studded with escutcheons. At nine in the evening it was placed in the carriage destined to transport it to Saint Denis. It was accompanied by the Count of Rochemore, master of ceremonies, the chief officers of the household, and all persons in the service of the Prince and Princess. The bells tolled when the convoy reached the abbey, the necropolis of the Kings of France. The royal guard formed a line on the right, and the National Guard of Saint Denis on the left. The Marquis of Dreux-Brézé, grand master of ceremonies, came to receive the body at the principal door of the church. The Duchess of Lévis and the Viscountess de Gontaut carried the corners of the pall. The entire interior of the nave and choir was hung with white draperies, sprinkled with lilies and the royal arms. The Abbé Bombelles, first almoner to the Duchess of Berry, said to the dean and canons of Saint Denis: "Gentlemen, on presenting, by the King's express command, S. A. R. Mademoiselle, in order to conduct her beneath these sacred arches to the last abode of the kings her ancestors, we will say with the Preacher: —

"She appeared like the bow which shines in a luminous sky, and like the rose that buds in springtime. But a few days have elapsed since this rose was born in the midst of all that is greatest on earth; by her beauty and freshness she promised all that could assure her preservation. Alas! in less than twelve hours she passed from the most perfect life into sufferings which hastened her death. Such an unexpected end rends the authors of her being with grief and overwhelms us with sadness. We share also the consolations imparted to a cherished race by the religion that penetrates them. Mademoiselle, regenerated in the waters of baptism, and never soiled by any imperfection, is henceforward the angel of the country, an angel who, reunited in heaven to the saints of her family, will draw upon them and us the blessings of the Lord."

The Duchess (then Viscountess) of Gontaut has written in her Memoirs: "I was appointed to accompany the convoy of the little Princess. It took place at midnight, escorted by body-guards carrying torches. The church was solitary and the royal vault open. This young scion of the royal race was laid at the foot of Louis XVI.'s tomb. A profound night, a pious silence interrupted only by the sound of footsteps and of weapons, saddened the heart. At her waking, Madame the Duchess of Angoulême summoned me, wishing to know the details of this sorrowful night. I said I had prayed near the coffin which contained the precious remains of the Martyr King; she took my hand, pressed it to her heart, and wept; I was profoundly affected."

In his powerful and judicious *Histoire de la Restauration*, Baron de Viel-Castel says concerning the death we have just narrated: —

"The royal infant, Mademoiselle, as she was called, had solemn obsequies at Saint Denis, and a court abbé pronounced even on this occasion a sort of funeral oration, in which, not being able to bestow other praises, he vaunted her beauty and freshness. The *Moniteur* deplored in emphatic terms a grief which could not have been felt very keenly by any but the Duchess of Berry. Even a poet was found to celebrate her death as if it had been a public calamity. These dull flatteries are part of the littlenesses inherent in all courts."

For once our sentiment is not wholly in accord with that of the eminent historian. Whether the mother be a princess or a woman of the people, the loss of a new-born child is a grief, a disappointment, a despair fitted to inspire profound compassion. France was in the right when it grew tender over the first sorrow of the amiable Duchess of Berry. The griefs of princesses are symbolic of those of other women. How many poor mothers, when they read the *Moniteur*, said to themselves: "And I too have suffered thus."

XIV

1818

THE Duchess of Berry possessed great elasticity of character and a fund of southern gaiety which quickly sprang up again, even after the most painful trials. Her gracious and amiable nature was not made for sad reflections and sombre meditations. Storms affected her keenly, but the rainbow soon came to brighten her heart and mind. August 6, 1817, for the first time after childbed, she walked out in the Elysée gardens, leaning on her husband's arm. On the 26th of the same month, a performance given at the Opera in aid of the pension fund was honored by her presence. The 31st, she went to Suresnes in a carriage drawn by eight horses, where the clergy formally received her, and where she crowned the *rosière*[1] in the village church. October 7 she visited the Sèvres manufactory, the 14th the Savonnerie carpet manufactory, the Gobelin manufactory on the 31st, and the Mint on November 14.

At the beginning of 1818 the young Princess, then more than ever esteemed by the court and the

---

[1] A young girl who has obtained a prize for virtuous conduct.

city, seemed happy and consoled. Her extreme kindliness made friends for her in all quarters. Her conversation, always agreeable and never affected, had charm and animation. Both in face and character, in ideas and impressions, she was very young. People found her simple, affable, and natural, and they liked to see her enjoy life and pleasure, and, in a word, full of the spirit natural to her youth. All those who formed part of her circle were sincerely devoted to her. One of her ladies-in-waiting, the Viscountess of Gontaut, became her lady of the bedchamber toward the middle of 1818. The position, which had at first been filled by the Countess of La Ferronnays, had been vacant for a year. The Duke of Berry wrote to Madame de Gontaut, whose daughter had married the Count of Bourbon-Busset: —

"I am delighted that Charlotte has become my cousin." (There was a very distant but perfectly authentic tie of kinship between the Bourbon-Bussets and the royal family.) "As to you, dear and excellent friend, you shall not be left alone. Come and live with us; we offer you the position of lady of the bedchamber. You will have your apartments in the Elysée. My wife is impatiently awaiting your reply. Come and give it to us yourself."

The Viscountess of Gontaut hastened at once to the Duke and Duchess. "I was filled with tender emotions," she says in her unpublished Memoirs. "They noticed this and were pleased by it. How is it possible not to love and devote one's self to princes who are worthy? They took delight in showing me the apartment intended for me, over that of the Duchess. The view across the Champs-Elysées was superb and gay. The rooms had been occupied by the King of Rome, and were full of traces of the care bestowed on his infancy: the panels were padded as high as the head of a child six or seven years old, and the entire apartment was hung with green silk, still beautiful and fresh, so as to preserve his eyes. The study of this human foresight, brought to nothing by the Supreme Will, made us thoughtful, and for an instant saddened even our Princess."

But the sunny Italian nature of the Duchess of Berry soon chased away all gloomy presentiments.

"Come," said she to her lady of the bedchamber, "let us think gayly of the future; I am happy, and I want to enjoy my happiness. Your quarters are spacious and charming; you have three salons; you can give balls which will be a hundred times more amusing than ours, for you have no such obligations as we have. Come, it is a promise, isn't it? You will give some balls?"

The Viscountess was about to reply, when the Duke of Berry remarked sadly: —

"Caroline, you think of nothing but amusing yourself."

"And why not?" returned the Princess. "I am so young."

Then, stamping, but smiling all the while, she closed the Duke's mouth with her pretty hand.

"Above all," added she, "don't talk to me any more about being a widow; it is the current jest, but I find it insupportable."

The Duke smiled in a melancholy way.

"I was wrong," said he, "but it is a fixed idea of mine; for some time past I have been thinking of your widowhood."

"A singular pleasantry!" returned the Princess, and taking her lady of the bedchamber by the arm she drew her out of the apartment.

Some time afterwards, the Duke, being alone in his study, had Madame de Gontaut summoned thither. "Look here," said he, "I am sure that this paper is poisoned. Don't touch it; when I opened it, I experienced a horrible sensation. The letter amounts to nothing and can give no clue; it is an appeal for aid, unsigned and not addressed." The Viscountess begged him to warn the police. He charged her to keep the thing secret, fearing to cause his wife anxiety. One might say he had a premonition of Louvel, who had been meditating and preparing his crime for more than four years.

Sadness passed quickly and enjoyment returned. The Duchess had had the good fortune to keep near her the friend of her childhood, Suzette de La Tour, the daughter of her former governess and the Count of La Tour, lieutenant-general and aide-de-camp of the King of Naples. This charming young girl of seventeen married the Count of Meffray in the Elysée chapel, and was soon afterwards appointed lady-in-waiting to the Duchess of Berry.

"Consider her, young women," said Madame de Gontaut of the Countess of Meffray; "amiable, witty, and pretty, surrounded and admired, yet slander cannot touch her."

During the summer the Duke and Duchess often dined *tête-à-tête* in the Elysée garden. Sometimes, when they knew that Madame de Gontaut was alone, they invited her. "Nothing could be more agreeable, pleasanter, and I may even say more friendly," she adds, "than these dinners *à trois*."

At the end of July, the Duchess of Berry went to Rambouillet with the royal family. We read in the *Moniteur*: —

"The little town of Rambouillet cannot contain all the curious persons who come from Paris and the neighboring communes; all the inns are full, and numbers who could obtain no lodgings have been obliged to sleep in their carriages. All the houses without exception are hung with white flags embroidered with lilies. The inscriptions are pretty much all alike: 'Long live the King! Long live the Bourbons! God and the King! May the King live a long time, and the Bourbons forever!'"

August 25, the statue of Henri IV. was solemnly inaugurated on the Pont Neuf. The Duchesses of Angoulême and Berry sat in the open carriage with the King. He reached the platform erected before his ancestor's statue at a quarter-past two. The Marquis Barbé de Marbois made an address, to which the King replied in these words: —

"I am affected by the sentiments you express. I accept with lively gratitude the gift of the French people, this monument erected by the offerings of the rich and the mite of widows. When they behold this image, Frenchmen will say: 'He loved us, and his children love us also.' And the descendants of the good King will say in their turn, 'Let us merit to be loved as he was.' We shall see in this the pledge of reunion between all parties, and the oblivion of all mistakes. We shall see the presage of the happiness of France. May Heaven grant these desires which are dearest of all to my heart." The thirteen legions of the National Guard marched past the statue. Popular representations were given during the day, and in the evening plays composed for the occasion.

The *Moniteur* had printed the following that morning: —

"It is on the feast of Saint Louis, the day on which the statue of Henri IV. is to be inaugurated, that it is sweet to be permitted to announce that the condition of S. A. R. the Duchess of Berry promises a new scion of the august Bourbon dynasty."

Like its predecessor, this hope was to end in a disappointment. The *Moniteur* thus announced the sad tidings: —

"S. A. R. the Duchess of Berry, had an accident

which made it necessary to bleed her in the arm and employ other remedies. Nevertheless, an untimely birth occurred this morning, September 13, at six o'clock. The child, which was of the male sex, lived nearly two hours. S. A. R. the Duchess of Berry is in a satisfactory condition."

This date, the 13th, reappeared at the interval of a year. On July 13, 1817, the Duchess had brought a daughter into the world who lived but a day. On September 13, 1818, she was brought to bed with a son who died at the end of two hours. The same date was to appear again two years and five months later. The Duke of Berry was assassinated by Louvel, February 13, 1820, and in the midst of his cruel agony the victim remarked the triple coincidence.

In spite of the Duchess's sufferings, she had the presence of mind to request the prelate to baptize at once the child who was about to die; "a veritable consolation for Her Royal Highness," said the *Moniteur*, "and the reward of the pious sentiments by which she is animated." The obsequies of the little Prince took place the same evening at half-past ten o'clock. The Bishop of Amiens and the Marquis of Anjorand, chief equerry to the Duke of Berry, got into a carriage drawn by six horses. The escort was composed of an officer, a brigadier, and four of Monsieur's guards. The body was received at Saint Denis by the canon in charge of the tombs, and deposited in the royal vault, beside that of the little Princess who died the year before. The Prince had been baptized, but given no name. This inscription was engraved on the coffin: "Here is the body of the very high and powerful Prince N. of Artois, grandson of France, son of the very high and very powerful Prince Charles Ferdinand of Artois, Duke of Berry, son of France, and of Caroline Ferdinande Louise, Princess of the Two Sicilies, who died at birth, September 13, 1818." It must be owned that this official phraseology is somewhat stilted. To describe a child who dies at birth as "very high and powerful" smacks of exaggeration.

The Duke of Berry was greatly afflicted. Possibly he had a presentiment that the death of this child would be the signal for his own. M. Alfred Nettement relates that a few days afterward the Duke of Berry went to the Palais Royal to call on the Duke of Orleans. The latter was in his study with the young Duke of Chartres. He made a movement as if to send away his son, fearing, doubtless, lest the sight of his own family prosperity might redouble his cousin's regrets, and that his blooming health might recall the empty cradle in which the elder branch had placed a hope which lasted only two hours. "But," adds M. Nettement, "the Duke of Berry gently detained the young Prince. He was a favorite with him and his wife, and was always welcome at the Elysée. Then, drawing him closer still, the Duke said, with an affectionate, though melancholy smile: 'Here is a fine fellow who possibly has a high fortune before him. My wife cannot give me any more children, or at any rate, nothing but daughters, and then the crown will pass to your son.' To this the Duke of Orleans replied: 'At least, Monseigneur, if some day he should obtain the crown, it will be you who will give it to him as a second father; for you are younger than I, and my son would receive all from your kindness.'"

The *Journal des Débats* published an article reproduced by the *Moniteur* of September 23, 1818, in which it was said: —

"No city has felt the shock of the events that have plunged France into mourning more than the faithful city of Bordeaux; none could welcome with more cordiality the new hopes offered us; the young Prince torn prematurely from our love was to have been called by its name. This signal honor was due, and had been granted by the King to the city which was the first of all to open its gates to the grandson of Henri IV., and which, at a disastrous epoch, was again the last asylum of that Princess whom France and Europe have styled the heroine of Bordeaux. The first scion of this august stem would have been a Duke of Bordeaux. Everything gives us the right to believe that this noble recompense of courage and fidelity is only delayed for several months, and that the moment is not far distant when Providence will consolidate, by another pledge, the glory of the faithful city and the destinies of France."

The Duchess of Berry was not more discouraged

by her second mourning than by her first. Almost immediately she resumed her habitual gaiety. On November 4, early morning serenades and military music announced, both at the Tuileries and the Elysée, the feast of Saint Charles Borromeo, the patron saint of both the Duke and the Duchess. A ball was given at the Elysée palace to celebrate this double fête, on November 7. It was opened by the young Princess, who danced with the Grand-duke Constantine of Russia, in a French quadrille. Dancing began anew after supper and was kept up until morning. The year 1818 finished prosperously and gaily.

XV.

1819

PROBABLY the Duchess of Berry, in all her changeful life, had no such calm and happy year as 1819. It was like a gleam of sunlight through an overclouded sky. The kindly young wife enjoyed her domestic happiness in peace, and lived only for her husband, the arts, and charity. At Palermo she had reproached herself for not having sufficiently cultivated the accomplishments. At the Elysée she took lessons. As the Duke of Berry loved music, she wished to become a good musician; he had fine galleries of pictures, and she wished to be able to appreciate them. She formed a choice and elegant society around her, in which the traditions of the old régime were united to a familiarity thoroughly modern. Small parties, private balls, and exquisite concerts animated the joyous winter. In the *Moniteur* of February 10, 1819, we read: —

"S. A. R. Madame the Duchess of Berry has just acquired possession of the fine picture of the Sybil, one of Madame Lebrun's masterpieces, which she has presented to Mgr. the Duke of Berry. One must be pleased to see this young Princess, in whom love for the fine arts is innate, seizing eagerly every occasion to encourage French artists, from whom she has already collected several interesting works, and seeking in the protection she grants them another means of increasing her affection for the things which interest her august spouse."

It is not without emotion that Madame de Gontaut has related her memories of this agreeable year 1819. She says that when spring came, the Duke and Duchess spent a part of their mornings in the garden. "They set up games there which amused them much; the wives, children, and husbands of the princely houses came there incessantly, especially on Sundays. Nothing could be gayer or more agreeable than Monseigneur's behavior to those around him; people amused themselves and were in harmony; they were happy and at ease."

The Duchess was then pregnant. She hoped greatly that this time the trouble of the two preceding years might not be renewed. She was forbidden to go out in a carriage. When she dined at the Tuileries with the King, she went on foot, leaning on her husband's arm. The *Moniteur* said in its issue of June 17, 1819: —

"The Duchess of Berry, whose condition, on which hang the hopes of France, obliges her to take great precautions, will be unable to accompany her august spouse in the Corpus Christi procession. Wishing, nevertheless, to contribute by her liberality to the magnificence of a ceremony to which her presence would have added so much brilliancy, this pious Princess has presented to her parish church, the Assumption, a superb canopy and an extremely rich ornament."

A short time before her delivery the Duchess was walking with her husband in the Elysée garden. She drew Madame de Gontaut into a thicket, and made the Duke tell her that she had been chosen as governess for the expected infant. The lady of the bedchamber thus relates the incident:—

"I was dumfounded; the first thing that presented itself to my mind was a long train of princes and princesses to bring up and superintend — the slavery, in a word, of all the rest of my life. The silence that ensued while my reply was delayed, amused and made them laugh; but reading in my eyes that I was sad, they kindly asked the reason. I said: 'I shall miss the happiness I enjoy with you now, free from trouble and vexation. I understand myself; I know I could never take lightly nor at my ease the charge you offer me; but I also know that it gives me still another means of proving my attachment to you. I will fulfil it as I did that which nature assigned me with regard to my own children.' Monseigneur, who was far from expecting me to be uncertain whether to accept a place much above that I then occupied, seemed disappointed; they both said the kindest and most encouraging things to me. I asked a few days' delay in which to consult my husband."

Not long afterwards Louis XVIII. gave the Viscountess an audience: "Sit down, god-daughter," he said to her, "and let us have a chat. Tell me, I beg you, why do you hesitate to accept the first place in the kingdom?" The King listened with his eyes, which, penetrating even to the conscience, obliged a truthful answer. "I have no ambition, Sire," replied the Viscountess; "I prefer liberty and independence to everything else." "Liberty!" exclaimed the King; "liberty and independence, senseless words! Devotion comes from the heart; yours has given proof of it and will never belie it. Believe me, and accept what is offered you with confidence, friendship, and my approbation." Louis XVIII.'s wish was a command. Madame de Gontaut obeyed.

It had been decided that if the child borne by the Duchess of Berry were a son, he should be called the Duke of Bordeaux. Hence the faithful city, as it was then called, attached special interest to the expected event. The *Moniteur* published a letter from Bordeaux, dated September 8, in which it was said: —

"We are expecting from one minute to another the news of the happy deliverance of Madame the Duchess of Berry. It seems that measures have been taken and orders given so that the result shall be made known directly after the arrival of the courier. If the news comes in the daytime, it will be announced by salvos of artillery; if at night, by the great bell of the Hôtel de Ville. Fifteen volleys will apprise the Bordelais of the birth of a prince; three volleys will announce the birth of a princess. The public edifices will be illuminated, and truly national fêtes will celebrate this memorable event."

On September 21, 1819, the Duchess of Berry brought into the world without accident, not the son so impatiently expected, but a daughter. Seeing evidence of disappointment on the faces of those surrounding her, the courageous Princess, instead of looking cast down, began to smile gaily: "After the girl, the boy," she exclaimed. Full of joy, she did not foresee the dismal future. She would have been greatly surprised had any one told her that the princess just born was to be, like herself, the wife of an assassinated prince, and like her also, the mother of a prince outlawed and deprived of his inheritance.

Here is a summary of the birth certificate of the future Duchess of Parma:—

"Certificate of birth of the very high and very powerful Princess Louise Marie Thérèse of Artois, Mademoiselle, granddaughter of France, born September 21, 1819, at thirty-five minutes past six in the morning, at the Elysée-Bourbon palace, signed by the King, Monsieur, the Duchess of Angoulême, the Duke of Angoulême, the Duke of Berry, the Duke and Duchess of Orleans, the dowager Duchess of Orleans, the Duke and Duchess of Bourbon, Mademoiselle d'Orleans, the Duke of Duras, the Duke of Reggio, General Marquis Dessolle, president of the

Ministerial Council; the Count of Pradel, director-general of the King's household, the Marquis of Dreux-Brézé, grand master of ceremonies; M. de Serre, Minister of Justice; Count Decazes, Minister of the Interior; Baron Portal, Minister of Marine; Baron Louis, Minister of Finances; Louis Dambray, Chancellor of France; the Marquis of Sémonville, grand referendary of the Chamber of Peers; M. Cauchy, keeper of the archives of the Chamber of Peers. Signed also, with the King's permission, the Duke of Gramont, the Marquis of Boisgelin, the Duke of Escars, the Duke of Sérent, the Marquis of Champenest, the Marquis of Rochemore, the Count of Puységur, the Count of Talleyrand, † J.-B., Bishop of Chartres, the Duke of Fitzjames, the Duke of Polignac, the Viscount of Agoult, the Duke of Damas, the Duke of Guiche, the Count of Nantouillet."

The Duke of Berry, always kind and affectionate toward his wife, wished to be the first to give her the new-born child. He did it with sincere feeling; no one could suspect from his expression that he was disappointed at having a daughter instead of a son. Afterwards, the grand master of ceremonies caused both leaves of the folding door to be thrown open, and the body-guards formed in double line up to the apartment of the little Princess. The Viscountess of Gontaut, governess of the children of France, carried her thither in great pomp. After the grand master had made a profound salute, the body-guards retired. "I hoped by this time," she says, "to have done with etiquette, when that of the chambermaids' began. I was sitting down, hugging my precious treasure in my arms, when the cradle-maid came forward to inform me, as she said, of the nature of her customary rights, which were to hold and to carry the child, the governess having merely to give orders and preside. Monseigneur came up just then, and smiling, asked me in English if he had quite understood the instructions which the serving-woman claimed to give me. We jested about it; he advised me to establish myself as mistress forthwith, so as to be able to enjoy with him and the Duchess a domestic happiness that might possibly be *bourgeois*, but was the only real one. So I told the elegant and pretentious maid that I would call her when I thought her services were needed. This being said in Monseigneur's presence, and evidently by his advice, produced an effect whose benefits I felt until the education of the Princess was ended.

The next day the Duke of Berry went to the Opera, where the public gave him an enthusiastic reception, and where Dérivis sang a cantata composed for the occasion by the celebrated ballad-writer, Désaugiers.

On the occasion of her daughter's birth, the Duchess of Berry received many marks of sympathy and interest from her aunt, the Duchess of Orleans. The Duchess was the sister of Queen Marie Antoinette, and daughter of Queen Marie Caroline, grandmother of the Duchess of Berry. The niece was very devoted to her aunt, and found it pleasant to renew in France her souvenirs of the Two Sicilies. On her arrival in France she had not met her aunt there; for, after the second Restoration she was relegated to a sort of exile in England with her husband and children. This disgrace lasted until April, 1817. The Duke of Orleans was then authorized by Louis XVIII. to return to France with his family, and he took up his residence again in the Palais Royal. The Duke of Berry had always entertained the friendliest sentiments toward his cousin, and energetically defended him against the rancor and suspicions of the *émigrés*. In London, one evening during the emigration, it had been necessary, in order to avoid disagreeable scenes, for the Duke of Berry to take the arm of his cousin of Orleans, and say in a severe tone to those surrounding them: —

"Is any one here more difficult to please than the Duke of Berry?"

After 1817, the relations between the Palais Royal and the Elysée became intimate and frequent. The Duchess of Orleans loved to tell how, in 1819, at the time of Mademoiselle's birth, the Duke of Chartres, hearing the first discharges of cannon, said: "Either my wife or my King has come into the world." After her recovery, the Duchess of Berry, as soon as she was permitted to go out, went to the Palais Royal with her husband to thank the Duchess of Orleans for her attentions. Mademoiselle was taken along. She was on the lap of the governess of the children of France when the Duke of Berry, recalling the reflection of the young Duke of Chartres, said to him: "Chartres, come here then, and embrace your wife." The young Prince reddened, but did not stir: his timidity was found amusing.

By degrees the Duchess of Berry resumed her occupations, the Elysée its amusements, the Duke of Berry his hunting, and everybody was happy. One may read in the *Moniteur* of October 29, 1819: —

"Since last Sunday, when S. A. R. the Duchess of Berry was churched, that Princess has dined at the Tuileries every day. Her Royal Highness, with the young Princess Mademoiselle d'Artois, her daughter, accompanied by her nurse, has gone out to Bagatelle for the last three days, from one o'clock to four."

The Duke of Berry was a very tender father. He often passed part of the morning in his daughter's room, and the Duchess frequently went to meet him there. She had appointed as cradle-woman the nurse who had attended her at the birth of her three children, Madame Lemoine. She was the daughter of the person who nursed the Empress Marie Louise when the King of Rome was born.

The Duchess of Berry seemed the happiest of women. Whenever she appeared, the public showed her a lively sympathy. The *Moniteur* of November 4, 1819, said: —

"About four o'clock on All Saints Day, the Duke

and Duchess of Berry made their appearance at the Salon. The crowd was still rather large and pressed about them, restrained less by the guardians of the museum, who preceded them, than by fear of incommoding the Princess, who, leaning on her husband's arm and following the balustrade, stopped before many of the charming *genre* pictures which line the Salon. On the same day Their Royal Highnesses were to visit the studio of M. Girodet to look at the picture of Pygmalion and Galatea."

While the Duke and Duchess of Berry, taking no part either in court intrigues or politics were thus leading a peaceful and happy life in the Elysée, the horizon was beginning to cloud over. November 23, 1819, Louis XVIII., in opening the session of the Chambers, said in his speech from the throne: —

"A vague but real anxiety pervades all minds; every one asks the present for pledges of its duration. As yet the nation enjoys very imperfectly the first fruits of peace and legalized government; it fears to see them torn away by the violence of factions; it is alarmed by their thirst for domination; it fears the too clear expression of their designs."

Count Grégoire, a regicide, had just been nominated deputy by the department of the Isère. "If it is decided that a regicide is admissible," cried M. de Corbière, "the entire Revolution will come out of its grave, hideous and bloody." M. de Marcellus said, in his indignation: "Such a nomination is an outrage on the majesty of the throne and the sanctity of the altar." M. Grégoire was not admitted. Thus opened the session which was to be the most stormy one of Louis XVIII.'s reign.

A few days afterward, the *Moniteur* said in its issue of December 18, 1819: —

"S. A. R. Madame the Duchess of Berry, accompanied by one of her ladies and her first equerry, mounts a horse nearly every day in the royal riding-school. The director of this school has the honor of attending her during her exercise, which appears to have a favorable effect upon her health, and at which S. A. R. Madame the Duchess of Angoulême and S. A. R. the Duke of Berry are often present."

The valiant Duchess doubtless said to herself that if the hour of danger arrived, she would like to be the first at the most dangerous posts, and mount on horseback, like an intrepid amazon, to defend the rights of her family and combat the Revolution.

XVI

COUNT DECAZES

THERE was a man in France at the beginning of 1820 who was probably more powerful than the King. This was Count Decazes, president of the Council of Ministers. The credit he enjoyed caused the ultras an exasperation bordering on convulsive rage. On ascertaining the omnipotence of a former favorite of the Empire, it was all the *émigrés* could do to refrain from treating Louis XVIII. as a disguised Bonapartist or crowned Jacobin.

Restorations, when accomplished, nearly always betray completely the expectations of those by whom they have been most ardently desired. The realization of their dream appears to them like a hoax on the part of destiny, and on seeing a court utterly different from what they had imagined, they experience a disgust and astonishment which make them lose their temper. Their resentment is all the sharper because they are forced to conceal it, and to smile at the very moment when they are ready to burst with rage.

The man who excited the jealousy and rancor of the courtiers of Louis XVIII. to such a pitch was not yet forty. Born September 28, 1780, at Saint-Martin-de-Laye, near Libourne, where his father was lieutenant of the presidial,[1] he had been first a barrister, and afterwards employed in the Ministry of Justice, under the Consulate. In 1805 his marriage with the daughter of Count Muraire, first president of the Court of Cassation, opened to him the career of the magistracy. Having been appointed judge of the Seine tribunal, he became a counsellor of the imperial court in 1806. He was called to the Hague the same year by King Louis Bonaparte, whose confidential counsellor he became. After the abdication of this Prince he filled the post of private secretary to Madame Mère from 1811 to the close of the Empire.

Under the Restoration he became an avowed royalist. He refused to keep his post in the magistracy during the Hundred Days, and Napoleon exiled him forty leagues from Paris. After Waterloo he became prefect of police to Louis XVIII. September 24, 1815, he entered the cabinet as Minister of Police, and from that day onward he was the confidant, the favorite, the *alter ego* of the sovereign.

Chateaubriand, who was so jealous of him, has said: —

"As soon as M. Decazes was appointed minister, carriages blocked up the quay Malaquais every evening, in order to bring all that was noble in the Fau-

---

[1] An inferior court of judicature.

bourg Saint-Germain to the salon of the parvenu. Do what he may, the Frenchman will never be anything but a courtier, no matter of whom, providing he is in power at the time. A coalition of follies in favor of the new favorite was speedily formed. In democratic society, prate about liberty, declare that you behold the advance of the human race and the future of things, throw in a few crosses of honor, and you are sure of your place. In aristocratic society play whist, utter commonplaces with an air of profundity, and get off witticisms carefully prepared in advance, and the fortune of your genius is assured. M. Decazes came to us from Napoleon's mother. He was familiar, obliging, and never insolent; he wanted to do me a favor, and I did not care about it; that was the beginning of my misfortune. It ought to have taught me that one should never fail in respect to a favorite."

The secret of the success of M. Decazes was that his conversation interested and amused Louis XVIII. He had been trained at a good school to make himself agreeable to the great ones of the earth. Having learned how to please King Louis Bonaparte, who was of a gloomy disposition, Madame Mère, who was easily provoked to anger, and Queen Hortense, who was very gay and amiable, but who was accustomed to much flattery as a queen, and more still as a woman, M. Decazes acquired early the suppleness necessary to court life. On the other hand, his term in the judiciary and his remarkable ability as president of the assize court had revealed to him both the strength and the weaknesses of the human heart. To this must be added that his functions as prefect of police, by initiating him into all the secrets of Parisian life, had given him clues to all the intrigues of the court and the city.

Louis XVIII., whose greatest pleasure was in conversation, and who was a talker of the first order, found his interviews with his young minister extremely charming. M. Decazes talked well, and, moreover, listened well, — a rarer accomplishment than one supposes. The King liked to tell stories. In his minister he found an enthusiastic auditor, careful to note the best points of each royal anecdote, and ready to give intelligent and respectful rejoinders to the sovereign, who considered himself a sort of crowned professor. "It was I, however," exclaimed Louis XVIII., "who recognized the merit of this young man, calculated his range, and formed him. He is my work, and people are still very far from knowing his full worth." He had arrived at the point of considering his favorite minister not merely as a faithful servant and friend, but as a son; so he styled him when speaking and writing to him.

Louis XVIII., whose infirmities forced him to be idle, dreaded the fatigue of labor. His ministers importuned him; M. Decazes was able to divert him. Through his past connections and present functions as Minister of Police, he knew better than any one else the secret histories of Napoleon's palace and those of the great lords and ladies of the new court. Even when discussing public affairs he would tell anecdotes which the King would cap by others. In this way the time passed agreeably. The matters to be discussed were prepared in concise notes, quickly read, which the King made a show of correcting as a professor does the exercises of his pupil.

If M. de Vaulabelle may be believed, Louis XVIII. had undertaken to teach his minister English. The latter, whose progress was very rapid, gave all the credit to his royal master, who evidently accepted it, never suspecting, it is added, that before going to the Tuileries, M. Decazes took an English lesson every day from one of the best teachers in Paris.

The King's affection for his minister became a real infatuation. He made him a count, a peer of France, Minister of the Interior, and President of the Council. As M. de Viel-Castel has very justly remarked, it was all the easier for M. Decazes to succeed in convincing the King of his absolute devotion, because, touched himself by the kindness with which he was treated and the affection displayed toward him by the sovereign, he responded to it by profound gratitude. After being a widower for twelve years, he had married in 1818, thanks to the royal protection, a young person of noble family, Mademoiselle de Saint-Aulaire, grandchild through her mother of the last reigning Prince of Nassau-Sarrebruck, and grandniece of the Duchess of Brunswick-Bevern, who obtained for the new married pair, from Frederick VI. of Denmark, the succession of the duchy of Glucksberg. In speaking of his favorite minister, Louis XVIII. said, "I will raise him so high that the greatest lords will envy him." Any criticism aimed at M. Decazes was considered by the sovereign as a seditious attempt against royal authority, and a sort of conspiracy or high treason.

The influence of the minister tended to favor ideas of moderation and compromise. It was he who made the conciliatory remark: "Whether we come to the King through the Charter or to the Charter through the King, we shall be equally welcome." It was he who brought about the celebrated decree of September 5, 1816, by which the reactionary Chamber had been dissolved. It was he who did most to end the White Terror. It was he who, through natural benevolence as much as through policy, had labored most efficaciously to open the prisons, recall the exiles, and those condemned in contumacy, and even not infrequently to procure for them governmental favors. It was he who decided Louis XVIII. to assume definitely the rôle of a liberal and constitutional monarch. "That such a man," says M. de Viel-Castel, "could have incurred the furious hatred by which he was pursued, would be incomprehensible if one did not know what has always been the fate of the favorites of kings in France whenever they have exercised great power." Excited by hatred, the imagination of the ultras went so far as to invent the most unlikely and absurd motives for the sovereign's affection for his minister. Still the *émigrés* said, "Long live the King!" all the same. But in their view, Louis XVIII., led astray by M. Decazes, was nothing but a revolutionist.

XVII

THE DUKE OF BERRY

THE Duke of Berry was not favorable to M. Decazes; but, being full of respect for the wishes of Louis XVIII., who imposed severe discipline on all his family, he refrained from opposition to the prime minister, and maintained a reserved attitude at court. The character of the Prince had changed for the better. Family life had softened his irascible temper. As he grew older he gained experience and judged men and things more wisely than in his early youth. His bluntness had become good nature; his rudeness, simplicity. "His countenance," says M. de Lamartine, "did not reveal his intelligence and goodness until it expanded in a smile. Then, in the frank and cordial penetration of his glance, the fixed contraction of his eyelids, the wrinkles around his mouth, the abandon of his gestures, and the sincere and animated tone of his voice, one divined the wit, felt the soldier, felt the good heart." Two eminent qualities he possessed in a high degree, — bravery and charity.

He was a good husband, a good friend, and a good master. Much beloved in his own house, he established perfect order there. When he learned that one of his servants had deposited money in the savings bank, he doubled the sum, so as to encourage his domestics to practise economy and make them provident for the future. Anecdotes were told about him which showed his natural goodness. One day the horse of a dragoon of the guard, who was accompanying the King, fell down, and the dragoon's leg was broken. The Duke of Berry, who was out driving with his wife, met the poor fellow. He alighted from the carriage at once, had the soldier put into it, ordered that he should be taken to the Elysée and cared for until he should be completely cured, and then walked home with the Princess under a burning sun.

Another day, as he was going to Bagatelle, in crossing the Bois de Boulogne he met a little child carrying a large basket. Stopping his cabriolet, he called out: "Little man, where are you going?"— "To La Muette, to carry this basket." "That basket is too heavy for you. Give it to me; I'll leave it as I go by." The basket was placed in the cabriolet, and the Prince left it at the given address. He went afterwards to find the child's father and said to him: "I met your little lad; you make him carry baskets that are too heavy; you will destroy his health, and prevent him from growing. Buy him a donkey to carry his basket." And he gave the father money to buy the donkey.

Another time, as he was out walking, he saw a

very animated group of charcoal-burners, who were trying to prevent one of their number from throwing himself into the Seine. Without being recognized, he approached them and inquired the cause of the despair of the poor devil who wanted to kill himself. It was the loss of some money which impelled him to suicide. The Prince opened his purse at once, and the charcoal-burner did not throw himself into the river. His comrades were greatly astonished when they learned that the man with whom they had just been talking so familiarly was the King's nephew.

The Duke of Berry practised charity intelligently and without ostentation. It has been calculated that in six years his alms had amounted to one million three hundred and eighty-eight thousand eight hundred and fifty-one francs. He visited the poor with his wife, and not only gave them money, but words of consolation. "Those who had the least good feeling toward the Prince," says Chateaubriand, "were disarmed as soon as they saw him; he never came out of a museum, studio, or manufactory without leaving a friend behind him there. If he saw an infant, he ran toward it, took it in his arms, caressed and embraced it, and behold a father and mother were wholly won. If a work of art were shown him, he examined it attentively; the artist or the connoisseur was charmed. In a word, he followed toward all the world, and through good nature, the counsel of Nestor, who recommended that every soldier should be called by his own name, in order to prove to him that he was known and his family esteemed."

As to the Duchess of Berry, happy, gay, in excellent health, rejoicing in another pregnancy, and hoping this time certainly to have a son, she beheld the future under the most glowing colors. Deeply attached to her husband and enjoying without a drawback the greatest happiness of life, a legitimate love, she thanked God for her lot.

Count de Mesnard writes in his *Souvenirs intimes*: "The Duchess of Berry, who prefers the freedom of private life to everything else, haunts the shops, promenades, and theatres. . . . She possesses beyond any one else the charm and grace which captivate. Nothing equals her kindness to all who surround her. Her ladies of honor are the objects of her entire solicitude. If there is a ball at the palace, she dresses them for it with her own hands; she takes pleasure in adorning them and thinking that they will be admired. One may add also, that she is adored in return for all the good she does." Alas! how short lived was this happiness! And what reason Chateaubriand had to say: "Happy is the man unknown to the world, who wakes up in a thatched cabin, in the midst of his children, who are not pursued by hatred, and of whom not one is lacking to the paternal embraces! At what a price must crowns be purchased nowadays? And what is to-day but an empire?"

The Duke of Berry was about to terminate his life

by a good action, — that of making generous reparation for a wrong done in a moment of anger to one of his servants named Soubriard. On Saturday, February 12, 1820, the Prince had hunted in the Bois de Boulogne. Everything went wrong; people passing back and forth disturbed the game. The Prince very unjustly accused Soubriard of all the mishaps of the chase, treated the poor man badly, and left him in consternation. But the Duke of Berry was good. He very quickly repented of his violence, and on his return to the Elysée he sadly remarked to Madame de Gontaut: "Pity me; I have just wounded the heart of a man whom I love and who would give his life for me. I have acted very badly; I have been very wicked." Just then he took his little girl in his arms to give her a kiss. She was frightened, and she cried. "She is right to be afraid of a sinner," said he. Madame de Gontaut seemed to find it impossible to believe that the Prince could have left the unfortunate servant without a word of consolation. "Alas," said he, "that is where you deceive yourself. Poor, poor Soubriard, I left him sad and unhappy. But I will not forget him; the day is not ended yet."

The next day, Sunday, February 13, the Duke of Berry came to see his daughter before going to the King's Mass. After embracing her he gave her back to her governess, saying: "Don't scold me any more; after leaving you yesterday I signed an order which will, I hope, secure Soubriard's happiness for the rest of his life. I confide the service of my daughter to him; he is to be my huntsman." Then, although in haste to get away, he stopped to tell Madame de Gontaut in confidence that he was certain that in a few months the Duchess, his wife, would contribute another infant to his happiness. His face shone with joy.

For some days anonymous letters had been announcing to him that a tragical death was impending over him. But, brave as his sword, the descendant of Henri IV. scorned such threats. When he was entreated to take precautions: "What would you have?" said he. "If any one has made the sacrifice of his own life in order to take mine, he will succeed in executing his project one day or other, whatever precautions one takes. In the contrary case I should have made myself needlessly unhappy." He considered politics as a battle-field, and was as calm in front of the poniards of assassins as in front of cannon-balls. For a long time he had not permitted the guards to form a double line when he went into or came out of a theatre. Not merely did he object to being guarded, but he complained at being the object of a surveillance which annoyed him. He especially desired to get rid of a man, belonging doubtless to the police, whom he found on his track wherever he went. He requested Baron d'Haussez to speak about it to M. Decazes. On February 13, M. d'Haussez came to tell the Prince about his interview with the minister. It turned out that the man in question, far from belonging to the police, was a suspected individual on whom they were going to keep their eyes. The Duke of Berry was satisfied with the explanation, and said, smiling, "I hope that my restoration to the minister's favor will last at least until next summer; for then I hope to go and chase the chamois and the bear in the Alps."

The Prince spent the remainder of the day gaily; he was happy as a prince, as a Frenchman, and as a husband. In the evening he went with his wife to the Opera.

XVIII

LOUVEL[1]

WHILE the Duke of Berry, holding himself aloof from political intrigues and agitations, was living peaceably at the Elysée with his amiable wife, and winning the approbation not merely of the friends, but the enemies of the Restoration by his circumspect attitude, a man to whom he had never done the slightest harm, a man who had never spoken to him, and who had no manner of acquaintance with him, was pursuing him with a ferocious and implacable hatred. This absolutely obscure individual was preparing to win for himself, at one stroke, the horrible celebrity of crime. He was a saddler named Louvel. Cold, taciturn, and solitary, he worked at his trade with the utmost punctuality. His comrades would have been greatly surprised had any one come to tell them that this workman was getting ready for a crime which would make an immense commotion throughout the world. Nothing in his relations, language, or habits could

---

[1] See M. de Nauroy's remarkable work, *Le Duc de Berry et Louvel*.

suggest anything of the sort. History abounds in dramatic strokes which no playwright could have invented.

What were the origin and antecedents of this unknown man who was about to change the whole political situation from top to bottom? Louis Pierre Louvel was born at Versailles, October 7, 1783, of Jean Pierre Louvel and his second wife, Françoise Moutier, both of them small shopkeepers. He lost his mother when he was two years old, and his father when he was twelve. An elder sister, Thérèse, entered him at the Institute of the Children of the Country, at Versailles, where, receiving gratuitous elementary instruction, as it was then understood, he learned to read in the Constitution of 1791, and the Declaration of the Rights of Man. Theophilanthropic hymns took the place of the catechism for him. He was apprenticed to a saddler at Montfort-l'Amaury, but being taken away again by his sister, who was alarmed by his weakly constitution, he assisted her for a time in her haberdashery shop. He was a sober, industrious, and steady child. He used to buy several four-pound loaves at a time, because, said he, one eats less bread when it is stale.

At eighteen, Louvel made his tour of France as a workman, and afterwards became a soldier. He entered an artillery regiment of the imperial guard, but was dismissed at the end of six months on account of the extreme weakness of his constitution. He grieved profoundly over the invasion of 1814 and the downfall of Napoleon. His brain was disordered by it. Thenceforward he considered himself as an avenger. He intended to strike Louis XVIII. at the moment when the King should land in France, and walked from Metz to Calais for that purpose. At the same epoch he had an idea of assassinating the Marshal Duke of Valmy for having acceded to the deposition; and the Count of Artois as guilty of emigration. From Calais he went to Paris. The triumphant entry of the Allies, and the ovations offered them by the royalists inflamed his exasperation to the fury of concentrated rage. He swore to himself to kill one or more of the men whom he regarded as public enemies and traitors to their country. But first he desired to see the Emperor, his hero, and he repaired to the island of Elba. The chief saddler of the imperial stables gave him employment from September to November, 1814, without Napoleon's surmising the devotion of this fanatical admirer. The economic reforms instituted in the household of the sovereign of Elba caused Louvel's dismission. He went to Leghorn, and from there to Chambéry, where he continued to work as a journeyman saddler. He was in the latter town when his employer's wife brought him a journal which announced that Napoleon had just landed in the Bay of Juan. At this news he rose without a word, and hanging his working-apron on a nail, went to rejoin the Emperor at Lyons. He went into the imperial stables as a saddler, and was admitted into the train of vehicles which followed Napoleon from Paris to Waterloo. He witnessed the final disaster with mortal anguish, and again followed the footsteps of the vanquished. The Emperor's equipages having stopped at Rochelle, he stopped also, and it was there that he caused a cutler to make with great care the knife with which he intended to slay a Bourbon. Lamartine describes him as "a little man, thin-limbed, wasted by internal consumption, yellow with bile, pale from incessant emotion, with a hard glance, compressed lips, and a tense, concentrated, and suspicious face; an image of fanaticism revolving in a narrow brain, an ill-comprehended idea, and suffering, until his fatal hand should have unburdened it by a crime, from the weight and the martyrdom of this idea."

In 1820 Louvel was employed as a saddler in the royal stables, and lived in the Place du Carrousel on that account. For a long time he had been possessed by his monomania; he had the madness of crime. "From the day when my resolution was definitely taken," he has said himself, "I avoided all intimate relations, wherein, without intending to do so, I might betray my secret. If, during my travels, I have always appeared solitary and taciturn, this would naturally be the character of a man whose life has always been roving and sedentary. Later on, I established myself at Paris; my plan entirely occupied me, and there was to be no further place for anything else in my life. I even kept away from women, although I might be fond of them. .... I was so far from giving away my secret to any one that I did not even once allow myself to speak against the Bourbons. That would have been a very useless imprudence."

After hesitating long over his choice of a victim, Louvel determined to strike the Duke of Berry, as the youngest and most energetic member of the royal family. But listen to his disclosures: "I followed the Duke of Berry during four consecutive years, to spectacles where I supposed he would be present, to the chase, to the public promenades, and in the churches. Several times I found good opportunities, but my courage always failed me; in 1817, 1818, and 1819, I was too feeble, and more than once I relinquished my project. But I was soon mastered by a sentiment which was stronger than I. I especially recall my thoughts one day when I was walking in the Bois de Boulogne and waiting for the Prince. I trembled with rage when thinking of the Bourbons; I had seen them returning with the foreigners, and I was horrified by it; then my thoughts took a different turn; I believed myself unjust towards them, and reproached myself for my designs; but my anger immediately returned. For more than an hour I remained fluctuating between these alternatives, and was not yet settled when the Prince passed by and was saved for that day. Neither was I without irresolution on February 13, although two or three days earlier I had sought to fortify myself by going to Père Lachaise to look at the graves of Lannes, Masséna, and the other warriors."

Louvel was not an ordinary assassin. He belonged to the same race as Brutus, Aristogeiton, Jacques Clément, and Ravaillac, those victims of a false conscience, a fixed idea; involuntary instruments of a sort of fatality, acting neither from interest, ambition, nor cupidity, pushed on to a specific crime, and perhaps to be pitied as well as blamed. Such criminals probably excite less horror than a wretch like Deutz. The man who kills a prince is not so vile as the man who betrays a woman.

Paris, meanwhile, was in the full tide of mirth and masquerading on the last Sunday before Lent, February 13, 1820. Forgetting party quarrels, all classes of society were amusing themselves. There had been a great ball the night before at the house of Count Greffulhe, at which the Duke and Duchess of Berry had been present. Small knives had been distributed to the ladies, in allusion to a play, the *Petites Danaïdes*, in which the comic actor, Potier, was then amusing all Paris. Were not these knives ominous?

It is said that, a few days before his death, Henri IV., disturbed by gloomy presentiments, remarked to Sully, "I shall die in this city; I shall never leave it; they will kill me!" and to the Queen, Maria de' Medicis, "Pass on, Madame the Regent." At the very moment when he was being warned of the conspiracies formed against his person, a rumor of his death was current in Spain and at Milan, and a week before his murder there passed through Liège, so they say, a courier who bore the news of his death to a German prince.

Similar signs had been occurring for some time with relation to the Duke of Berry. Every day he received anonymous letters containing horrible threats. His death had been announced in London at the beginning of February. But the Prince was bravery itself. The invisible poniard whose point he instinctively felt to be aimed at him, caused him neither fear nor trouble. He was one of those men whose good nature and even whose gaiety are not disturbed by danger. At this time he thought of nothing but amusing himself while amusing his young wife, always so eager for pleasures and diversions.

During the day the Parisians had enjoyed one of their favorite sights, the fat ox led in procession round the city at Shrovetide. After watching the procession, Louvel returned home to get a second poniard, and then went to dinner in a restaurant where he boarded. In the evening there were two aristocratic balls, — one at the house of Marshal Suchet, Duke of Albuféra, in the rue du Faubourg Saint-Honoré; and the other, a masquerade, at the house of Madame de La Briche, in the rue de la Ville l'Evêque. It was supposed that the Duke and Duchess of Berry would not attend these balls, but would go to the Opera, where there was to be an extraordinary representation which promised to be very brilliant.

The *Noces de Gamache*, the *Rossignol*, and the *Carnaval de Venise* were to be given. The latter piece was a ballet whose music was composed by Persuis and Lesueur. Albert and La Bigottini interpreted the principal rôles. A dancer named Elie, who was to replace Mérante in the rôle of Polichinello, and who wished to surpass him, was the subject of much comment: people said he had studied with Séraphin, by watching the artificial movements of his little wooden puppets.

The Opera-house was at this time in the rue Richelieu, opposite the Royal Library. It was inaugurated August 7, 1794, and occupied the site of the present Louvois Square. It had five tiers of boxes, including those on a level with the pit. It could seat something like sixteen hundred and fifty persons; and while its exterior was not at all imposing, the interior was a masterpiece of elegance.

A special entrance on one side of the edifice, just opposite the rue Rameau, was reserved for the royal family. It was there that Louvel awaited the coming of his victim. "Great personages," said he later on, "make a mistake in taking so few precautions as they do, especially when they have sins on their consciences. In this respect the German princes are more prudent than our own. When they are getting into a carriage, the soldiers, instead of presenting arms to them, as ours do, turn their backs; they are quite in the right, for nobody can then approach without being seen. I have noticed another thing: when the Prince entered the Opera, towards eight o'clock, the servants cried out to the coachman in such a way that I understood them perfectly: 'Come back at a quarter before eleven.' This was an imprudence, and I profited by it."

The Duke and Duchess of Berry had just entered the hall. Louvel, possibly hesitating still, wandered up and down between the Opera and the Palais Royal, awaiting the moment when the Duke should leave the theatre.

XIX

THE MURDER OF THE DUKE OF BERRY

IT is eight o'clock in the evening. The Duke and Duchess of Berry have just entered the Opera-house, and all the lorgnettes are levelled at them. The audience is very large. The boxes are filled with women covered with diamonds. Everything wears an air of festivity. The representation is to be more brilliant and elegant than the others. The joy of the spectators is depicted on their faces. The Duke and Duchess of Orleans, who are in a box with their family, exchange friendly signs with the Duke and Duchess of Berry. The *Rossignol* and the *Noces de Gamache* are successful. The spectacle is to terminate with the ballet of the *Carnaval de Venise*, the principal attraction of the evening.

What is Louvel doing all this time? He roams about in the neighborhood of the theatre, still pondering whether to strike or to spare the object of his hatred. "At eight o'clock," he will say afterwards, "I was in front of the Opera-house, and I could have killed the Prince when he entered, but at that moment my courage failed me. I heard the rendezvous given for a quarter before eleven; but nevertheless I went away, fully resolved to go to bed. In the Palais Royal, my thoughts returned more forcibly than ever. I reflected that I must return to Versailles at the end of the month, and that then my project would be adjourned for a long time. I began to ponder, and I said to myself: 'If I am right, why does my courage fail me? If I am wrong, why do not these ideas leave me?' I decided then upon that very evening. It was barely nine o'clock, and while awaiting the given hour, I walked up and down between the Palais Royal and the Opera-house without my resolution weakening, unless it might be at long intervals, and then for a few instants only."

Meanwhile the performance is going on. Between the acts the Duke and Duchess of Berry go to pay a visit to the box of the Duke and Duchess of Orleans. The Duke of Berry, who is very fond of children, caresses those of his cousin. He bestows especial attention on the Duke of Chartres, his favorite, and is seen passing his hand often through the little Prince's fair hair. The audience, pleased with the cordial relations existing between the two branches of the Bourbon family, applaud them several times. On returning to her box, the Duchess of Berry is jostled with some violence by the door of another box. She had gone to bed very late the night before, and her husband proposes that she shall return home. He will attend her to her carriage and then return to the hall to see the end of the ballet. The Princess accepts this offer, and goes down the stairway of the theatre, leaning on her husband's arm. It wants some minutes of eleven.

Louvel is before the door. Posted near a cabriolet which follows the carriage of the Prince, and standing at the horse's head, he seems to be a domestic, and attracts nobody's attention. The Duke's carriage draws up before the Princes' door, opposite the rue Rameau. The guards beneath the vestibule and the sentry who has his back toward the rue Richelieu present arms. Here are the Duke and Duchess under the penthouse of the portico. The Count of Choiseul, aide-de-camp to the Prince, is at the sentry's right, in the angle of the entrance door. The Count of Mesnard, chief equerry to the Duchess, offers his left hand first to her and afterwards to her lady-in-waiting, the Countess of Béthisy, to assist them in entering the carriage. The Duke gives them his right hand. One of the servants shuts up the steps of the carriage.

Still standing under the penthouse, the Duke waves his hand to his wife, and says, "Adieu, Caroline; we shall see each other presently." All of a sudden, just as he is about to re-enter the hall, a man throws himself upon him, and seizing his left shoulder with one hand, gives him a poniard thrust under the right breast with the other. The Count of Choiseul, thinking that this man has involuntarily jostled against the Prince while running, pushes him back, saying, "Take care what you are doing."

The murderer takes flight, leaving his poniard in the wound. "I am assassinated!" cries the Prince. And as those about him question him, he cries a second time, in a loud voice, "I am a dead man; I have the poniard in me!" Then he tears the knife from his wound and gives it into the hands of the Count of Mesnard. The Princess, whose carriage has not yet started, has heard her husband's cry of anguish, and while others are running in pursuit of the assassin, she flings herself out of the door, which is opened by a footman. Madame de Béthisy tries to hold her back. The Duke of Berry, summoning all his strength, calls out, "Wife, I beg you not to get out." But she, springing over the carriage steps, and pushing away with both hand Madame de Béthisy and the footman, cries, "Let me alone, let me alone; I order you to let me alone." Alighting from the carriage, she receives her husband in her arms at the very moment when he had just handed the bloody knife to M. de Mesnard, and as he was exclaiming, "I am dying; a priest; come, wife, let me die in your arms." They made him sit down on a bench in the passageway where the guards were, leaned his back against the wall, and opened his clothes to look for the wound. The blood flowed so abundantly that the Princess tried in vain to staunch it. Her robe and that of Madame de Béthisy were covered with it.

Meanwhile the assassin was fleeing, hotly pursued by the Count of Choiseul, Count Clermont-Lodève,

Desbiès the sentry, a footman, and several other persons. What would Louvel have done, had he not been arrested? He will tell us himself later on. "If I had succeeded in escaping on the evening when I struck the Prince," he will say, "I should have returned to sleep at my usual lodgings in the King's stables, where certainly nobody would have suspected me, and I should have continued to carry out my plans on some other member of the family. Perhaps I should have stopped after Monsieur; because, as to the King, I do not think he has ever borne arms against France. And the only thing I regret to-day is that I was taken so soon."

Louvel is taken. At the moment when he was running at full speed in the rue Richelieu, toward the boulevard, the street lights showed him as he upset in his flight a lemonade-seller, Paulmier by name, who was passing near the Colbert Arcade, carrying a tray, on which his beverages were spread, to the Opera-house. This fellow runs after the man who had thrown down his tray. Louvel is arrested, and taken to the watch-house of the Opera. M. de Clermont is the first one who spoke to him. "Monster," says he, "who could have induced you to commit such a crime?" The murderer replies, "The most cruel enemies of France." They fancy he is about to make avowals and name his accomplices. Not at all. Louvel's phrase is neither an expression of repentance nor an allusion to accomplices. It is merely an insult offered by the assassin to the family of his victim. He is searched, and they find on him the sheath of the weapon he had left in the Prince's wound, and also a sort of stiletto of a different shape.

During this time, the Duke of Berry has been taken up stairs to the little salon behind his box. He is placed on a sofa, with his head resting on his wife's shoulder. The Duke and Duchess of Orleans, and also Mademoiselle d'Orleans, who have just been notified in their box, hasten to this little salon. There the Count of Clermont announces that the assassin has been arrested. "Is he a foreigner?" asks the Prince. As some one answers no, he exclaims, "It is very cruel to die by the hand of a Frenchman."

Meanwhile the performance continues. The audience does not know what has just happened. The ballet is a wonderful success. From the salon where the Prince is agonizing, one can hear the music, and through a large window which opens into the box from this salon, even the dancing women on the stage can be seen. Truly a Shakespearean contrast between the death agony and pleasure.

Two doctors, MM. Lacroix and Caseneuve, had arrived instantly. They have bled him in the arm and tried to enlarge the wound so as to make a passage for the extravasated blood. Another physician, Doctor Blancheton, is there. "Is the wound mortal?" the Duchess of Berry says to him. "I have courage, I have plenty of it; I can endure anything, and I ask you for the truth." The doctor dares not express his opinion.

The Prince asks to see his daughter and the Bishop of Amyclée. M. de Clermont hastens to the Tuileries in search of the prelate. Some one else goes to the Elysée to give the tidings to Madame de Gontaut, Mademoiselle's governess. M. de Mesnard undertakes to apprise Monsieur, and also the Duke and Duchess of Angoulême.

One of the first places to which the fatal news arrives is the salon of Marshal Suchet, Duke of Albuféra, where a magnificent ball is going on. The Duchess of Reggio, who is present, quits the ball-room in great haste. The dances are stopped. I recall Victor Hugo's verses on the death of the Duke of Berry: —

"Calm down the transports of insensate madness;
  'Tween joy and sorrow short the passage of the hours;
Death loves to lay his hand so fraught with sadness,
  Ice-cold, on foreheads crowned with flowers.

"To-morrow, soiled with ashes, humbled, bowed to earth,
  The vain remembrance of our mirth
    Shall haunt us almost like remorse.
Sepulchral pomps shall follow on our plays;
For with us, wretches! Saturnalian lays
    But usher in the chant above the corse."

The guests of Madame de La Briche, the mother-in-law of the Count of Molé, among whom were several members of the Prince's household, are in full masquerade when they learn the news. Listen to the account of an eye-witness, M. de Rémusat: "Some thirty persons in society," says he, "had dropped in on Madame de La Briche in more or less grotesque costumes and accompanied by fiddlers. They were dancing when some one came to look for M. de Béthisy, who commanded the guard at the palace, and for M. F. de Chabot, who was aide-de-camp to the Prince. The news spread at once; the dancing stopped, and everybody found themselves on their feet and talking in undertones; a dull murmur succeeded the noise that had been going on; the musicians had disappeared without my being able to guess how. It was one of the most dramatic effects I ever saw. Some men had gone out and come in again; various accounts had been related. The effect they produced was curious. More than one face hid, under an expression of grief, another of malignant joy and the famous 'I told you so!' Some even said, 'If he is not very badly wounded, all this is fortunate.' Others added, '*For the country*, was engraved on the poniard.' Still others said, 'It is all very simple, considering how things are going.' A friend of mine was obliged to retire in tears over the revolting absurdity of certain reflections that were made. A young man remarked naïvely, thinking, apparently, of the balls that he would lose, 'Eh! what a horrible thing, to choose Shrove Sunday for it!' And it was odd enough to see a peer of the realm, M. de M . . . , dressed as a woman, with a toque and a great bare neck, talking very seriously and sadly in that costume."

At the Elysée some one has just rudely awakened the Viscountess of Gontaut, the governess of Mademoiselle, who must be taken to her dying father. The vestibule is already filled with maskers, people, and ladies in ball dresses, who are crying and weeping. Madame de Gontaut perceives M. Decazes and M. de Sémonville in this crowd. "Calm yourself," the latter says to her, "Monsieur the Duke of Berry has been wounded by an assassin, but he is not dead." She entreats M. Decazes to tell her what he knows the moment she approaches him. "Oh, speak, speak!" she exclaims; "I have a right to know all, and in the place you occupy nothing can be a secret for you. For mercy's sake, speak!" M. Decazes answers, "The Duke of Berry has been assassinated as he was leaving the Opera; he is still living, and if the poniard was not poisoned, his wound may not be mortal." — "But you are here. Monseigneur is here too, then?" "No; he is at the Opera. I came to assure myself of his safety in case he had been brought back; I find nobody to take my orders." — "I will give them; everything shall be lighted up and ready. . . . But as I was approaching just now, I thought I heard you say poison." "True; I fear lest the poniard may have been poisoned. The assassin has been arrested, and I am going to question him."

Madame de Gontaut gets into a carriage with the

little Princess in the midst of an immense crowd, filled with consternation and lighted up by dismal torches; not a word, an almost religious silence, an expression of chagrin on all faces. She reaches the chamber of sadness with the poor child.

The Duke of Berry is no longer in the small salon near his box. He has been carried to a hall used by the directors of the Opera; he is lying on a bed where, by a strange coincidence, he had passed the first night of his stay in France, at the beginning of the Restoration. This bed belongs to M. Grandsire, secretary to the Opera, who, living in Cherbourg in April, 1814, had lent it for the accommodation of the Duke of Berry when the Prince landed at that port. Monsieur, the dying man's father, the Duke of Angoulême, his brother, and the Duchess of Angoulême, his sister-in-law, are standing near him. When Madame de Gontaut enters with the little Princess, the Duchess of Berry takes her daughter and presents her to the unfortunate Prince. He makes an effort to embrace her. "Poor child!" he exclaims, "mayst thou be less unhappy than thy father!" He extends his arms and tries to give her his blessing.

Still, all hope of saving the Prince is not yet relinquished. The best surgeons of Paris, among others MM. Dupuytren and Dubois have been summoned. Deep incisions have been made, and the wound unbandaged; the application of numerous leeches and cupping-glasses has resulted in streams of blood; and as the burdened chest seems relieved for a moment, there is a momentary hope. Every one who comes out of the bloody laboratory is besieged for news. General Alexandre de Girardin is heard relating that he had been left for dead on the battle-field, and nevertheless had recovered from his wounds. But the Prince is not under the slightest illusion. "Your efforts, for which I thank you," he says to the surgeons, "cannot prolong my existence; my wound is mortal."

The Duchess of Berry does not leave her husband for an instant. Before beginning his surgical operations, M. Dupuytren had asked Monsieur to remove the Princess. "Father," she exclaims, "do not force me to disobey you." Then, addressing herself to the surgeon, "I shall not interrupt you, sir; go on." Kneeling on the side of the bed during the operation, she holds the Prince's left hand, which she waters with her tears. When, feeling the iron in his wound, he cries, "Let me alone, since I must die," she says to him, "Suffer for love of me, my dear," and the dying man makes not another complaint. "My dear," he says to her, "don't allow yourself to be overcome by grief; take care of yourself for the sake of the child you have yet to bear." Several times he asks to see his assassin. "What have I done to that man?" he exclaims; "could I have offended him without intending it?" — "No," answers his father; "you have never seen him, and he has no personal hatred whatever against you." "He is a lunatic then." And thereafter his fixed idea is to save the life of his assassin. "The King does not come," he kept on saying; "I shall not have time to ask for the man's pardon."

The Prince is about to die like a saint. Listen to Lamartine: —

"The Duke of Berry's first word is to ask, not for a doctor, but for a priest. Struck down in the midst of the delirium of youth and pleasure, there is no transition in his soul between the thoughts of time and the thoughts of eternity. In one second he passes from the spectacle of an entertainment to the contemplation of his last end, like those men whom immersion in a vessel of cold water suddenly arouses from the hot delirium of drunkenness. In this instantaneous revival, free from any weakness of mind, he shows the deliberate courage of a soldier. He shows now the faith of a Christian and the anxious impatience of a man who does not fear to die, but only to die before having confessed his faults and received the pledge of a second life. His education, imbibed in a family not less incorporated with the Church than with the throne, discovers itself in the depths of his soul in proportion as the effervescence of life subsides with his blood. He never ceases asking in a low voice if the priest he has asked for has not arrived."

The priest comes at last. It is Mgr. de Latil, Bishop of Chartres, Monsieur's first almoner. "The Duke of Berry," relates Madame de Gontaut, "had long experienced an aversion for this prelate, which he said he could not even explain; but as soon as he saw him, he said to M. de Clermont-Lodève, who had fetched him: 'That is well! God is giving me a trial for which I thank Him. I must make painful avowals to the Abbé de Latil, and receive from him hope and consolation." The dying man had a long interview with the priest, and then, calm and resigned, he asked pardon of God for his sins, and of the persons surrounding him for the scandal he might have given them. A few moments later, the Curé of Saint-Roch brought the holy oils. The Prince received the last sacraments with the most lively piety. "Ah!" exclaimed the Duchess, "I knew well that this beautiful soul was born for heaven and would return there."

During his emigration in England, two daughters whom he cherished had been borne to the Prince by a pretty and ladylike young Englishwoman, Miss Amy Brown. He wishes to embrace them before he dies. He speaks in a whisper to his wife, who answers aloud: "Let them come! I want to prove to you that I will not abandon them." She orders M. Clermont-Lodève to go and find the two young girls. They arrive toward the end of the night. The poor little things are trembling greatly. Their father talks to them in English; they kiss his hand, and then, turning to the Duchess of Berry, they kneel down. The Princess raises them, and leading them to Mademoiselle, says, "Embrace your sister."

Then, leaning over her husband, she says several times, "Charles, Charles, I have three children now." And she will keep her word; she will be a second mother to the young girls, of whom one will marry the Count of Faucigny, Prince of Lucinge, father of the present deputy, and the other the Colonel Baron of Charette, father of the general of that name.

The Duke of Berry has but one more anxiety: he wants to obtain the King's pardon for Louvel. The hours go by, and the King does not come. This delay causes more pain to the dying man than the death-struggle itself. Every noise in the street makes him think that Louis XVIII. is arriving. "I hear the escort," he says. But no; the King is still at the Tuileries. At midnight he received the first warning; but the gravity of his nephew's condition was at first concealed from him. A second bulletin was sent him. He wished to set out, but they detained him through fear of a conspiracy which might break out on his way. At last every precaution having been taken for guarding the road between the Tuileries and the Opera-house, he leaves the palace and repairs to the dying man. It is five o'clock in the morning. "Father! father!" cries the Prince, "the King is not coming! Cannot you promise, in his name, that this man's life shall be spared?" Just as he is pronouncing these words he shudders. He hears the tread of horses in the distance. "At last," says he, "here comes the King.

Oh! that he would come quickly! I am dying!" Louis XVIII. enters. "Mercy!" cries the dying, the death-rattle in his throat, "mercy for the man who struck me!" And in a faint and muffled voice repeats, "At least spare the man's life!"

The King embraces his nephew, and replies, "We will talk about that another time; be calm; you are not so ill as you suppose." Then he sits down near the bed. Presently he perceives Miss Brown's two daughters. The Duchess of Berry says a word to him in an undertone; then, presenting the two young girls, she says, "I have promised to adopt these children, and I ask the King, in the name of him whom we cherish, to deign to bestow his bounties on them." Louis XVIII. reflects for an instant, and then, reminding himself of other reigns, he says, "I will give the title of Countess of Vierzon to one, and Countess of Issoudun to the other." It is uncertain whether the dying man can hear this promise, which would have been a consolation to him. The agony is making terrible progress; but he is still able to articulate once more, "Mercy, mercy for the man." It is his last word. It is thirty-five minutes past six in the morning. The Duke of Berry exists no longer.

They wanted to remove the Duchess, in order to spare her the horror of such a sight. But she escapes from the hands of those who seek to keep her back, and throws herself upon the inanimate body of her husband; then, casting herself at the King's feet,

"Sire," she exclaims, "I have one favor to ask of Your Majesty. You will not refuse me. It is permission to return to Sicily. I cannot live here after my husband's death." Louis XVIII. tries to calm her. She is carried fainting to her carriage, and taken back to the Elysée. The courtiers try to induce the King to depart also. "I am not afraid of the sight of death," he says; "I have a last duty to perform towards my nephew." And, leaning on M. Dupuytren's arm, he approaches the bed, closes the eyes and mouth of the Prince, kisses his hand and retires, to return to the palace of the Tuileries. The fatal night is ended. Day is breaking.

XX

THE DAY AFTER THE MURDER

THE Duchess of Berry returned to the Elysée, alas! without her husband. Let us listen to Madame de Gontaut, an eye-witness of this doleful return: "I sat down beside her; her head fell on my shoulder; the Duchess of Angoulême, who was on the front seat of the carriage, supported both of us. The ride was brief. Madame regained consciousness when we entered the court of the Elysée; with her icy hands she groped for him from whom she had just been separated; to find herself apart from him gave her a moment of terrible despair. We wanted to take her to her apartment; she refused this and went straight to that of Monseigneur. This was another agony for her. Everything was in readiness to receive him who was no more; his armchair drawn up, his dressing-gown spread out; all except himself, except life. She clung to me convulsively, and pressed her daughter to her heart: the poor little thing was frightened and cried. I entrusted her to Madame Lemoine, Madame having told me to remain with her. She wept over everything belonging to him; no longer restraining the outbreak of her sorrow, her cries were heartrending. She was determined to stay in this chamber, and remained on her knees beside the bed, which she clutched with her nervously contracted fingers. She, so calm, so courageous, during the dreadful night, now abandoned herself to the very excess of despair. She wished to be entirely alone with me; I gently entreated her to undress herself, for her clothes were still wet with blood. They brought me her nightdress, and I was able to persuade her to take some repose."

Madame de Gontaut sat down on the steps of the bed, where for several hours the Princess slept the sleep of fatigue and youth. Her awakening was cruel. While she was sleeping, her women had been preparing her widow's weeds. No one proposed it to her, but as soon as she perceived the costume she put it on. Then she went to the Elysée chapel to assist at the Mass offered by her almoner for the repose of her husband's soul. It was in this widow's dress and in this chapel that a painter caught a glimpse of her and made a portrait which she gave to her daughter's governess. After some painful hours, passed partly in prayer, always in sobs, she was persuaded to take a little nourishment. They spoke to her of the infant yet to be born. She promised to take care of herself.

Her father-in-law came to the Elysée, promising her his solicitude and assistance, and seeking to sustain her courage. But in her despair she asked nothing but to leave France and return to Sicily, to go as far as possible, so she said, from the place where he who alone could make her happy had been caused to perish. Monsieur succeeded in calming her and induced her to go to Saint Cloud, whither she went that very evening with her daughter.

At Paris the excitement was general. The majority of its inhabitants did not learn until next morning the crime of the previous night. The *Moniteur* of Monday, February 14, said not a word about it. It contained these lines, which were like the irony of fate: —

"To-morrow, Tuesday, there will be theatricals at the palace of the Tuileries, in the Gallery of Diana. The Opéra Comique will play *Picaros et Diego;* the *Vaudeville,* the *Château de mon oncle;* and the Variétés, the farcical comedy which is having a run at this theatre at present, *l' Ours et le Pacha."*

Instead of the pleasures announced there was universal mourning and consternation. Not only were the courts, the Bourse, and the theatres closed, but the balls, entertainments, and reunions of every description, even those that were most insignificant, to which the last days of the Carnival were devoted, were countermanded. The most sinister rumors were spread abroad. The murder of the Duke of Berry was said to be only the prelude to other crimes. A vast conspiracy was believed to exist. The royalists of every shade were in the utmost fury. The liberals thought they were ruined, because a reaction seemed inevitable. On that very day M. Decazes wrote to M. de Serre, who was ill at Nice: "We are all assassinated." And M. de Rémusat wrote to his mother: —

"Shortly before the Prince's last sigh they had sent away his wife; she could not endure it and returned. Monsieur stood at the door to keep her out; she gave him a violent push, and he fell, and she too, and there they both were, the father and the wife, rolling about the floor in the wounded man's chamber. I don't know anything so heartrending as that. And what a spectacle! A whole royal family assembled, and where? At the Opera-house, near an assassinated prince lying on the very mattresses used by the dancers when they fling themselves down from a high place. This is exact; for at the first moment these mattresses were the first that came to hand, and they were not changed again, for fear of disturbing him. And finally, to complete the strangeness and the grandeur of the spectacle, the Blessed Sacrament brought to and received in such a place! And this in presence of that old King, and of an entire family which has seen six of its members perish by violent deaths within thirty years! And what a barrier does not this new crime raise between the people and the Kings! How many ties have been sundered at a blow! In what relations of suspicion and shame does not one behold the family which has received the blows and the nation from which the blows proceeded!"

At eleven in the morning the tribunes of the Chamber of Deputies were already filled, and an immense crowd thronged the avenues of the Palais-Bourbon. Blended anxiety and wrath were depicted on all faces. Then a motion was made which proves to what a height the fury and injustice of party spirit can rise. Without having taken counsel with any members of the Right, M. Clausel de Coussergues ascended the tribune, and exclaimed: —

"Gentlemen, there is no law which fixes the mode in which ministers shall be accused, but it belongs to the nature of such a deliberation that it shall take place in public session. I propose to the Chamber to bring an act of accusation against M. Decazes, Minister of the Interior, as accomplice in the assassination of the Duke of Berry, and I ask to develop my proposition." Cries of "Order" proceeded from many benches. "That is my opinion, gentlemen," said M. Clausel de Coussergues, returning to his place on the right.

During the entire day Monsieur had refused to see visitors. At eight o'clock in the evening he consented to receive the Baron of Vitrolles. He embraced him, and fell to weeping. After some time M. de Vitrolles began talking politics. Supposing the infant now expected by the Duchess of Berry should prove to be a girl, he asked what was to become of the monarchy. The possible accession of the Orleans branch alarmed all the royalists. The Spanish branch, moreover, might think of making good its rights, notwithstanding its renunciations, the validity of which had often been contested. To avert the dangers of such a situation, Monsieur ought to marry again. At these words the Count of Artois experienced a sort of shock. "What!" exclaimed he, "and it is you who do not fear to speak to me of marriage at such a moment!"—"I am in despair at being obliged to do so," replied M. de Vitrolles; "but Monsieur's unhappy position is such that in him the father, even at this moment, ought to give place to the political man, and that France and the monarchy should take precedence of his grief." The adviser of the Count of Artois went on to say that the woman who seemed most suitable for the Prince was the Duchess of Lucca, Marie Louise de Bourbon, former Queen of Etruria, daughter of Charles IV., King of Spain, sister of Ferdinand VII., widow of a Bourbon of the Parma branch, and mother of a son aged twenty; this young man might be summoned to France and made colonel of a regiment of the guard, and if the Duchess of Berry did not bring a son into the world, he might be made the heir of the elder branch of the Bourbons. M. de Vitrolles has claimed that, far from disapproving, Monsieur pressed him with questions concerning the age, appearance, and habits of the Duchess of Lucca. Such a scheme shows how disturbed the minds of royalists were.

Their rage against M. Decazes, from whom Louis XVIII. persisted in his unwillingness to separate, rose to madness, to frenzy. Their journals, on February 15, contained an avalanche of insults, a torrent of anathemas against the favorite.

According to the *Gazette de France*, ministers whose complicity with Louvel was incontestable could not be left at the head of the government. The *Drapeau blanc* declared that the real criminals were the seditious writers who had for a long time been preaching revolt and sacrilege, the unworthy and perjured deputies who had defended a priestly assassin, and above all the fatal man who had warmed, nourished, caressed, and unchained the revolutionary tiger. "Yes, M. Decazes," added the author of the article, "it is you who have slain the Duke of Berry. Weep tears of blood, obtain the pardon of Heaven, but the country will never forgive you."

The same day, M. de Sainte-Aulaire, the father-in-law of the calumniated minister, ascended the tribune of the Chamber of Deputies and said: "Since M. Clausel de Coussergues, instead of permitting his proceeding of yesterday to be attributed to an only too legitimate grief, persists in an accusation which is simply the monument of his insanity, I do not oppose his proposition being placed on the minutes. I limit myself to demanding that my response to it shall also be placed there. This response will not be lengthy. I shall merely say to him: You are a calumniator." M. Clausel de Coussergues, without leaving his seat, contented himself with replying, "France will judge." During the same session, M. Decazes, remaining impassible in the face of so many outrages, submitted to the Chamber a bill suspending individual liberty.

The ultras, seeing that their enemy was not yet overthrown, pushed their fury beyond all bounds. The rage of the women, especially, was almost epileptic. When the salons break loose, their violence is not outdone by that of the most ferocious clubs. Court ladies were heard to exclaim, "What a pity that the relaxation of the penal laws no longer permits tortures proportionate to the enormity of his crime to be applied to Louvel,— tortures which would wring from him the name of his accomplices!" Nobody would believe that the crime was an isolated crime. Any one who should have expressed the notion that there had been no conspiracy, that the assassin had no accomplices, would have been set down as an ill-disposed person, a traitor. The royalist press waxed into a formidable crescendo of hatred and exasperation. The *Journal des Débats* thundered against the minister "whose policy dismayed kings and peoples, all powerful against fidelity, impotent against perfidy." It called him a froward child, an expectant Bonaparte. The *Drapeau blanc* stated that on the night of the murder the president of the Council had said something in Louvel's ear, "doubtless to give him some secret instruction." The *Gazette de France* declared that if he remained minister, "civilization was compromised, and hell broken loose." M. de Chateaubriand wrote that the guiltiest hand was not that which struck the blow, and that he should pity M. Decazes if that minister consented to "dye his dictatorial purple in the blood of the Duke of Berry." On all sides, the ultras exclaimed, "If this man remains in power, we are all ruined, the monarchy is ended, the King and all his family will be assassinated." — "Yes, Sire," said President Séguier, speaking on behalf of the magistrates of the royal court of Paris, "there exists a permanent conspiracy against the Bourbons, and ferocious joy has shown itself amid the general consternation. May not the pure blood which has flowed merely irritate thirst?"

The more his favorite minister was attacked, the more bent was Louis XVIII. on his defence. "The wolves," said he, "ask nothing of the shepherd but to sacrifice the dog." To him, the dismission of M. Decazes would have seemed an abdication. Four days had gone by since the murder of the Duke of Berry, and the minister still held office. Word had been sent him that if he dared present himself at the house of the victim's father, he would never leave the hall of the body-guards alive. And yet he dared go thither. And the ultras said to each other, despairingly, that Monsieur had been weak enough to receive him politely, and even to say to him, "I am greatly touched by your sympathy."

On the morning of February 18 M. de Vitrolles was visited by several officers of the royal guard.

"Things ought not to go on in this way any longer," said they; "the reign of M. Decazes cannot be prolonged; an end must be put to it. Is not Monsieur going to give us any orders?" The same day a rumor got about that the minister would be killed at the Tuileries, in the hall of the body-guards, when he should be passing through it on his way to the King. An ultra, M. Mathieu de Montmorency, was so convinced of this that he had the loyalty to warn M. Decazes, through M. de Saint-Cricq, by imploring him to keep away from the Tuileries in the evening. The minister paid no attention to these warnings. But his position became constantly more unsettled. "This political struggle succeeding the veritable death-struggle," says the late Duke of Broglie in his *Souvenirs*, "this warfare of influences above a corpse, between the morbid tenderness of a poor infirm King and the ascendancy of an heir presumptive, dangling the bloody shirt of his son in his hand, could not last long."

The Duke and Duchess of Angoulême came to dine with Louis XVIII. at the Tuileries in the evening of February 18. A solemn interview between the King and his family took place after the repast. The attendants having retired, Monsieur and the Duchess of Angoulême threw themselves on their knees before the sovereign and entreated him to banish M. Decazes. "We make this request," exclaimed the daughter of Louis XVI., "to avoid another crime." Misunderstanding this remark,

Louis XVIII. replied that he would risk the poniards. ' "Ah! Sire," replied the Duchess of Angoulême, "thanks be to God, my fears do not extend to Your Majesty, but to a person who is dear to you." —"I shall be as brave for my friend as for myself," returned the King; "and I defy the crime for him as I do for me." The Duke of Angoulême, who was very timid and very respectful toward his uncle, kept silence, but his wife and his father insisted with great energy. Louis XVIII. was overcome. "Sire," said the Count of Artois, "it is impossible for me to remain at the Tuileries if M. Decazes, publicly accused by M. Clausel de Coussergues of complicity in the death of my son, continues there as minister. Your Majesty will permit me to retire to the Elysée-Bourbon." The King replied nearly in these terms: "Eh! what! it is because he is pursued by a calumny whose extravagance equals its atrocity that you want me to smite a man who is so devoted to me! Even the deputies who are opposed to him have repelled this calumny with horror, and shall I, I only, appear to believe it, when, on the contrary, it revolts every faculty of my soul? I declare to you that I have never known a heart more candid, nor one endowed with a more active and genuine sensibility, than Count Decazes. I am convinced that he would have given his life to save my nephew, as he would give it for you. I respect the extravagance of your grief; mine is not less heart-rending, but does not render me unjust." Then the

Duchess of Angoulême made a final effort to convince her uncle: "Sire," said she, "our family has been greatly united by misfortune. Let our union at least console us! Do not refuse this favor!" "I ask it," exclaimed Monsieur, "I ask it as a sacrifice to the manes of my son."—"You will have it," returned the King; "very well! I will see that you are satisfied."

Duke Victor de Broglie says in his *Souvenirs:* "Louis XVIII. abdicated by dismissing his darling child, *invitus invitum*, without ceasing to send him three letters a day." The *Moniteur* of February 21, announced that Count Decazes was no longer minister, and that the Duke of Richelieu had formed a new cabinet. The favorite was compensated by the title of duke and the embassy from France to London. The King, possibly, was more afflicted by the absence of this friend than by the murder of his nephew. "Such," says M. de Viel-Castel in his *Histoire de la Restauration*, "was the termination of the ministerial existence of a man who had scarcely attained his fortieth year, and who was to live for more than forty more, without a return to power ever being granted him. For nearly five years he had exerted an influence over France which very few have equalled. An act which does honor to his memory is the decree of September 5, by which, it could be affirmed, he added fifteen years to the life of the Bourbon royalty."

M. Decazes had not disarmed the hatred of his enemies by quitting the ministry. More than ten days afterwards, M. de Chateaubriand wrote in the *Conservateur:* "What precautions were taken before and since the death of the Duke of Berry? Is it not true that the prefect of police was deprived six months ago of some of his means of surveillance? and that on the very day of the crime several agents of public safety were absent from the place where it was committed? The barriers have not been closed, passports have not been demanded, mail-bags and parcels have not been searched, nor carriages and diligences. Not a proclamation, nothing to console or enlighten the people. It has been said they feared to excite indignation. But those who still struggled against public hatred have not been able to resist public grief. Our tears, our groans, our sobs, have astonished an imprudent minister whose feet have slipped in blood." It is true that in the same article the author of the *Génie du Christianisme* spoke of "the good natural sentiments of M. Decazes, perverted by the *little creatures* who surround him," adding that, the royalists being without rancor, the King's favorite ought to recognize in his generous enemies the friends whom he should have chosen for his own glory and the welfare of France. Despite this cloaking over of hatred, the last sentence was that which struck the reader most. Chateaubriand, to judge by this passage from the *Mémoires d' Outre-*

Tombe, seems to have repented of it: "I said that his feet had slipped in blood, which did not signify, God forbid! that he was guilty of murder, but that he had fallen in the red pool that formed under Louvel's knife."

XXI

THE OBSEQUIES OF THE DUKE OF BERRY

EVERYTHING that concerned the murder of the Duke of Berry was calculated to impress the imagination. In passing the Opera-house, which had been used for the last time on the day of the crime, and was about to be demolished from top to bottom as an accursed spot, every one made his own reflections on the emptiness of human grandeur and pleasures. "Let one imagine," says Chateaubriand, "an empty theatre after the catastrophe of a tragedy, the orchestra deserted, the lights extinguished, the scenery moveless, the decorations stationary and smoky, the comedians, the singers, and dancers all vanished through traps and secret passages." Thus pass away, thus vanish, the vanities of the world. Even the living are phantoms.

As soon as the King had closed the Duke of Berry's eyes, the mortal remains of the Prince had been carried to the Louvre and deposited in the apartments of the manager. During the entire day the priests of Saint-Germain-l'Auxerrois prayed beside the deceased. Detachments of the body-guards were on duty there. The doors of the Louvre were closed. As for the assassin, he had been taken from the theatre of his crime to the Conciergerie and put into a strait-jacket to prevent him from committing suicide. For twenty-four hours he refused all nourishment, but in the end he resigned himself to his fate. In the morning of February 15 he was brought from the Conciergerie to the Louvre. He was taken into a lower room, hung with black, and in front of a bed from which the sheet was suddenly drawn. This sheet had hidden the body of the Prince, still covered with the bloody shirt, the wound gaping in the side. Some one said to the murderer: "Do you recognize this wound and the poniard which made it?" — "Yes," he answered, without the least sign of emotion. "Have you any accomplices?" — "None."

On returning to his prison, Louvel said to one of his keepers: "This morning they inflicted a rough spectacle on me; they took me to the Louvre into the presence of the Duke of Berry's corpse. I was greatly moved, but I did not let them see it. I did not know the Prince, and I had no personal grudge against him; but he was one of those who had borne arms against France and brought in foreigners. I do not repent of what I have done; and yet it is a horrible thing for a man to throw himself on another and poniard him from behind when he is defenceless. I know very well that I have committed a crime; through ill-understood and insane patriotism, if you like; but people would be wrong to believe it was cowardly. If they knew what force of mind it required at the moment of performing it, they would have a very different notion. They want to make me commit a second crime by trying to force me to name my accomplices, when I have none."

The next day, February 16, the body of the Duke of Berry lay in state at the Louvre, and three days afterwards the coffin was placed on a catafalque surrounded with burning tapers, erected in the south gallery of the palace, which was hung with funeral draperies. Two altars were erected, one on each side of the catafalque, where Mass was said in the mornings and the Office of the Dead at night. All classes of society, from the princes and the Duke of Orleans, who sprinkled the holy water as representative of the King, down to workmen and the humblest of the common people, were admitted to pass in front of this coffin. The people experienced more curiosity than sadness. As Chateaubriand has said: "Men love whatever is spectacular, especially death, when it is the ·death of a great personage." The multitude that thronged the Louvre complained because the Prince's face had been covered so soon; they would have liked above all things to see the wound.

The corpse of the Duke of Berry was transported from the Louvre to the Abbey of Saint Denis, February 22. At five in the morning the drums of the National Guard beat the call to arms, and the National Guards repaired to the posts assigned them in the Louvre and on the quays. The Duke of Orleans headed the procession, in which four hundred poor men carried the candles. The market porters and the charcoal men of Paris walked in the procession. The houses and thatched cabins in the villages it passed through had been hung with the best the inhabitants possessed. On arriving at the basilica of Saint Denis, the coffin was again surrounded with burning tapers and exposed until March 14, the day fixed on for the funeral.

Rarely has a funeral ceremony presented a character at once so lugubrious and so grandiose. The King, the Duke and Duchess of Angoulême, the Duke and Duchess of Orleans, Mademoiselle d'Orléans, the Duke of Chartres, and the Prince. of Condé were present. As all classes of society were to be represented, thirty places had been reserved in the church for the charcoal men, the market porters, and market-women. The old basilica, hung with black throughout its whole extent, resembled an immense tomb. Bands of light outlined themselves against the funereal draperies. The King occupied a tribune almost opposite the catafalque, with the daughter of Louis XVI. Mgr. de Quélen, coadjutor to the Archbishop of Paris, pronounced the funeral oration. He had taken this verse of the Bible as his text: —

Convertam, Israel, festivitates vestras in luctum, et jubila vestra, in planctum.

Monsieur's body-guards lifted the coffin and carried

it toward the vault. As they passed in front of the tribunes, the King and the Duchess of Angoulême kneeled down. Tears flowed from every eye.

Listen to an eye-witness, the author of the *Génie du Christianisme:* "It was not yet two months since I had seen the Prince, full of life, sitting, January 21, in front of the catafalque of Louis XVI. One looked for him in vain on the bench near his brother, the Duke of Angoulême, and found him only on the same catafalque, before which his brother was weeping. One's eyes turned with emotion towards the royal family, already so small, and still diminishing; on the King, who seemed to be meditating amidst the ruins of the monarchy; on Madame, wrapped in a long crape garment as if it were her usual attire; on the Duke of Angoulême, who was chief mourner, and who, bowing to the altar and the coffin by turns, seemed asking from the first strength to behold the second. . . . They chanted, they tolled the bells, they discharged cannon; there was such grandeur in this pageant that one might fancy he was assisting at the obsequies of the monarchy."

Placed in the very centre of the crypt, the royal vault of the Bourbons is its most sombre and impressive point; the eye cannot penetrate into this lugubrious enclosure save through a grated window, and then only by the aid of a torch. There were the coffins of Louis XVI. and Marie Antoinette, of Madame Adelaide and Madame Victoire, daughters of Louis XV.; of the two children of the Duke of

Berry, who died a few hours after they were born; of the Prince of Condé, who died in 1818. There the body of Louvel's victim was about to repose.

The king-at-arms called for the honors in this order: "Monsieur the Count of Mesnard, performing the functions of chief equerry to Mgr. the Duke of Berry, bring hither his sword.

"Monsieur the Count of Choiseul, aide-de-camp to Mgr. the Duke of Berry, bring hither the collar of the Order of the Golden Fleece.

"Monsieur the Viscount of Montlégier, gentleman of honor to Mgr. the Duke of Berry, bring hither the star and the ribbon of grand cross of the royal Order of the Legion of Honor.

"Monsieur the Count of Brissac, gentleman of honor to Mgr. the Duke of Berry, bring hither the star and the ribbon of grand cross of the royal and military Order of Saint Louis.

"Monsieur the Count of Rohan-Chabot, gentleman of honor to Mgr. the Duke of Berry, bring hither the collar of the Order of the Holy Ghost.

"Monsieur the Count of Clermont-Lodève, gentleman of honor to Mgr. the Duke of Berry, bring hither the kingly mantle.

"Monsieur the Count of Nautouillet, performing the functions of first gentleman of the bedchamber to Mgr. the Duke of Berry, bring hither the crown."

As fast as the king-at-arms received one of the honors, he gave it to the first herald, stationed on one of the steps, and he passed it on to the second, who laid it on the coffin. The vault having been opened in presence of the great officers of the crown, the Duke of Angoulême, as chief mourner, went down into it. The Duke of Berry's coffin was afterwards lowered. Then the Duke of Angoulême came up alone. Twenty-one cannons announced this moment.

The Count of Nautouillet, as performing the functions of first gentleman of the bedchamber to the defunct, stood in the entrance of the royal vault and addressed the officers of the Prince in these words: "Monseigneur the Duke of Berry, your master and mine, is dead. Officers, provide for yourselves." And finally, the king-at-arms cried twice: "Very high, very powerful Prince Charles Ferdinand of Artois, Duke of Berry, son of France, is dead!" adding after the second time, "Pray God for the repose of his soul."

XXII

THE WIDOW

A LEGEND of poesy and sadness was about to form around the young widow who, at twenty-one years of age, had been so cruelly stricken. The very day of the murder she cut off her hair, — "her hair," said she, "which her husband loved." She gave the tresses to Madame de Gontaut, saying: "Take them; one day you shall give them to my daughter; she will learn that her mother cut off her hair on the day her father was assassinated." The Elysée palace, where she had been so happy, and where she no longer found her husband, horrified her thenceforward. She went to hide her sorrow in the palace of Saint Cloud. Her father-in-law came there to visit her. She was haunted by the idea that the murder of the Duke of Berry was an act of vengeance. In order to divert her from this thought, the Count of Artois related to her that one day the Duke of Berry, returning from the chase, and slowly ascending the mountain in the forest of Fontainebleau, noticed a man who seemed fatigued. The Prince summoned his huntsman, told him to take the man up behind the carriage and ask him if he were suffering and what was his name. "He is not sick," answered the huntsman, "he is only tired. His name is Louvel, and he works in the King's stables at Versailles, where he lives with his sister." On reaching the summit of the mountain, Louvel got down from the carriage, and no more was thought about him.

After the lapse of several days, the Duchess of Berry left Saint Cloud and installed herself, with her little daughter, at the Tuileries, in the Pavilion of Marsan, close to her father-in-law. Her new apartment was not entirely strange to her. She had already slept there one night, at the time of her entry into Paris on the eve of her marriage at Notre Dame. How happy she was then! What joyous rays were dispersed in all directions by the prism of hope! What a fairylike abode the Tuileries had seemed! What confidence in the future! What youth, enthusiasm, and gaiety! And in less than four years what a change! The young widow's apartment was like a mortuary chapel; in accordance with the mourning ceremonial of princesses the walls were draped in black. Mirrors, armchairs, sofas, footstools, all were covered with crape. None but yellow wax candles were lighted. The various objects of luxury resembled the ornaments of a catafalque. The Princess had ordered a full-length portrait of her husband from the painter Gérard, wishing to have it constantly before her eyes.

The Parisians saw her on March 20 for the first

time since the fatal day. She was taking a walk with her daughter on the terrace beside the water. The sight of her caused a profound impression. Women, holding their children in their arms, pointed out to them the widow of the assassinated Prince and the little orphan dressed all in white. Crowds would wait several hours together for the moment when the Princess would issue from the Tuileries, in order to salute her as she passed. It was suggested to her to go by the underground passages which formed a means of communication between the palace and the terrace bordering the water. "I will not," she replied; "they would think I am afraid." She was convinced that she had a mission, and that she bore the saviour of France in her womb. At the court she no longer appeared as a mournful widow, but as a sort of amazon, ready to brave all perils and defy all storms. In this most energetic of young women there was something virile which the French character takes delight in. Even the adversaries of the monarchy recognized in her the worthy daughter of Henri IV.

At eleven in the evening, April 28, 1820, a petard, the match of which was already lighted, was flung under one of the wickets which separate the Place Carrousel from the rue Rivoli, opposite the rue Echelle. The explosion produced by it resembled that of a heavily loaded musket. When she heard it, the Duchess of Berry said with great coolness: "They would like very well to frighten me, but they will not succeed." The guard had taken up arms at the sound of the explosion, but the guilty person had escaped.

Hoping that an alarm might bring about a miscarriage for the Princess, the criminal renewed his attempt at the same place in the night of May 6-7. But this time he was arrested just as he was lighting a much larger fire-cracker. It was a former officer named Gravier, who had an accomplice named Bouton.

Far from allowing herself to be intimidated by such menaces, the Duchess of Berry felt an intimate conviction that her delivery would be fortunate, and that the child would be a boy. She had had a dream, an account of which she wrote with her own hand in the following lines, which she sent to the Count of Brissac, and which have been preserved by his family: —

"About the fourth month of my pregnancy, being asleep, I saw Saint Louis enter my room, just as he is painted, his crown on his head, his large royal mantle with the lilies, and his venerable face. I presented my little girl to him. He opened his mantle and presented me with the prettiest little boy. He took off his own crown and placed it on his head.

"For my part, I kept pushing Louise forward; nevertheless, he persisted in keeping the crown on the boy's head, although he sheltered my daughter also under his mantle. Saint Louis then disappeared with my two children, and I awoke, convinced from that time that I would have a boy, and since then not a single doubt on that head has occurred to me during the whole time of my pregnancy.

"MARIE CAROLINE."

To the young Princess whose Italian imagination was so easily impressed, this dream was more than a promise; it was a certitude. She believed in it as if it had been an article of faith. As Monsieur said to her that perhaps it would be a daughter she would bring forth, she replied, "Saint Louis knows more than you do about that, father."

Royalist society, so menaced and unsettled, which felt the earth trembling under its feet and dreaded volcanic explosions both in France and elsewhere, had no longer any hope save in an infant, in a cradle. Already people were comparing the child of the young Princess to Moses. Victor Hugo had composed, directly after the Duke of Berry's death, a poem entitled *Moïse sur le Nil*, which ended thus: —

> "Mortals, whose pride the Eternal disavows,
> Bow down: a cradle shall deliver Israel,
> A cradle is to save the world."

All royalist France adored the woman who was to perpetuate the race of Bourbons. A religious sentiment blended with the enthusiasm and tenderness she excited. One might have said that in her was incarnated the cause of the altar and the throne. The calm and confidence she manifested contrasted with the revolutionary agitations and profound troubles which showed themselves everywhere else. Never, since the Revolution, had there been such turmoils in the streets of Paris. The discussion on the law of electoral reform which opened in the Chamber of Deputies, May 15, summed up anew the struggle between the liberals and the reactionists, and excited the wrath and the passions of the populace to the highest degree.

General Lafayette said from the tribune: "Let no one oblige the generations, by threatening them with the loss of the fruits of the Revolution, to seize anew the sacred forces of the principles of eternal verity and sovereign justice." And M. de Serre, alluding to October 6, 1789, replied: "The honorable member must have experienced several times, he must have felt, with death in his soul and a blush on his forehead, that, after having roused up the masses of the people, not merely is it not always possible to arrest them when they plunge into crime, but that one is often forced to follow them; sometimes to lead them." Hostile groups and tumultuous gatherings collected in the approaches to the Palais Bourbon, where the Chamber was sitting. Officers of the guard in citizen's dress mingled with the crowd and shouted, "Long live the King!" in response to the cries of "Long live the Charter!" The armed force was obliged to intervene. In one of the collisions a student named Lallemand was shot and killed. The populace cried out that it was intended to massacre them. On both sides the fury reached its height.

June 4, M. Camille Jordan asked for a provisional suspension of the parliamentary debates. M. de Serre, after maintaining that the threatened riot was occasioned by nothing but the appeal to revolt made by the journals of the Left, reassured the Right by detailing the measures adopted for putting an end to the disturbances, and obtain' a prolongation of the debate. Out of doors, the cavalry were charging on the crowd. A retired colonel named Duvergier led those manifestly disaffected as far as the Bastille, whence the stream of rioters, swelled by the population of the faubourgs, returned toward the Tuileries by the rue Saint-Antoine and the quays. Cuirassiers and gendarmes were sent to meet them and succeeded in dispersing them. Louis XVIII. could see from his palace windows the manœuvres of the troops, the cavalry charges, the movements of the groups of curious spectators or rioters, flying before the galloping horses and the sabres of the soldiers. The cries of fright or fury from the crowd reached the ears of the Duchess of Berry and the Duchess of Angoulême. The daughter of Louis XVI. recalled the dismal scenes of 1792, — the 20th of June, the 10th of August.

The troubles continued the following day. Thousands of students, wearing white cravats, armed with heavy canes, and marching two and two, assembled on the quai d'Orsay, before the Chamber of Deputies. The gendarmes having repulsed them, they reassembled on Place Louis XV., where their ranks were swelled by a multitude of agitators and half-pay officers. From the terraces of the Tuileries, the windows of the Ministry of Marine and other hotels on Place Louis XV., numerous spectators were watching these popular scenes, which evoked the spectre of the great Revolution, with a curiosity mingled with anxiety. The mounted gendarmes and the dragoons of the guard charged. Voices were heard crying, "To the faubourgs!" Some groups bearing a red flag attempted a diversion in the direction of the Palais Royal. The crowd rushed into the rue Saint-Antoine to return upon the Hôtel de Ville. But a regiment of cuirassiers, coming from the Arsenal, pursued them. A pelting rain prevented a collision, and the rioters withdrew.

The situation was more menacing still the next day, June 6. It was the day when young Lallemand was buried, and the Chamber of Peers was about to pronounce its sentence against Louvel. The rioters were going in crowds through the boulevards toward the rue Saint-Antoine. Meantime, Louvel was reading before his judges this declaration, in which may be felt the ferocious hatred of the enemies of the Restoration, a régime which had at the same time enthusiastic admirers and fanatical detractors.

"To-day I have to blush for a crime which I alone committed. I have the consolation of believing, in dying, that I have dishonored neither my nation nor my family. Nothing need be seen in me but a Frenchman who vowed to sacrifice himself in order to destroy, in pursuit of his system, a part of the men who have taken up arms against his country. I am accused of having taken the life of a prince; I alone am guilty; but among the men who compose the government there are many as guilty as I am. They have, according to me, recognized crimes as virtues; the worst governments France has ever had have always punished the men who have betrayed it, or who have borne arms against the nation.

"In my view, I cannot avoid believing that if the battle of Waterloo has been so fatal to France, it is because there were Frenchmen at Ghent who disseminated treason in the army and gave assistance to the enemy.

"According to me and to my system, the death of Louis XVI. was necessary because the nation had consented to it. If it had been a handful of intriguers who had gone to the Tuileries and taken his life on the moment, it would have been different; but as Louis XVI. and his family were under arrest for a long time, it is inconceivable that it should not have been by the consent of the nation. . . . To-day the Bourbons claim to be the masters; but, according to me, they are criminals, and the nation would be dishonored if it allowed itself to be governed by them." The Chamber of Peers listened with stupor to this coldly disdainful language, and unanimously condemned Louvel to death.

More favorable to the liberals than to the partisans of the Ministry, the Duchess Victor de Broglie, daughter of Madame de Staël, has thus described the sombre day of June 6, 1820: "What a sight Paris presented at that time! At the Chamber of Peers a criminal trial in progress, a man who was a sort of prodigy of crime and fatality, condemned that day to be executed on the morrow. A wretched victim stricken down by the royal guard. The entire *bourgeois* class in revolt, crying murder, and in dread for its children. All the young men in revolt. A furious Chamber; a slavish and hypocritical Ministry. Inside the Tuileries that unhappy Duchess of Berry, beside herself, pursued by the thought that her husband's last will would not be respected; Madame listening to the cries of the populace that had caused her family to perish; indignation and pity swaying from one side to the other, from the victors to the vanquished, without anywhere finding a place to rest."

The next day, June 7, the agitation in Paris continued. At six in the evening, Louvel ascended the scaffold. An immense crowd covered the Place de Grève and its approaches. A large force of military had been put under arms. They say that up to the last moment the condemned man hoped to be rescued by the rioters. He looked and listened as if he were expecting a signal. When he saw that none was coming, he calmly mounted the steps of the guillotine; then his head fell beneath the knife. The government finally quelled the disturbance which had been grumbling for several days. The electoral law was passed, June 12, and the Chambers adjourned.

Abroad, the revolutionary spirit was making gigantic strides. On the other side of the Pyrenees and the other side of the Alps all was aflame. The Bourbons of Spain and of Naples were threatened still more than the Bourbons of France. Pronunciamientos and popular risings brought the dynasties within a hair's-breadth of their ruin. Ferdinand VII., King of Spain, was obliged to take oath to the constitution of 1812, and he opened the revolutionary Cortes, July 9. People said it was his 1789, the prelude to a 1793. Almost at the same moment General Pépé made his triumphal entry into Naples at the head of a revolted regiment. King Ferdinand I., grandfather of the Duchess of Berry, was obliged to resign his royal powers to her father, the heir-apparent, who proclaimed the Spanish Constitution of 1812, that ultra-liberal constitution of which, notwithstanding, not a single copy was to be found in the Kingdom of the Two Sicilies.

The rebound of the agitations in Spain and Italy made itself felt in France in the barracks and secret societies. In August some Bonapartist officers, acting in concert with the democrats and the directing revolutionary committee, in which sat General Lafayette, organized a grand conspiracy. They had an understanding with many regiments, several deputies, and numerous officers of all grades. Their aim was to seize the fort of Vincennes, the Hôtel de Ville, and the Tuileries, to arrest the royal family, raise the tricolored flag, establish a provisional government, and then make an appeal to the people, who would decide either for Napoleon II. or the Republic. The conspirators had arranged to strike the blow during the night of August 19-20, 1820. But they were betrayed by some of their accomplices, and the military authorities, warned in due time, arrested the officers who were most compromised, and notably Colonel Fabvier, formerly aide-de-camp to Marshal Marmont. The government esteemed itself most happy to have escaped so grave a peril; it felt itself too weak to dare attempt to prosecute the deputies secretly affiliated to the conspiracy.

The royalists told themselves that their saviour against such ambushes and dangers would be the child the Duchess of Berry bore in her womb. He was compared already, not merely to Moses, but to the Messias himself. Monarchical bombast treated the mother of such an impatiently awaited son as a supernatural being, a second Blessed Virgin. Encouraged by such protestations of devotion, the young Princess fancied that her little foot would have small difficulty in stamping out the monsters. She believed in the prediction addressed to her by Victor Hugo, that poet who was then a courtier: —

"Yet, of the royal stem, O frail support,
If God through thy aid show His majesty,
Thou mayst save France, and once again make sport
O' the hellish hydra's foul expectancy.
Thus, when the serpent, author of all woe,
Would thrust into the black abyss below
Man, whom his sin had ruinèd,
The Lord abased his sullen arrogance;
A woman came, weak and without defence,
Who bruised his cursèd head."

XXIII

THE BIRTH OF THE DUKE OF BORDEAUX

ALL royalist France was in commotion. The Duchess of Berry was nearing her time. The municipal councils of cities and the owners of castles had Masses said and novenas made to implore Heaven for her safe delivery. It had been decided that if she brought a prince into the world, he was to be styled the Duke of Bordeaux. Three market-women of that city, Mesdames Dasté, Duranton, and Aniche, were sent in deputation to the Tuileries to thank the King for the honor done to their city, and to offer a cradle intended for the expected child. "These dames," says Chateaubriand, "selected me to present them and their cradle to Madame the Duchess of Berry. I made haste to ask the gentleman-in-waiting for a formal audience. But lo, M. de Sèze thought that such an honor rightly belonged to him; it was said that I would never succeed at court. I was not yet reconciled with the Ministry, and I did not seem worthy to act as introducer of my humble ambassadresses." When the cradle was presented, the three Bordelais entreated the Princess to lie in at Bordeaux, where she would be safer than in Paris.

Was it not just, moreover, that the young duke should be born in the town whose name he was to bear? "This is to lay our prince in," said the market-women, pointing to the cradle. "We women will wash his swaddling-clothes, and our men will take good care that the Jacobins do not prevent him from sleeping."

Some one sent from Béarn the chanson of Jeanne d'Albret, of which the following is a translation: —

> "Our Lady of the end of the bridge,
> Assist me now.
> Pray God who is in heaven,
> That He will graciously deliver me soon.
> That He will grant me a son.
> All even to the tops of the mountains implore it.
> Our Lady of the end of the bridge,
> Assist me now."

To this was added a bottle of Jurançon wine and a clove of garlic, in memory of that which had been rubbed on the lips of Henri IV. as he was born.

On September 28th, the dowager Duchess of Orléans, the widow of Philippe-Égalité, went over to the chapel of the *Missionnaires* and piously assisted at the Mass offered for the happy deliverance of the Duchess of Berry.

The young Princess was calmly and courageously awaiting the solemn moment. Foreseeing the possibility that nature might be rebellious, she had said to the accoucheur, M. Deneux: "I know that in case of a dangerous delivery it is usual to save the mother at the risk of losing the child. I do not know whether Heaven has willed that my delivery shall be dangerous. However it may be, remember that the child I am bearing belongs to France; in case of danger, do not hesitate to save him, even at the expense of my life." She proposed to be brought to bed in her salon. Over her head was to be the full-length portrait of the Duke of Berry, painted by Gérard, and before her eyes a picture by Kinson which represented her weeping, her daughter at her side, before the bust of her husband.

Party spirit had at this time reached such a pitch of violence that many of the enemies of the Restoration obstinately refused to believe that the Princess was pregnant at all, and pretended that there was to be a supposititious child. Every precaution was taken to demonstrate the absurdity of such a calumny. As the time drew near, Louis XVIII. appointed the Marshal Duke of Coigny and Marshal Suchet, Duke of Albuféra, as witnesses, enjoining both of them to establish themselves at the Tuileries immediately, as well as the accoucheur and the doctors who formed part of the household of the Princess. Marshal Marmont says in his Memoirs: —

"The usual precautions had been taken to certify the birth of the child. They had been redoubled, so to say, by the choice of the individuals called to be witnesses. If only certain old nobles of the court, attached to the Bourbons, had been selected, their testimony might have been suspected; but one of them was Marshal Suchet, Duke of Albuféra, who was above suspicion by reason of his origin and his alliance with the Bonapartes. Installed beforehand at the Tuileries, he was to be stationed in the chamber of Madame the Duchess of Berry at the moment when the child was to be born."

September 28th, 1820, at nine in the evening, the King had said when giving the countersign, "I do not believe that Madame the Duchess of Berry will be delivered for five or six days yet." · Let us listen to Madame de Gontaut, governess of the children of France: "I spent nearly all my days with the Duchess of Berry; but one evening (September 28th), having had company in our little salon, I had not seen her, and as she was suffering somewhat, she waited until the visitors had gone before coming to me. She owned to me then that she had felt slight pains during the evening. I informed her of all the precautions that had been taken; I wanted to stay with her, but she said, 'Rest easy; at the least indication you shall be notified.' She left me, and before going to bed I went softly to her chamber door; all was quiet and reposing. I was doing the same when, in the middle of the night, Madame de Vathaire, first chambermaid to Madame, who occupied a chamber close to hers with Madame Bourgeois, another of her women, and kept the door of communication habitually open, arrived at mine. Finding it locked, she knocked repeatedly, and called me in a loud voice, saying, 'Come quick, quick! Madame is delivered.

Send the guard. Hurry up! I gave the order to go to Madame Lemoine, whom I told last evening to be ready in case she was called: she ran there at once.'

"Already prepared to rise at the least signal, I merely took time enough to slip on a dressing-gown. I arrived near Madame. As soon as she saw me, she held out her arms to me and exclaimed, 'It is Henri!' We embraced each other with one of those joyful cries that come but once in a lifetime.

"The infant was crying, and I examined it; it seemed to me strong and well. The nurse said to me, 'The child is doing well; he can stay just so for some instants.' Madame then exclaimed, 'Quick! quick! the witnesses!' My valet de chambre had followed me in this moment of confusion. I said, 'Here is one.'—'He will not answer,' replied Madame, 'as he is in your pay.' But she gave orders to light up everything and everywhere.

"Madame de Vathaire had already gone to look for the accoucheur, the Faculty, and to wake up everybody. I went across a passage which led to the vestibule of the court. Two sentries were at the door, one belonging to the royal guard and the other to the National Guard; I called them and bade them follow me; they hesitated, and talked of their instructions. 'Come,' I said to them, 'and save him who will one day be your king.' They did not comprehend me, but at this name of king, and encouraged by a sergeant, they followed me; the sergeant himself joined us (his name was Dauphinot). To make sure of them, I held them securely by the arms.

"At this moment the Duchess of Reggio, who had been notified, was coming down-stairs. She saw me in a dressing-gown flying open, a short petticoat, and black stockings, dragging along these two men, astounded but submissive. She assured me, laughing, that she should never forget it as long as she lived. I made them enter the narrow little corridor, which we got through with difficulty. On arriving near Madame, they were the first witnesses; then I put them in a corner of the room and kept my eye on them."

The infant was not yet separated from its mother. When the accoucheur came in, the Princess said to him, "Monsieur Deneux, we have a prince; I am well; don't concern yourself about me, but take care of my child; is there no danger in leaving him in that condition?" The accoucheur replied, "The child is very strong, he breathes freely, and he is so well that he may remain just so until the delivery, even though that should not happen for an hour." — "In that case," said the courageous mother, "let him be. I want to have him seen still attached to me. I want people to see that he is really mine."

It was then thirty-five minutes past two in the morning. Three National Guards, MM. Lainé, a grocer, Paigné, a druggist, and Dauphinot, an employé, all belonging to the Ninth Legion, and M. d'Hardivilliers, captain of the grenadiers of the royal guard, were in the chamber. "Gentlemen," said the Princess to them, "you are witnesses that it is a prince. See, he is not yet separated from his mother." She repeated the same phrase to the Marshal Duke of Albuféra, who came a few minutes later, and it was not until he had seen with his own eyes what the Princess said, that the umbilical cord was cut.

Concerning this, Marshal Marmont has said in his Memoirs: "The Duchess of Berry objected to have the cord cut before the arrival of the official witnesses, an act of courage and presence of mind which merits universal admiration. Some silly Parisian women have criticised this conduct on the ground of modesty. Miserable objection! Before the interests of a dynasty and the repose of a nation such considerations should disappear; and the Duchess of Berry rose to the level of circumstances. She was sublime. On the whole, she has great courage, great moral force, and a great instinct for government. If fortune had placed her in more favorable circumstances, it is probable that she would have succeeded in her enterprises and made herself a great name."

Meanwhile the King and the royal family had arrived. "God be thanked!" exclaimed Louis XVIII., "you have a son." And he handed a magnificent spray of diamonds to the mother, saying, "This is for you, and that is for me." As he spoke, he took the newborn child in his arms; then, calling for the clove of garlic and the bottle of Jurançon wine, he rubbed the infant's lips with the one and moistened its mouth with a few drops of the other. "Sire," said the Princess, "I wish I knew the air of Jeanne d'Albret's chanson, so that everything might be just as it was at the birth of Henri IV."

Learning that the marshals, generals, etc., were asking to be admitted to the presence of the newly born, the Viscountess de Gontaut carried him into the grand salon. "The Duke of Orleans came at last," says she in her Memoirs; "he looked attentively at the Duke of Bordeaux, and then said to the Duke of Albuféra, 'Monsieur the Marshal, I summon you to declare what you have seen. Is this child really the son of the Duchess of Berry?' I confess I had a moment of great impatience. 'Speak, Monsieur the Marshal,' I cried; 'tell all that you have seen!' The Marshal energetically testified to the legitimacy of the child, and added, 'I swear it on my honor! I am surer that the Duke of Bordeaux, here present, is the child of Madame the Duchess of Berry than I am that my own son is the child of his mother.' Silence ensued. After such incontestable proof, the Duke of Orleans departed to offer his felicitations to Madame the Duchess of Berry."

At half-past three in the morning, Mgr. de Bombelles, Bishop of Amiens, administered private baptism to the little Prince, and M. Dambray, Chancellor of France, fulfilling the functions of registrar to the royal household, wrote the certificate of birth.

Outside of the palace the house of the body-guards

and the barracks of the royal guard were suddenly illumined as if by magic.

Five o'clock in the morning. The cannon of the Invalides began to thunder. Several persons had advised that these bronze messengers should wait for daybreak before speaking, but the Duke of Richelieu responded, —

"For such a piece of news it is daybreak at any hour."

The Parisian population, suddenly awakened, anxiously count the discharges. Twelve were to be fired if it were a princess, twenty-four if it were a prince. At the thirteenth there is an explosion of joy. The royalists rise and hasten in crowds underneath the windows of the Pavilion of Marsan, where the Duchess has just been delivered, on the first story, looking down the rue Rivoli.

Six o'clock in the morning. The Duchess of Berry orders that all the military who present themselves shall be admitted. Officers, subalterns, and soldiers, more than five hundred, file in. "I bless thee," says an old Vendéan, looking at the little Prince, "and I enlist for six years longer." A soldier with three chevrons exclaims, "Ah, my Prince, why am I so old? I cannot serve under your orders." — "Keep up your heart, my hero," says the Princess; "he will begin early." Another soldier cries, "He is surely the child of the army, that fellow. He is born in the midst of cannonading and grenadiers' caps, and my captain is his first nurse."

The crowd constantly grows larger in the rue Rivoli, under the windows of the Princess's apartment. Enthusiastic acclamations resound. People who are unknown to each other carry on long conversations. Everybody is inquiring for news. They hope to get a glimpse of the little Prince. At the same time the churches are thronged by the faithful who come to return thanks to God.

Ten o'clock. The marshals, generals, and great officials are admitted to the King's cabinet. The Duke of La Châtre presents a young poet, M. Mennechet, who reads the following impromptu verses set to the air of the *Premier Pas*, on which the King and the Duchess of Angoulême congratulate him: —

> "France, 'tis a Bourbon has been born to thee!
> 'Tis of thy kings august the late-born son!
> And from his cradle this weak child shall be
> The traitor's terror and the brave man's glee.
> 'Tis a Bourbon.
>
> "It is a Bourbon whom thy tears besought:
> Heaven heard and the auspicious gift sent down;
> The glory of thy arms sustain shall he,
> And dry the tears of helpless misery.
> 'Tis a Bourbon.
>
> "It is a Bourbon, happy mother; leave
> Thy sadness, and thy widow's weeds lay down.
> It is a husband rises from the tomb,
> This noble child restores him to his home.
> 'Tis a Bourbon."

Noon. A Mass of thanksgiving and the *Te Deum* in the chapel of Tuileries. Louis XVIII. and all the royal family are present at it.

One o'clock. On returning from Mass, the King stops on the balcony of the Pavilion of the Horloge. Addressing the crowd that fills the garden, he says in a strong voice: "My friends, your joy increases mine a hundredfold. A child is born to all of us. This child will one day become your father; he will love you as I do, and as you love all who belong to me."

Two o'clock. Monsieur receives the officers of the Duke of Berry's household. With the King's permission, he had said to them on the day of the murder, "If my daughter-in-law brings forth a son, you will all resume towards him the same functions you fulfilled toward his father." The hour has come for the realization of this promise. "My friends," says Monsieur, "I announce to you with pleasure that you are in the service of the Duke of Bordeaux; I am very sure that you will be as tenderly attached to the son as you were to the father."

The household of the little Prince was constituted thus: governess, the Viscountess of Gontaut; under-governess, the Marchioness of Foresta; first gentleman of the chamber, the Count of Nantouillet; gentlemen of honor and aides-de-camp, the Prince of Léon, the Count of Brissac, the Viscount of Montlégier; aides-de-camp, the Count of Mesnard, the Count of Clermont-Lodève, the Count of Choiseul, Count

Eugène d'Astorg, the Prince of Bauffremont, the Marquis of Coligny, the Count of Mailly.

All Paris spends the entire day in jollity. They sing, they dance farandoles. They hum a refrain like this in the streets: —

> "It is a boy! I in my happiness
>   Counted twice twelve discharges of the guns.
> All Paris is in motion; each one runs,
>   Yet each the other stops, to say with joy,
>   It is a boy!
>
> "It is a boy! And if he wear the crown,
>   We'll see him worthy of so great a name.
> Noble and generous his soul will be,
>   And to no man will he desire annoy.
>   It is a boy!"

The rue Rivoli, opposite the Pavilion of Marsan, is constantly thronged by an immense and enthusiastic crowd. It is with difficulty that the Duchess of Berry is prevented from rising in order to show herself standing with her infant in her arms. They want to give her a composing draught to quiet her. "Let it alone," says she, and, listening to the clamor of the populace: "that is the real sedative."

Evening has come. The promenaders are innumerable. The weather is magnificent. The stars rival the illuminations. The garrison of Paris, having obtained the honor of offering the young mother a luminous bouquet, the troops assemble beneath her windows. The bouquet is composed of a great many rockets which explode at a given signal. The noise is prodigious and the effect splendid. The Princess is ravished with delight. She has her windows opened and her bed drawn close up to them in order to see and be seen. She applauds with childish joy. The soldiers who can perceive her admire her animation and her courage, and they are heard exclaiming, "She is worthy to be the mother of a king."

The theatres are livelier than ever. At the Opera, *Athalie* is given with the choruses, and in the work of Racine the public find allusions to the newly born, who is already called the child of miracle, which raise their enthusiasm to its highest pitch. After the tragedy, M. Mennechet's verses, *C'est un Bourbon*, are sung. At the Feydeau theatre the entire audience join in the air, *Vive Henri IV.* At the Variétés a rondo is sung alluding to the twenty-four volleys of cannon fired in the morning. At the Gaîté, a plump and fresh-looking nurse arrives at the close of the *Fanfan la Tulipe*, and furnishes the occasion for a very joyous entertainment.

To sum up, the 29th of September was but one continual ovation for the Duchess of Berry. After so much emotion and so much happiness, the valiant mother needed repose. But listen to Madame de Gontaut: —

"After the evening reception Madame was tired; the Faculty interposed and ordered absolute quiet; she consented to it on condition that she might have her children near her. I had the two cradles and my bed set up in the gallery. Madame Lemoine not only took care of Monseigneur, but acted as nurse to Madame. This citizen-like simplicity pleased her. On this first night, Madame, who was very uneasy, often summoned her nurse; at such times I remained alone in that badly lighted gallery, still hung with black, where everything was dismal and the image of a tomb. — Poor, fatherless infant, I said to myself; a prey to the most frightful attempts even before his birth (for that of Gravier was fresh in my remembrance)! — Oh, how fervent were the prayers I addressed to Heaven! I shall never forget that first night. When day began to break, it seemed to me that I gained more confidence; the name the Nuncio had given to the Prince recurred to my mind. No, said I; God does not work a miracle without an end in view."

XXIV

THE REJOICINGS

THE newly born had received the Christian names of Henri Charles Ferdinand Dieudonné (God-given): the first in memory of the most popular of his ancestors; the second, in memory of his father, the Duke of Berry; the third, on account of his great-grandfather and sponsor, King Ferdinand of the Two Sicilies; and the fourth, in allusion to Heaven, to whom thanks were offered for the birth of an heir to so many kings. As to his title of Duke of Bordeaux, this was a recompense granted to the city which boasted of having been the first to proclaim the Bourbon Restoration, in 1814. The young Prince was born on September 29, 1820, feast of Saint Michael the Archangel, one of the protectors of France. The courtiers never stopped saying that this was a presage of good fortune, a proof of the divine favor. Chateaubriand has made this remark: "When Henri was born, on Saint Michael's Day, did not people say that the archangel was going to put the dragon under his feet? It is to be feared, on the contrary, that the flaming sword was only drawn from the scabbard to banish the innocent from the terrestrial paradise, and to guard its doors against him."

Meanwhile the joy of the royalists rose to delirium. They triumphed noisily and proudly. One of their journals termed the little Prince the Messias of legitimacy. Another said one would have to be an atheist not to see the finger of God in his birth. Those were held up to public indignation " whose criminal silence and guilty reticence disclosed odious sentiments." The following appeared in the *Débats:* " Young infant, object of so much love and so many prayers, in the midst of political storms you appear to us as a star appears as the last sign of hope to the mariner beaten by the tempest. May the efforts of honest men rally around your cradle! May all the efforts of the wicked come to naught against that sacred cradle! Grow up to imitate the virtues of the noble family that surrounds you! Grow up to console a mother who conceived you in sadness! Grow up to render happy a people who received you with so much joy!"

Although the birth of a posthumous child is in nowise a miraculous event, people persisted in calling the Duke of Bordeaux the child of miracle. The address of the National Guard of Paris was thus expressed: —

" The happiness of the King is that of France; our hearts have no words whereby to express the sentiment which transports us. Sire, you have in us subjects faithful to their King, children who will cherish a father, and soldiers ready to shed their blood for the defence of the throne. The child of miracle is a certain pledge of the altogether special mercy which watches over France. Your enemies, Sire, are those of the human species; the Duke of Bordeaux, worthy scion of so many kings, has vanquished them on the day of his birth. May the love of the French people efface the tears which cruel souvenirs mingle with so much joy!"

Royalist gladness manifested itself in popular demonstrations. On Sunday, October 1, at eleven o'clock in the morning, the market porters and the charcoal men of Paris, all dressed in new clothes, executed several dances in front of the Duchess of Berry's windows. They hurrahed for the Princess, who, having had her bed drawn near a window, showed them her son, whom she held in her arms. Then she ordered that the doors of her apartments should be thrown open to them, and all, entering by twos, contemplated the mother and the child.

October 3, there were public fêtes and rejoicings, a *Te Deum* at Notre Dame, a free distribution of eatables, and a hundred barrels of wine in the Champs Elysées, balls and spectacles on the Square Marigny, fireworks and general illuminations.

On the same day, after the Mass in the chapel of the Tuileries, the diplomatic corps having presented its homage to the King and the Duke of Bordeaux, Monseigneur Machi, the Papal Nuncio, spoke as follows: "Sire, the diplomatic corps comes to join its felicitations to those of all France for the great benefit which a most favorable Providence has deigned to grant to the paternal tenderness of Your Majesty. This child of sorrows, of souvenirs, and regrets, is also the child of Europe; he is the herald and the guarantee of the peace and repose which must follow so many agitations."

Louis XVIII. responded: "Never have I received with so much satisfaction the congratulations of the diplomatic corps. I am persuaded that your sovereigns share the joy that fills my heart; it is all the more vivid because I behold in this great event the most signal benefit of Providence, and the pledge of the repose which He will at last deign to bestow upon the world. I recommend this dear child to the prayers of the Holy Father, to those of the whole Church, and to the friendship of all sovereigns."

Popular festivities continued. In virtue of a resolution taken, October 2, by the municipal council, the prefect of the Seine had been invited to assemble at banquets the market-women, the corporation of market-porters, and also that of the charcoal-burners. The banquets took place on Sunday, October 8, that of the "Ladies of the market" at the market of *Blancs-Manteaux*, those of "Messieurs the porters of the markets and the wharves" in the premises of the storage granaries, boulevard of the Arsenal, and that of "Messieurs the charcoal-burners" at the Saint-Martin market. The honors of each table were done by the mayors of Paris, and a ball followed each banquet.

At this time the Duchess of Berry excited universal enthusiasm. A witty woman said, "The Duchess of Berry has brought forth not only the Duke of Bordeaux, but a great number of royalists also." Never has there been a princess more the fashion in the salons or more popular with the masses. The letter by which she obtained pardon for Bouton and Gravier, who had been condemned to death for attempts against her person, received unanimous praise. This beautiful and generous letter is thus expressed: —

"SIRE: As I cannot see the King to-day, I write to him to ask pardon for two unfortunate men who were condemned to death yesterday for an attempt against my person. I should be in despair if there were Frenchmen who must die for me. The angel whom I mourn asked pardon as he was dying for his murderer; he shall be the arbiter of my life. Will you permit me, uncle, to imitate him, and to implore Your Majesty to grant the favor of life to these two unfortunates? The King's august example has accustomed us to clemency. Will he deign to permit that the first instants of the existence of my Henri, my dear son, be marked by a pardon? Excuse, my dear uncle, the liberty I dare take of opening my heart to you; on all occasions your indulgent goodness has encouraged me. I supplicate the King to excuse my boldness, and to believe in the respect, as profound as the sentiments with which I am, of Your Majesty, the most humble and most obedient and most submissive niece.

"CAROLINE."

The royalists, satisfied with the present and looking tranquilly towards the future, thought themselves in possession of the promised land. To read their journals, one would think that the age of gold had returned to earth. They published sentimental anecdotes like the story of old Huet, a man of a hundred and sixteen years, who had been born in the corps to which his father belonged towards the close of the reign of Louis XIV. Having been received by the Duchess of Berry, he blessed the little Prince, saying, "I have the happiness to see the sixth generation of the Bourbons." A glass of the Jurançon wine with which the lips of the Duke of Bordeaux had been moistened at his birth was poured out for the good old man, and a gold medal given him, representing France and the Prince, with this motto: "Frenchmen, I give him to you; swear to defend him."

Felicitations, addresses, protestations of devotion, arrived from every corner of the realm. Balls, rejoicings, and entertainments were given everywhere. The King distributed thirty-four ribbons of the Order of the Holy Ghost. MM. Decazes, Pasquier, Lainé, de Serre, Dessoles, Marshals Moncey, Victor, Macdonald, Oudinot, Marmont, and Suchet figured in the promotion, beside Prince Talleyrand, the Dukes of Luxembourg, de Gramont, de Lévis, de Mouchy, de Montmorency, the Abbé de Montesquiou, and Cardinals de Beausset and de La Luzerne.

We read in the *Moniteur* of October 22: —

"After the audience with the King, the whole diplomatic corps were introduced into the apartments of S. A. R. the Duchess of Berry, who was on a couch placed beneath the full-length portrait of the spouse whom she daily mourns. On her knees lay the son, the successor of so many illustrious monarchs; in a word, the new Henri whom Heaven has given to be the consolation of his heroic mother and the hope of the country. Her entire household, ranged around her, shared her doleful situation; tears were in every eye. But in the midst of this general affliction the Princess pressed to her bosom, with tender affection, the gift she has received from Heaven, while her august daughter seemed, by her grace and that expression of kindliness which belongs to her family, to be saying to those who were present, 'Love me; I shall merit it some day, like all my relatives.'

"It was under these circumstances that the Nuncio Apostolic addressed the following discourse to her in the name of the diplomatic body: —

"'Madame, Heaven has deigned to accord Your Royal Highness the greatest of all consolations.. This precious infant, who makes the happiness of France and staunches so many tears, is a recompense of the eminent virtues which honor Your Royal Highness, and of the truly heroic courage which distinguishes you. The diplomatic corps, overwhelmed with joy, has the honor to present the homage of its felicitations to the august mother, and to offer the most ardent prayers for the preservation of a prince who is the object of so many hopes and so many interests.'

"A new Jeanne d'Albret, the august Princess replied, with as much greatness of soul as nobility: 'I thank the sovereigns for the sentiments you have just expressed. I am proud of the title you have given to my son, of *Child of Europe.* Accept also my thanks for your participation in my sorrows.'"

The Emperor Alexander had written to Louis XVIII.: —

"The birth of the Duke of Bordeaux is an event which I regard as very auspicious for peace, and which conveys just consolation to the bosom of your family. I beg Your Majesty to believe that I ratify the title of Child of Europe with which Monseigneur the Duke of Bordeaux has been saluted."

Naturally, the poets joined the party. Victor Hugo wrote a dithyramb in honor of the young Prince, in the month of October, 1820. Lamartine's enthusiasm was not less lyrical. Alas! there was nothing new in these adulations; read the *Moniteur* of 1811, and you will find just such lyrics and hyperboles concerning the King of Rome and the Empress Marie Louise. Casimir Delavigne, essaying his adolescent muse, had saluted the heir of the Empire as a "child dear to Heaven, awaited by earth, promised to posterity." M. Lemaire, a professor known by his talent for Latin verse, had carried his enthusiasm so far as to compare Marie Louise to another Marie, this other being the Blessed Virgin. One of these two sovereigns, he said, reigns in heaven, the other on earth, —

"*Hæc cœlo regina micat; micat altera terris.*"

Among the courtiers now weeping with joy before the cradle of the Duke of Bordeaux were many men who, nine years before, had been shedding enthusiastic tears before the cradle of the King of Rome, and who, eighteen years later, would display the same emotion before the cradle of the Count of Paris. Strange epoch, bizarre commingling of opposing ideas and principles! How many retractations among the prose-writers and the poets! One of the two bards who sang with Biblical emotion the birth of the child of miracle became the founder of the Second Republic, and the other has had a burial without religious rites. What would these enthusiastic defenders of the throne and the altar, these mystical poets to whom royalty was a dogma, a divine right, have said had the vicissitudes in their opinions and their career been predicted to them?

However, even in 1820, there was more than one discordant note in the concert of adulations going on around a cradle. M. de Lally wrote to the Duke Decazes the following letter, in which Orleanist tendencies are already perceptible:—

"When I say to you that I have been pleased with this birth chiefly on the King's account, it is because I am daily more inclined to doubt whether it is the combination most desirable for France, for the monarchy, and for this dynasty which is so dear to us; whether the birth of a Princess who might have been affianced in her cradle to that admirably trained Prince" (the Duke of Chartres, then ten years old) "would not have been more propitious to these great interests, more calculated to settle minds, to consolidate the Charter, to dissipate gloom, and to make conciliation necessary. The turn affairs are taking gives room to fear lest new discords may issue from this cradle which was to be the ark of the covenant and the symbol of reunion." It seems that when he heard the cannon that announced the birth of the child so impatiently expected, the Duke of Wellington exclaimed, "There is the death-knell of legitimacy!" At bottom, France was wavering betwixt opposing sentiments. The Duchess Victor de Broglie wrote, October 18, 1820: "The birth of the Duke of Bordeaux has given the Bourbons a momentary popularity; the people are really delighted. No one can say whether they are loved or hated, so fluctuating and uncertain is opinion." Who could be surprised at the scepticism of people who had witnessed so many metamorphoses? They believed in nothing, especially not in themselves.

XXV

CHAMBORD

THREE leagues from the Loire, on the banks of the Cosson, near the waste lands of Sologne, rises one of the most beautiful and picturesque castles in the world, the marvellous and fantastic Chambord. It is an immense feudal manor, flanked by four enormous towers, each sixty feet in diameter. In its architecture the Moorish and Gothic styles are united with exquisite elegance. What historian, what artist, what man of taste, could contemplate this magnificent efflorescence of art without emotion? The best view of it is obtained from the middle of the esplanade that separates it from the ruin. There all can be seen at once, — the towers, the pavilions, the chimneys, the terraces, the arcaded galleries, the myriads of bell turrets and caryatides, and the cupola which crowns the celebrated staircase where two flights of steps, crossing each other, turn around the same spiral of stone in such a manner that two visitors might ascend to the very top at the same time without meeting each other. At every one of its four landings, four immense halls in the form of a Greek cross surround this superb stairway with its wide and easily ascended steps. Victor Hugo has described it as "beautiful as a palace of fairies and grand as a palace of kings." From the balconies, which surmount the roof of the castle, the eye reaches to an immense distance, and takes in Blois, Beaugency, Orleans, the flat plains of Sologne and the smiling valley of the Loire.

Coppices, heather, woods, meadows, lakes, make up the vast park, seven leagues in extent, and surrounded by walls. It is inhabited by a rural population who form a commune. When the park gates are closed in the evening, the commune, with its municipal council and its town hall, are literally under lock and key.

A swarm of historical souvenirs gather round this legendary castle. Chambord was originally owned by the Counts of Blois, belonging to the family of Champagne, but it was then merely a rendezvous for huntsmen. At the end of the fourteenth century it came into the possession of the Orleans family. A century later, Louis of Orleans having become King of France under the title of Louis XII., Chambord became crown property. Its splendor dates from Francis I. On his return from captivity in Madrid, the most artistic sovereign who has ever reigned in France ordered the construction of the existing castle. Louis XIV. sojourned there nine times. Two of Molière's plays were given there for the first time, *Monsieur de Pourceaugnac* in 1669, and *Le Bourgeois Gentilhomme* in 1670. The ex-King of

Poland, Stanislas Leszinski, the father-in-law of Louis XV., took up his residence at Chambord, and built the delightful chapel which is still called the chapel of the Queen of Poland. Maurice de Saxe was endowed with Chambord after the peace of Aix la Chapelle. The victor of Fontenoy caused two barracks to be constructed beside the castle for his two regiments of uhlans. The Ukraine horses, left free in the park, ran up of their own accord at the hour of drill, when the trumpets gave the signal from the terraces.

Under the Revolution, Chambord having become national property, the interior of the chapel was mutilated and defaced. The furniture, which was of royal magnificence, disappeared. It was sold at auction to the second-hand furniture-dealers of the neighborhood, who carried off everything, even to the chimney-pieces. The beautiful Arras and Gobelin tapestries, which decorated the apartments of Francis I., were burned for the sake of the small quantity of gold and silver they contained.

At the time the Legion of Honor was instituted, Chambord became the headquarters of the 15th cohort, and was comprised in the property set apart as its endowment. In 1809 it became, for the benefit of Marshal Berthier, the seat of the principality of Wagram, with an annual allotment of five hundred thousand francs. After the fall of Napoleon this allotment was suppressed. Marshal Berthier's widow was no longer able to keep up the expenses of so large a domain, and by a decree dated August 31, 1819, she was permitted to sell the castle of Chambord.

The exterior of the edifice was still superb; but the interior presented an appearance of complete dilapidation. Ruined by the rains which filtered through the soft stone of the roofs from which the lead had been stripped, the apartments were but the shadow of their former selves. The four hundred and forty rooms of which the French Alhambra was composed were entirely bare. Of Maurice de Saxe's bedchamber nothing remained but the ruins of the gallery which had surrounded the platform on which his bed had stood. The altar and the pictures had disappeared from the Queen of Poland's chapel, and nothing indicated that it had been a holy place. The roofs were everywhere sinking in, the balconies were cracked, the ceilings and floors destroyed, the parquetry broken by the fall of joists and timbers. The doors and windows, without panels, shutters, or panes, left the apartments exposed to all the inclemency of the weather. The fine barracks which Marshal de Saxe had constructed in the park, near the chateau, were falling into ruins.

This was the time when the Black Band, that society of iconoclasts, attacked all the castles and razed to the ground the most admirable monuments of the past as a matter of speculation. Royalist society, instead of combining against this work of destruction, remained inert, and even the King himself never thought of saving such a marvel as Chambord. The castle so dear to Francis I. was about to disappear like an ordinary house. The pickaxe of the demolisher was getting ready to sack and tear down without pity the masterpiece of sixteenth century architecture. A part of the old trees in the park were already cut down. The day for selling the domain at auction was already fixed. The purest gem of the Renaissance was to be sold by weight. The Black Band was about to fall upon its prey, when, by mere chance, a conversation which caused the redemption of Chambord took place between Count Adrien de Calonne, quartermaster of the King's cavalry, and General Baron Du Casse, commandant of the department of the Somme. M. de Calonne, on returning from a journey in the west, had just visited the castle, and described to General Du Casse the deplorable condition of that magnificent edifice.

"But, my dear Calonne," exclaimed the general, "you must put a stop to this act of vandalism."

"How can I do that, general?"

"I will tell you; it occurred to me while I was listening to you. You must open a subscription to buy Chambord and present it to the Duke of Bordeaux."

"That is an excellent idea, general, I admit; but why not put it into execution yourself?"

"No; I can't do it; it would seem as if I were an ambitious soldier who wanted to advance himself with money belonging to the public. I might be accused of having ransomed Chambord and bought my epaulettes as lieutenant-general at one stroke.... You are evidently the right man; don't shrink from it."

M. de Calonne allowed himself to be persuaded, and became the promoter of the subscription.

At first the idea was not welcomed by either Louis XVIII. or his ministers. But at this period a great part of France was more royalist than the King, and M. de Calonne's proposition was cordially approved in the departments and at Paris. Caen was the first city which gave in its adhesion. Its municipal council voted an address, October 11, 1820, in which it was said: —

"Sire, Your Majesty has deigned to accept from certain respectable but not rich mothers of one of your cities (the market-women of Bordeaux) the cradle of the heir to so many kings. Why should not the whole country be permitted to redeem for a son of France the fields of his fathers, the manor where his ancestors reposed, the noble asylum of the victor of Fontenoy, and thus, with the aid of the fine arts, to found a magnificent monument of love? For, Sire, to preserve is to build up."

The movement spread so rapidly in every commune of the realm that Count Siméon, Minister of the Interior, who at first looked unfavorably at the scheme, soon recommended the King to approve it. In a report dated December 20, 1820, he wrote: —

"How cold one would seem in the midst of universal gladness, if, under pretext of economy, one should refuse to allow the French people to offer the young Prince who rekindles all their hopes a trifling tax on their revenues, when they are ready to sacrifice for him, if need be, their property and their lives, when they would count among their riches the honor of having furnished their quota of the free gift which will forever prove their attachment and their love! It is for Your Majesty alone to refuse, in the name of your august ward, a present which he does not need. He will have plenty of castles at his disposal some day, and the Chambers, in the name of the nation, will settle his allowance. Meanwhile, would it not afflict good and faithful subjects if Your Majesty were to accept the good wishes which certainly reach his heart, and yet refuse the homage which accompanies them? Your Majesty would perhaps show as much generosity as kindness by condescending to their wishes. So many resolutions press one upon another that it is no longer a question of private affairs to be examined according to administrative rules. It is a universal and national prayer which asks to be heard. To grant it would be a sweet satisfaction for Your Majesty, and a new benefit for your subjects."

This obsequious language was a sign of the times. To credit the minister's report, the King was bestowing a favor on his subjects by deigning to accept their present, and he was thanked for a generosity which consisted, not in giving, but in receiving.

The opposition tried in vain to arrest the movement. Paul Louis Courier, in his "Simple discourse of a vine-dresser of the Chavannière to the members of the Municipal Council of Veretz " (Indre-et-Loire), tried without avail to combat the idea of the subscription. It made progress notwithstanding. All the communes of France emulated each other in zeal and generosity. A committee, with the Marquis of Herbouville as president and M. Berryer as secretary, organized the undertaking, and in the name of the subscribers, bought the domain of Chambord for the Duke of Bordeaux. It was sold at auction, March 5, 1821, for 1,542,000 francs, independent of costs.

The news reached Chambord two days later, in the evening. The inhabitants of the park and the neighboring villages had been anxiously awaiting the results of the bidding. A general outburst of joy greeted the tidings. There were fireworks on the Place d' Armes, and all the guards of the park assembled to salute the new master of the castle by discharges of musketry.

What is really strange is that less satisfaction was felt at the Tuileries. We are assured that the Count of Artois was but half pleased with the homage offered to his grandson, and that he said to some one who made haste to inform him of the result of the sale, "What business is that of yours, sir?" More than one ambitious person was secretly jealous of the initiative taken by M. de Calonne. Chambord was in no great esteem, moreover, because for the last century and a half the court had not journeyed thither. One courtier was heard to exclaim anxiously that the apartment formerly called the King's cabinet would not be large enough for the present grand receptions.

A royalist writer, M. Merle, who had brought back some views, drawings, and notes concerning Chambord, undertook to defend the calumniated castle to the Duchess of Berry, and as the amiable Princess had the soul of an artist, he had no difficulty in convincing her. After having examined the drawings, she said to the Duchess of Reggio, her lady of honor: "They told me Chambord was nothing but a heap of ruins. How they deceived me!" As soon as she learned that the buildings were intact and the sculptures in a state of perfect preservation, she became most enthusiastic, and asked M. Merle a host of questions concerning the historical origins and the magnificence of the castle just presented to her son.

Some weeks afterward the Count of Marcellus, after making a sort of royalist pilgrimage to Chambord, published an article in the *Ruche d'Aquitaine*, which was republished in the *Moniteur* of August 30, 1821.

"I confess," said he in this article, "that I forgot Henri II. and Marshal Saxe, and even Francis I., at Chambord, and thought of no one but the Duke of Bordeaux. I saw him only. To me, that beautiful solitude awoke to new life. Chambord became Versailles. I already saw the superb castle resplendent with the pomps of royal majesty. I saw its stairs, its galleries and columns, its gardens, cascades, and sheets of water, and, in the midst of all these marvels, the marvellous child, become a great Prince, walking in the splendid alleys and meditating, to the sound of ever-flowing fountains, on the means whereby to renew the welfare and the happiness of the country which had restored Chambord to him, how to alleviate the woes of France, and to recall the days of its power and glory to the realm of Francis I. and Henri the Great."

What has remained of all these projects, of all these hopes? Nothing, unless it be the memory of a dream.

XXVI

THE BAPTISM OF THE DUKE OF BORDEAUX

THE baptism of the Duke of Bordeaux took place with the greatest pomp at Notre Dame, May 1, 1821. The old basilica was resplendent. An immense portico, the whole width of the front of the church, had been erected which reached as high as the upper galleries of the edifice. In the middle of its front, a porch, forming the principal entry, was covered with a large pointed archway, richly decorated with the escutcheons and monograms of Louis XVIII. and the Duke of Bordeaux. Below were four gilded statues representing Clovis, Charlemagne, Saint Louis, and Henri IV. Enormous banners displaying the arms of France floated from the towers. Seats had been arranged in form of an amphitheatre in the open space before the church. The interior of the cathedral was hung with magnificent draperies and sparkled with a myriad of lights.

Listen to the account given by Madame de Gontaut, governess of the children of France:—

"The household of M. the Duke of Berry, already styled the household of M. the Duke of Bordeaux, accompanied him to the palace of the King, where all the princes were assembled. The grand master of ceremonies then went to receive the commands of His Majesty as to the moment of departure; the aides-de-camp of M. the Duke of Bordeaux escorted him to his carriage; I sat down on the right, carrying Monseigneur, with Madame de Foresta (under-governess) carrying Mademoiselle; on the left was the nurse, facing her; Madame Lemoine was opposite Monseigneur; we were surrounded by body-guards, and an officer stood at each of the carriage doors.

"At this moment a man brought a letter addressed to me and then vanished: it was handed to me. I can recollect every word of this note, which commenced in this way: 'Urgent and important: Look out when you approach the Pont-Neuf, where there is to be a halt. Take care of the Prince then.' At these words, 'Take care of the Prince,' I handed the note to the officer of the body-guards, saying, 'This concerns you.' He read it, and laying his hand on his sword, said to me, 'Fear nothing.'

"For some years, the King, who suffered from gout, had not walked any: but, being still active, he went out every day in an armchair rolling on a springboard adapted to the height of a carriage. It was thus His Majesty set out from the Tuileries for Notre Dame."

The grand procession started at noon. Three salvos of artillery, of twenty-one guns each, announced its departure. The King's carriages, fifteen in all, and those of the princes and princesses of the royal family, amounting to twelve, were drawn down by eight horses apiece. That of the Duke of Bordeaux went in front of the King's, which was preceded by pages, four heralds, and the king-at-arms. Louis XVIII. and the Duchess of Angoulême sat on the back seat of the royal carriage, and the Duchess of Berry and the Duke of Angoulême on the front. An immense crowd thronged the quays and squares all along the route. All the windows were decked with white flags and flowers. The procession was to pass through the Carrousel, the Louvre quay, the quay l'École, the Orfèvres, the rue Marché-Neuf, the rue Neuve-Notre Dame, and the Place of the Parvis-Notre Dame.

The nearer it drew to the Pont-Neuf, the more Madame de Gontaut pondered on the mysterious billet that had been sent her. Let us return to her account: —

"There was a halt at the Pont-Neuf, the market-women having received permission to present a bouquet to Monseigneur and an address to the King, during which, I confess, I held Monseigneur close to my heart, which was beating very hard, and gave those dames a view of my broad shoulders."

The anxieties of the governess were not yet ended. "The good and gentle Madame de Foresta," she adds, "who was tormented by timidity, implored me not to abandon her during the imposing ceremony which was at hand. I explained to her that she had nothing to do except to keep near Madame the Duchess of Berry. I told the nurse to assist her in getting out of the carriage and lead her to the cathedral, which she did; then I asked Madame Lemoine to roll up the bottom of my robe, which was over eight yards in length, and heavy with silver, and be careful in throwing it after me at the moment I alighted (which she happily did). When we reached the open space in front of Notre Dame, a footman opened the carriage door; Madame de Foresta and the nurse alighted; but as I was still standing on the steps, with the Duke of Bordeaux in my arms, I felt and saw the two front horses of the King's carriage coming up to me at full speed. It was too late to draw back, and I sprang out with the force and skill given by a danger which must be escaped. I saw M. the Duke of Orleans, who had already arrived to receive the King, and I called him in a terrified voice. A footman had caught up the bottom of my robe with much presence of mind; the Duke of Orleans, prompt and attentive, supported me, and said, 'The Duke of Bordeaux is safe; go into the cathedral; they are waiting for you there.'

"At this moment, M. de Brézé came to look for me. The church was dazzling; every pillar was covered with gold and silver gauze; the raised seats were filled with elegant women; nothing could be finer. I advanced alone, holding Monseigneur in my arms so that everybody could see him. The organ began as soon as he appeared. Monseigneur was not frightened. He sat up and began to look for the place the beautiful sound came from. He was charming then. The cries of 'Long live the Duke of Bordeaux!' were unanimous."

Cardinal Périgord, the Archbishop of Paris, was old and infirm, and as little able to walk as Louis XVIII. He was therefore obliged to remain at the altar, and it was his coadjutor, Mgr. de Quélen, who went to the threshold of the cathedral to receive the King: "Sire," said he, "our venerable Archbishop is now at the foot of the holy altar, imploring celestial blessings on the King, his august family, and France. He has sent me to beg Your Majesty to graciously permit his old age to borrow, to-day, the voice of his coadjutor whereby to offer Your Majesty his profound and respectful homage, and that of his chapter and diocesan clergy."

Louis XVIII. replied: "Your venerable Archbishop could not express his sentiments to me through a more worthy interpreter. It is consoling for me, in my infirmities, to be able to enter the Lord's temple and offer Him the child of Saint Louis, the child of France, my child, the inheritor of my throne. Let us seek for him the protection of the Mother of God, the Queen of Angels. Let us pray her to watch over his life, to avert from his cradle the misfortunes by which it pleased Providence to try his parents, and to conduct him, by a less difficult path than mine, to eternal happiness."

Surrounded by the princes and princesses and the officers of his household, Louis XVIII., drawn in his armchair, slowly approached the choir, and then his *prie-Dieu.* On his right were the Count of Artois, the Duke of Angoulême, the Duke of Bordeaux, in the arms of his governess, the Duke of Orleans and the Duke of Bourbon; on his left, the Duchess of Angoulême, the Duchess of Berry, Mademoiselle, carried by the under-governess, the Duchess of Orleans and Mademoiselle of Orleans. Cardinal Périgord, Archbishop of Paris, intoned the *Veni Creator.* Then the princes and princesses of the royal family and of the blood approached the steps of the Sanctuary, and the baptism was celebrated. Monsieur represented the King of the Two Sicilies, the godfather. The Duchess of Angoulême represented the Duchess of Calabria, hereditary Princess of the Two Sicilies, the godmother. After the baptism, the governess of the children of France ascended the altar steps and laid the little Prince thereon for an instant, then, turning and holding him up in her arms, she presented him to the audience, who greeted him with acclamations.

Cardinal Périgord. said afterwards to the King: "Sire, when this royal infant was given to God to console France in its misfortunes, Religion saluted him with transports of gratitude. It cannot, without profound emotion, see Your Majesty coming in person to consecrate him to the Lord in His temple and to lay him on His altar, as if to recognize in a more solemn manner the miracle of so great a blessing. Religion, Sire, gives back into your hands this precious deposit, laden with its blessings and its hopes; it confides him to Your Majesty to be taught, by your lessons and examples, what the Church has the right to expect from a most Christian King."

Louis XVIII. replied: "What better could I do than to come and present this precious infant to the Lord, to invoke for him the protection of the most Holy Virgin, and to dare adjoin my blessing to that which you have just poured out upon his head? Pray for him, Monsieur the Cardinal; I beg you most urgently to do so. Let the metropolitan clergy and all the clergy of France pray for him, that he may render himself worthy of the blessing bestowed on us by Heaven in his birth, and that his life may be devoted to the welfare of France and the glory of our holy religion."

After this discourse, the Duke of Bordeaux and Mademoiselle his sister, "whose graces had been much noticed by the public during the ceremony," said the next day's *Quotidienne*, were taken back to the palace with a special cortège composed of the Duchess of Berry's three carriages. A half-squadron of light cavalry rode in front; eight of Monsieur's body-guards and a brigadier preceded the carriage of the Prince, at the right door of which was stationed a commanding officer of a detachment of the royal guard, and an officer of Monsieur's guard, and at the left door another officer of the same guards; behind the carriage came a squadron of body-guards and a half-squadron of the royal guards.

During this return, the governess of the children of France experienced another vivid emotion. "Monseigneur was asleep on my lap on the way," says she. "On re-entering the quays in the court of the Tuileries, the officer of the guards being unable to pass under the wicket at the same time as the carriage without danger of being crushed, I had placed myself (as was my habit) in the middle of the carriage window, so as to preserve Monseigneur from injury, when I received a blow on my shoulder which made me jump; I put my hand to it, and saw a stain of blood on my glove. Delighted to have saved Monseigneur by my precaution, I said loftily, 'I am wounded; he is saved.' And I added, laughing, 'I shall have the cross of Saint Louis; that is the object of my ambition.'

"On alighting at the Pavilion of Marsan, I had a search made for the thing that had struck me; an unsigned petition was found written on a piece of parchment twisted into the form of a cornet, at the end of which was a very small and sharply pointed bit of iron; the woman who threw it had been seen; but this method of presenting petitions being known, no attention had been paid to it."

To sum up, everything had passed off to the entire satisfaction of the royal family. In the morning, a deputation of charcoal-men and market porters had laid at the base of the statue of Henri IV. on the Pont-Neuf, a tablet with this inscription: "Frenchmen, love my grandson as I have loved your fathers. — Jeanne d'Albret, 1553 — Caroline, 1820." Fireworks were displayed during the evening, the whole city was illuminated, and bands went through the streets with white flags, greeted by cries of "Long live the King! long live the Duke of Bordeaux!"

A grand fête was given at the Hôtel de Ville by the municipal council the following day, May 2. M. de Chabrol, prefect of the Seine, said, while regretting the King's absence: "August monarch, cherished father, the eager crowd looks on every side for your venerated features; it offers you its benedictions and its transports." Monsieur exclaimed with emotion: "For my part, a Frenchman and the son of a Frenchman, born of a family altogether French, what is not my happiness to find myself thus in the midst of my compatriots. And how can my prayers be for aught except their happiness? Be assured, gentlemen, that my family and I will always labor for it with all our hearts." The banquet of the princes and princesses was served in the hall of Saint John. Twelve dames designated by the King from different classes of the citizens sat down at it. After the repast, the guests passed on into the hall of the Holy Spirit, where an interlude called *Les Arts rivaux* was performed, the words of which were by M. Alissan de Chazet and the music by Berton and Boïeldieu. After this interlude, executed by artists from the Opéra-Comique, a curtain was lifted and an allegoric transparency exposed, which represented the Duke of Bordeaux, lying as in a cradle, in the vessel of the arms of Paris, *Fluctuat, nec mergitur.* "How like it is!" cried the Duchess of Berry, joyfully, and then she showed

Madame de Chabrol a bracelet containing a portrait of the little Prince, so that she might judge of the merits of the likeness. During this time a romance entitled "God gave him," was sung by the tenor Ponchard, accompanied by the violinist Lafon.

The Princess afterwards looked with great pleasure at two transparencies by Ciceri, one of which represented a view of Palermo, and the other her triumphant arrival at Marseilles in 1816. The artists of the Opéra and the Opéra-Comique joined their forces to execute in the Throne-room a cantata the words of which were composed by Baour-Lormian and the music by Cherubini. The princes and princesses then repaired to the large ballroom which had been constructed in the court of the Hôtel de Ville; it rose to the height of the first story and connected with the other apartments. Six hundred women were sitting on benches which had been arranged in the form of an amphitheatre. The men were ranged behind them. The decorations consisted of arcades of mirrors enshrined in garlands of flowers. The middle of the hall was entirely empty. The princes and princesses promenaded there, the assembly standing meanwhile and applauding them enthusiastically. Then the ball opened, and was kept up until seven o'clock in the morning. Five thousand persons had been spectators of this admirably organized entertainment.

The following day, May 3, there were popular balls and other amusements to celebrate the seventh anniversary of the King's re-entry into Paris. May 6, the general and supreme officers of the royal guard and the body-guards, the ordinary foot-guards of the King and those of Monsieur, gave a fête to the princes in the Odéon theatre. This was not organized without some difficulty; for there is a limit to the enthusiasm for princes, especially when the question of expense arises. Consider, on this head, the avowals made by Marshal Marmont, Duke of Ragusa, who says in his Memoirs: "It was in good taste for the guard, which had been loaded with benefits by the King, to celebrate the immense happiness of the royal family with brilliancy and splendor. Being on duty, I advanced that opinion. The generals and other officers did not take to it kindly. A mean parsimony stood in its way. I overruled these considerations and ordered the fête at their expense. But I had calculated so that the sum should not exceed their means. The King promised me to pay half the expense in his capacity as colonel-general of the guard. The King's household joined us, and one day's pay was all that was required to provide for all the rest. The hall of the Odéon was selected. Four thousand persons assembled there. A play written for the occasion in the first place, afterwards an admirable cantata, *Dieu l'a donné!* and a magnificent ball, followed by an excellent and abundant supper, composed this entertainment, which succeeded as well as could be desired." A military character had been given it. The front of the boxes was hung with silver gauze sown with the crosses of Saint Louis and of the Legion of Honor. Weapons and flags were displayed on all sides. The arrivals of Monsieur, the Duchess of Berry, and the Duke and Duchess of Angoulême were greeted by noisy bursts of music.

There were theatricals at court on the 1st, the 4th, and the 5th of May. May 5th! Napoleon died on the rock of Saint Helena that day. The news did not reach Paris until early in July. The court of France had the good taste not to rejoice publicly over it. One of the Emperor's former aides-de-camp, General Count Rapp, was on duty at the time as first chamberlain and master of the wardrobe to Louis XVIII., and in that capacity he was on his way to breakfast with the King when he was informed of the news. At first he refused to believe it; but when doubt could no longer be entertained, he was unable to restrain his tears, and retired, saying that he could not be unmoved by the death of him to whom he had been attached for fifteen years, as he was not an ingrate. As the general did not breakfast at the royal table, Louis XVIII. had him summoned after Mass.

"I know," he said to him, "that the news I have received has afflicted you deeply. That does honor to your heart; I love and esteem you all the more for it."

"Sire," replied General Rapp, "I owe everything to Napoleon, and above all, the esteem and kindness of Your Majesty."

Thenceforward the Bourbon monarchy believed itself invulnerable. The Duchess of Berry had taken in serious earnest a present from the city of Bordeaux — the faithful city, as it was then called — which had offered her a counterpane representing not merely the Child of Miracle, but the Archangel Michael overthrowing the Evil One. The most ardent revolutionists were discouraged. The recent conspiracies were forgotten. No further thought was given to the seething agitations in Spain and Italy.

If one desires an idea of the pitch to which laudation had risen, he should re-read the ode composed by Victor Hugo in May, 1821, to celebrate the baptism of the Prince. We quote several stanzas: —

"Peoples, doubt not! Chant your victory,
   A saviour is born, vested with power and glory.
   The sceptre and the sword he binds together.
   Days of prosperity shall rise from the lessons of misfortune,
     For the uncoffined shades of sixty Kings,
   His fathers, watch above his cradle.

      "Let all tremble and be abashed!
      Mortal pride speaks in vain;
      The royal lion bends beneath
      The yoke of the Divine Lamb.
      The father, encircled by stars,
      Toward the feeble and unveiled child
      Descends, borne upon the winds.
      The Holy Ghost bathes him in fire.
      He is born into the world
      But to be born again into eternity!

> "Marie of the modest halo,
> Happy and ever praying,
> Guides the celestial virgins
> Toward her ancient temple of two towers.
> All the heavenly hosts,
> Dispread among the stars,
> Follow her triumphal car.
> Charity goes before them;
> Faith shines, and holy Hope
> Sits near the humble child."

And yet, at the close of this triumphal hymn, of this resounding canticle of thanksgiving, there comes a melancholy note, as if the poet had had the gift of prophecy: —

> "I go, O Muse, whither thou sendest me.
> I know only how to shed tears!
> But may this lute, faithful to their woes,
> Be faithful also to their joys.
> My voice has not learned
> From their recent history
> How to praise the Lord
> In the accents of victory.
> O Kings, crowned victims,
> When one sings your destinies
> He little knows how to sing of happiness."

At this same period Béranger bethought himself of another baptism, which had also been celebrated at Notre Dame, — that of June 7, 1811, — and he composed his famous chanson, "The Two Cousins, or a letter from a little King to a little Duke." The little King was the King of Rome; the little Duke, the Duke of Bordeaux: —

> "Hail! little cousin german;
> From a land of exile I dare write you;
> Fortune extends her hand to you.
> Your birthday makes her smile.
> My first day was fine also,
> As every Frenchman will agree;
> Kings adored me in my cradle,
> And yet I am at Vienna. . . .
>
> "If you grow up near the throne,
> If I vegetate without power,
> Confound those cursèd courtiers
> By reminding them of my birth.
> Tell them: — 'I may have my turn.
> Remember my cousin!
> You promised him your love,
> And yet he is at Vienna.'"

In 1821 the Duchess of Berry did not believe that her son likewise would go to Vienna. She banished all dark forebodings and thanked God from the bottom of her heart. Some days after the baptism of the Duke of Bordeaux, she made a pilgrimage of thanksgiving to the shrine of Our Lady of Liesse. A letter, addressed to the Baron of Frémilly, by the Marquis of Montreton, which has been communicated to us by the Marquis of Pimodan, gives certain details on this subject which delineate extremely well the spirit of the time: —

"This Saturday, May 26, 1821. — I promised you, my dear, an account of Madame the Duchess of Berry's pilgrimage, and I hasten to keep my word. On Tuesday, Madame arrived at Laon, where all the people of the environs were assembled. The whole city was hung with white flags, and she was greeted with repeated cries of 'Long live the King! Long live the Duchess of Berry! Long live the Bourbons!' The prefect, the officer of the regiment of Berry cuirassiers, and the authorities received the Princess at the foot of the mountain. There she got into an open carriage. The entire road was lined with people. The mountain, covered with men and women, was an admirable sight. She viewed the regiment and then went to the prefecture, where all the ladies of the city were presented to her. A commercial deputation from Saint Quentin offered her cambrics, dresses, and other products of the industries of that town. The Princess went on her way again after having visited the cathedral and prayed there. . . . Nothing has been more affecting than Tuesday's journey. The Princess reached Liesse at seven o'clock, and went at once to the parish church to hear Mass and receive Communion. Twenty young girls performed the same duty. Madame was dressed in a simple white robe, with a veil on her head. After her Communion the Princess kneeled down again on her *prie-Dieu*, which was placed in the middle of the choir of the church. There the memory of her eternal sorrow again assailed her, and her tears flowed freely. All who were in the church were as deeply moved as she. I saw some of the cuirassiers wiping away the tears they could not keep back. This spectacle of a young princess, widowed by an atrocious crime, weeping at the foot of the altar for the object of her affection, thanking Heaven for the consolation it had given her, and imploring for her son the protection of the Blessed Virgin, was the most imposing and the most affecting that can be conceived."

Two days later, the Duchess of Berry visited the mirror manufactory, where a workman made a play on words to her which had a great success: "Madame, everything is ice [*glace*, meaning in French both "ice" and "mirror"] here, except our hearts." The Marquis of Montreton ends his letter thus : —

"This four days' journey has convinced me more than ever that the mass of the people are royalists, and that the Bourbons need only to show themselves, in order to win all hearts. You are right in thinking that the Princess has given abundant alms on this sacred journey. She has been as amiable as possible to all who have had the honor to approach her. The National Guard of Laon, both foot and horse, who were on duty about her person, are enchanted, and from being lukewarm, as they were, I believe, on my word, they have become ultra."

XXVII

THE COUNTESS OF CAYLA

ALTHOUGH not affectionate by nature, Louis XVIII. had need of a special kind of affection. He must have near him a person in whom he had absolute trust, who saw him at any moment, who received all his confidences, all his secrets, and with whom he could think aloud. This friendship of a particular kind did not last indefinitely, but, so long as it did last, it possessed an exclusive character which made it a veritable passion. Any attack on the object of this favoritism was like high treason in the eyes of the King, and the greater were the jealousies excited by the person thus preferred, the more did the monarch please himself by heaping up and overwhelming him with favors. In aggrandizing him, he thought he aggrandized himself, and he identified himself with the object of his choice. Unable to hunt, and incapable of many pleasures, nailed to his armchair by sufferings, he had no resource but this impassioned friendship into which he cast all he possessed of mind and heart. It was thus that he loved, one after the other, the Countess of Balbi, the Count of Avaray during the emigration, the Duke Decazes from 1816 to 1820, and the Countess of Cayla from 1820 till his latest hour.

M. Decazes was still in high favor when he introduced to Louis XVIII. the woman who was to replace him in the monarch's favor. Zoé Victoire Talon, Countess of Cayla, was born in 1784. Her father, who belonged to an ancient family of advocates, had taken part in the struggle between the court and the Revolution from 1789 to 1792, and was mixed up, so it was said, with the policy of the Count of Provence. At the time when the unfortunate Marquis of Favras was condemned to death, without having revealed anything concerning his real or supposed relations with the brother of Louis XVI., M. Talon, it was also said, had received the compromising confidences of the condemned man, and a packet of documents inculpating the Count of Provence. During the emigration of her father, Zoé Talon had remained in France. She had been educated there by Madame Campan, and had profited by that elegant education which Lamartine has called a school of feminine diplomacy. She was intimate with Hortense de Beauharnais and the brilliant young persons who were the fashionable women of the Consulate and the Empire. Pretty, amiable, and intelligent, she possessed all that could make her pleasing.

She was married to a man of high birth, belonging to the little court of the Condés, Count du Cayla, who became a peer of France in 1815. This union was not a happy one, and the pair separated on the ground of incompatibility of temper. But the Countess was skilful enough to secure the sympathy of the Condés and that of her mother-in-law, who had belonged to the household of Madame the Countess of Provence, wife of Louis XVIII.

The dowager Countess of Cayla was altogether on the side of her daughter-in-law. Before dying, she sent her a letter, which, in case of necessity, would become a talisman. She addressed it to the King, whom she had always found full of good will toward her, and in words which her approaching death rendered solemn and affecting, she supplicated the monarch to protect her son's wife against the resentment of her son.

The dowager Countess was already dead when her daughter-in-law was obliged to make use of this precious letter. Her husband brought suits to force her to live with him again, or, failing that, to take their children from under her care (a son who had not attained to manhood, and a daughter who became the Princess of Craon). The unhappy Countess thought of escape, of leaving the country, of hiding herself, when the idea of throwing herself at the King's feet as a suppliant occurred to her. The Prince of Condé himself conducted her to the door of the Tuileries.

At the same time, the ultra-royalist party, which detested M. Decazes, and wanted to inaugurate a reactionist policy at any cost, conceived the scheme of utilizing the beautiful Countess in order to gain influence over the mind of Louis XVIII. Many persons renowned for their piety and gravity entered into this sort of conspiracy. One of the best and oldest friends of the Countess, Viscount Sosthène de La Rochefoucauld, boasts in his Memoirs of having overcome, and not without difficulty, the resistance she herself offered to this project.

Lamartine, accustomed to see things in rose color, and very favorable to the attractive Countess, has written : —

"Madame du Cayla's letters to the Viscount La Rochefoucauld, tender and pious at the same time, like all feminine confidences, nevertheless attest by their clear notions concerning the events of the day, a power of reflection and a breadth of judgment which would not have been surprising in a Sévigné or an Orsini princess. These letters, many of which have since been published, doubtless suggested, either to M. de La Rochefoucauld or his set, the first notion of that plan of alluring influence which it was sought to exercise over the eyes, the mind, and the heart of the King. An Esther, as Madame du Cayla herself said sportively, was necessary to this Ahasuerus."

The get-up of the presentation was planned in the most skilful manner. The beautiful Countess appeared as a suppliant. She was a persecuted woman who needed a defender. She was a weeping mother who desired to keep her children. She had all the charm of emotion and of grief. Her gentle eyes swam in tears. She brought the letter of a dead woman, her mother-in-law, who from the depths of the tomb pleaded her cause with the King. Louis XVIII. found himself affected, fascinated. The imagination of this old man retained a juvenile freshness. M. de Vitrolles relates that when the suppliant came to say that her husband wanted to take away her children, Louis XVIII. exclaimed, alluding to the incessant efforts made to remove his dear minister, M. Decazes: "Me too, Madame; they want to take away my child!" Spite of her perspicacity, Madame du Cayla did not at once understand the King's meaning, and supposed he alluded to some plot against the life of the Duke of Angoulême. But Louis XVIII. explained himself more clearly, and the clever Countess took good care to speak deferentially of *the child* she was about to supersede in the royal favor. From that moment her cause was gained. The beautiful solicitress obtained the favor that her children should be put out of her husband's reach, and the Minister of Police received orders to conceal them from all eyes.

Louis XVIII. fell in love . . . as much in love as was possible for him. To credit M. de Lamartine, "the King's sentiment for this attractive woman had from the first the character of a love which hides from itself, under the name of friendship, what the age of the King and the reserve of the woman did not permit to be avowed; he felt an affection for her which he styled paternal, and he called her his daughter, not daring, through respect for himself and respect for her, to call her by any other name." What is certain is, that the sympathy of Louis XVIII. for the Countess was soon transformed into a real infatuation. Far from ostentatiously displaying itself, the new favoritism began timidly at first; except the ushers and a few courtiers more familiar than the others, no one was informed of it; the Ministers themselves knew nothing about it. Little by little the thing got about at court. Two or three audiences a week, at certain days and hours, no longer sufficed the eagerness of the King. He began to write frequently to Madame du Cayla, then every day, then several times a day. He spoke of everything to her, consulted her on everything. M. Decazes was forgotten.

The ultra-royalists were in ecstasies over this result. The Abbé Liautard, adviser to the Countess, has written: "One can understand without difficulty what care and minute attentions were necessary in order to despoil the King of his own ideas, to make over, so to say, his brains, his memory, all his faculties and all his affections." And the Viscount Sosthène de la Rochefoucauld exclaims in his Memoirs: —

"It was necessary to combat a faction as active as it was perfidious, to change the thoughts and feelings of the King, and to wrest him from the always dangerous influence of M. Decazes.... It was a contest between the angel of good and the spirit of evil."

Louis XVIII. finally put his Ministers on the alert by requesting them not to attempt to transact business with him at certain hours which he named, and which were precisely those of his interviews with his new friend. Madame du Cayla became a political woman. M. Ernest Daudet says in his excellent *Histoire de la Restauration:*—

"When Madame du Cayla wrote or spoke to Louis XVIII. it was the extreme Right that expressed itself by her mouth or held her pen. The more and more decided inclination manifested by the King toward this young woman, caused the favor she enjoyed to be a force for her friends, and her influence became so powerful that we shall soon see the austere and serious Villèle obliged to reckon with her, or, rather, with the political personages whose inspirations she received and whose counsels she followed." M. Ernest Daudet adds this reflection:—

"When one studies the great events of history and goes back to their beginnings, it is not a rare thing to find apparently futile causes, which, notwithstanding their futility, the historian cannot leave in their obscurity. It is on this account that it is necessary in passing to outline this favorite, who had nothing in common with her predecessors, who was simply an agreeable intellectual pastime for the infirm monarch, but whose action was more than once exercised in politics during the last years of his reign."

The court was concerned about Madame du Cayla, but the public hardly considered her. As M. de

Vitrolles has remarked: "Kings have lost the prestige which once lent all their actions the interest of public events. Moreover, the age of Louis XVIII. forbade all suspicion of commonplace gallantry." Nevertheless, M. de Vitrolles adds that there was some jesting on the subject among the courtiers at the Tuileries. He says: "It seems she was very reserved about accepting his gifts, and her fortune was so modest that her disinterestedness was all the more creditable. We are assured that in the beginning of their relations he offered her a roll containing one hundred banknotes of a thousand francs each, but was never able to induce her to accept them. He did better than that in the long run."

The high favor enjoyed by Madame du Cayla was soon an open secret. Louis XVIII. had bought the park of Saint Ouen. He had a fine residence built there, and it was generally supposed that he intended to present it to the Duchess of Angoulême. Suddenly it became known that the Countess of Cayla was to be its owner. He thought that after his death the beautiful eyes of the Countess could be continually turned from its windows toward the church of Saint Denis, where he would be buried, and this melancholy idea had for him a sad and nameless charm. On the other hand, Saint Ouen, where he had promulgated the liberal Declaration of 1814, reminded him of what he considered the best monument of his wisdom, and it pleased him to adorn himself, in the eyes of his favorite, with the most glorious souvenir of his reign. He personally supervised even the least details of the construction and furnishing of the elegant residence by which he was to pay homage to his fair friend. Gérard had painted a magnificent portrait of him. This masterpiece was hung in the grand salon. Opposite to it the King caused a large slab of marble to be placed, with the following inscription in letters of gold: "Here began a new era, May 2, 1814." It was the date of the Dedication of Saint Ouen. "Everything was choice and perfect," says the Baron of Vitrolles. "Nothing was lacking but a dedication. I should have liked to put this verse from *Athalie* over the entrance wicket:—

"'I have built her a temple and taken pains to adorn it.'

"But I was far from being in such favor as would have permitted me to suggest it."

Like almost all women who have concerned themselves in politics, the Countess of Cayla has been the object of the most widely diverse criticism. Marshal Marmont has aimed a violent and insulting remark against her in his Memoirs. Béranger also attacked her in 1823, in his cruel ballad, *Octavie*. On the other hand, the favorite has been exalted by the Viscount Sosthène de La Rochefoucauld, and by M. de Lamartine. The Count of Artois made her promise "not to mind the things that might be said against her by spite and folly, and to rest peacefully in the noble use she made of the confidence and affection of the King." It is thus that, accordingly as party spirit moved them, this woman seemed to some eyes an intriguer, a selfish person, a guilty favorite; and to others, a pious Esther, a subject of edification, a friend of the Church, and a protectress of the good cause.

XXVIII

THE END OF THE REIGN

THE favor enjoyed by the Countess of Cayla did not cast the Duchess of Berry into the shade. The Countess, who resembled the favorites of Louis XIV. no more than Louis XVIII. resembled the Sun-King, took good care not to put on airs of triumph, and did not even appear at the receptions of the Tuileries and Saint Cloud. The Duchess Victor de Broglie wrote, September 27, 1821: —

"Madame d'Hénin told me that the King decidedly has a passion for Madame du Cayla; he receives her in private three hours at a time; when he drives along the quay, she is at the window of her house; he puts his head out through the door of the carriage to look lovingly at her."

But this favor remained in the shade; its only theatre was the cabinet of the King; it never put itself in evidence in the greater apartments of the palace. The Duchess of Berry, on the other hand, flattered, venerated, adored, shone in the fullest lustre, and received homage which was almost a cult.

The mother of the Duke of Bordeaux did not then seek to dominate; she thought only of pleasing, and always succeeded in it. Whenever there was any question of her the rival parties concluded, as it were, a truce of God. There were no calumnies, no slanders, against the amiable Princess; even the most hostile pamphlets may be searched in vain for a line, a word of criticism, against her. Although living at the Tuileries in the same pavilion with her father-in-law, she took no part whatever in the intrigues of the palace. She occupied herself in the education of her children, the cultivation of the arts, private entertainments, always elegant and select, and excursions where at every step she received ovations. Not having forgotten the wish often expressed by the Duke of Berry, that she should preserve a taste for study, she had again summoned the professors indicated by her husband. Her aptitude for music was admired by Paër, her instructor. She only needed to hear an air once in order to retain it. The piano and the harp, which succeeded each other, did not interfere with lessons in all other branches.

The journey she made to Mont-Dore, early in September, 1821, delighted the young Princess. By night the mountaineers accompanied her with fireworks and torches. She rode on horseback most courageously. She wore the costume of an Auvergnat peasant which she had made for her. People sang ballads in patois for her and danced before her to the sounds of the bagpipe. She had a little beggar brought up to her apartment and amused herself with his chatter. Some one wrote to the *Moniteur* from Mont-Dore: —

".When we saw the august Princess lightly scrambling up the sharp peaks of our mountains, we remembered that she had been born at the foot of Vesuvius, and found still another link between her and our Béarnais."

The Duchess of Berry at the end of Louis XVIII.'s reign was what the Duchess of Burgundy had been in the last years of that of Louis XIV.: the radiance, the poetry, the smile, of an old and severe court. She represented the future, hope, the rising sun. In a ceremonious, cold, and self-contained society, she was the living symbol of gaiety, recreation, and pleasure.

The Duchess Victor de Broglie, who saw the royal family at the end of September, 1821, gave at the time the following description of it: —

"Day before yesterday I was at court, and found myself all alone amongst those old figures, which rather frightened me. The King was rolled in in his armchair. He has a singular physiognomy. In spite of his size, he has a great deal of dignity; in spite of his round, red face, he has the royal air. There is no sort of agreement between his mouth and his eyes; his smile is constant, but his glance is so severe as to be hard. He is a witty man after the fashion of the old régime; he says characteristic things, but that is all. Madame the Duchess of Angoulême has nobility without grace; she holds herself awkwardly; her voice sounds rough; she is badly dressed, and yet she has dignity. Her eyes are red, perhaps because she has wept so much, but that increases the grave impression her face produces. The Duke of Angoulême is ungainly and awkward; he is always on the move, and tries to be facetious, but his intentions are more kindly than those of the others."

Then comes a portrait of the Duchess of Berry, whose attraction the Duchess Victor de Broglie could not fail to recognize, notwithstanding her unfavorable opinion of the elder branch of the Bourbons: —

"As to the Duchess of Berry, she no longer looks at all unhappy; but it is difficult to conceive how greatly sorrow has developed her; she is much more graceful; she is less timid. Although her eyes squint, they are not disagreeable; her color is beautiful, and her shoulders charming; although a blonde, there is something southern about her which attracts."

The Duchess of Berry was proud of her son, who must, as she thought, procure the welfare and glory of France. She did not consider the dove, bearing in its beak an olive branch, which figured in the ark-shaped cradle offered to the little Prince by the city of Bordeaux, as an idle symbol. On her son's first birthday, September 29, 1821, she received a picture which represented him as parting the clouds above a misty sphere, and treading on the serpent of discord. In November of the same year there was talk of a pretended conspiracy, which was to break out in the Bois de Boulogne at the time when the little Prince and his sister were taking their usual promenade. The governess of the children of France did not think it her duty to countermand their promenade. When the Duchess of Berry was informed of it, she exclaimed, "Madame de Gontaut did perfectly right! The Duke of Bordeaux ought never to flinch at anything, not even at a year old."

Naturally inclined to optimism, the Princess looked forward to the future with perfect confidence. Her family had just been firmly established on the throne of the Two Sicilies. An Austrian army had entered Naples, March 23, 1821, and King Ferdinand had resumed the exercise of absolute power there. On the 2d of May following, a handful of Austrian soldiers had extinguished the Piedmontese insurrection. The reaction was triumphant throughout Italy, and reactionary politics were likewise going to prevail in France.

The year 1822 was troubled at first. Military conspiracies, the introduction of Carbonarism into France, the alliance between the Liberals and the Bonapartists, the agitation in the schools, the violence of parliamentary discussions, the profound emotion caused by the execution of the four sergeants of Rochelle, all revealed a grave situation. But the Right got the ascendency, and the Restoration seemed more solid than ever. "The bloody holocausts attained their end," says Duke Victor de Broglie in his *Souvenirs;* "there were no more plots when it was well understood that one risked his head in them; the more recklessness the official conspirators had shown about engaging in these foolhardy enterprises, the more haste they now showed in retiring from them or disavowing them."

The birth of the Duke of Bordeaux had greatly discouraged the revolutionary party. On September 29, 1822, Count de Chabrol, prefect of the Seine, presented to the King the medals which the city of Paris had caused to be struck for the second anniversary of this celebrated birth.

"Sire," said the prefect, "there are some memorable epochs the souvenir of which the city of Paris likes to preserve in an imperishable manner. The medal it has caused to be struck for the birth of the Duke of Bordeaux represents this noble city as offering to France the noble child granted to our prayers. He seems to have issued from the bosom of the grave. He comes to gladden royal Majesty, to console sorrows, and to pierce with a mild radiance the funereal crape which covers our native land. Brought up beside his mother, and under the eyes of the wisest monarchs, this young son of kings will learn from your example, Sire, the difficult art of cementing the union and founding the prosperity of a people. Live long for his sake! Live long for the sake of France."

Louis XVIII. replied: —

"I receive with lively satisfaction the expression of the sentiments of my good city of Paris. The day whose anniversary it celebrates was the most fortunate of my life. In France also it began an era of happiness. I hope that we shall long enjoy it."

The year 1823, when Bourbons simultaneously triumphed at Madrid, Paris, and Naples, and when the family compact seemed renewed by victory, was the apogee of royalty. Chateaubriand has said, not without some exaggeration: —

"My Spanish war, the great event of my life, was a gigantic enterprise. Legitimacy was for the first time to burn powder under the white flag, to discharge its first cannon after the artillery of the Empire, which the latest posterity will hear. To stride across the Spains at one step, to succeed on the same soil where the armies of a conqueror had but lately met reverses, to do in six months what he had not been able to do in seven years, who could have dared aspire to such a prodigy? Yet that is what I did."

The success of the war in Spain flattered the royalists all the more because the Opposition had loudly declared that such a success was impossible. This war had from the first excited the ardent enthusiasm of the Right. What acclamations, what transports, had greeted Louis XVIII. when, in opening the session at the Louvre, in the hall of the guards of Henri IV., he had said: "One hundred thousand Frenchmen, commanded by a prince of my family, him whom my heart takes pleasure in styling my son, are ready to march, invoking the God of Saint Louis to preserve the throne of Spain for a grandson of Henri IV., . . . I have consulted the dignity of my crown and the honor and dignity of France.

We are Frenchmen, gentlemen; we are always of one mind in defending such interests."

The Duchess Victor de Broglie, always sarcastic, was present at this session, which she has thus described: —

"I was surrounded by women who seemed very much excited; the hall had been filled with people belonging to the court.

"When the diplomatic corps arrived, it was remarked that the English ambassador was not among them; several women near me said, 'Do you see? he is not there; he would not come!' Others said, 'We must hope it is an accident.' There was complete anarchy among all these women; they stood up on the benches, although the ushers ordered them down; all this seemed the image of a party at once arrogant and popular.

. "The King was announced; presently a great noise was heard; it was his armchair being rolled into the hall. Then all the women began trying to shout, as if they had been in the street. . . . The King pretended to be moved when he said the Duke of Angoulême and one hundred thousand Frenchmen were ready to march. That was a farce; but what was real was the ridiculous yet tragical contrast of that bowed head, half stricken with apoplexy; that impotent figure, dragged about in an armchair; that cracked voice, which spoke of delivering battle and imposing its laws on its neighbors. The shouts redoubled afterwards, especially those of the women.

The Duchess of Berry was all the time applauding the King's discourse. The Duchess of Angoulême said nothing, and was very sad."

The war in Spain was a victorious walk-over for the army of the Duke of Angoulême. That modest Prince might have said like the haughty Cæsar, "*Veni, vidi, vici.*" While he was advancing to the other side of the Pyrenees, his virtuous wife was making a journey in the west and south of France, which was a series of ovations for her. She left Paris for Bordeaux, April 2, 1823, after bidding an affectionate farewell to the children of France, who were dear to her. Bordeaux, her favorite city, received her as a sort of divinity. They took the horses from her carriage and drew it themselves. Her bust was carried through the streets to the beating of drums. At the Custom House she saw that of her husband under a triumphal arch, with this inscription: —

"Spain welcomed him; in his turn he saves her."

At Montauban, May 3, she learned that Saragossa was taken. She entered the former city of the Popes under a triumphal arch on which this motto was graven: —

"Avignon receives with transport the guardian angel of France."

The same ovations were repeated at Nîmes, Aix, Montpellier, Cette, Narbonne, and Marseilles. On visiting at Pau, June 27, the chamber in which

Henri IV. was born, the Princess said: "It was here that Queen Jeanne sang her little chanson; afterwards, they rubbed the Prince's lips with garlic, and made him drink Jurançon wine. They did the same thing to the Duke of Bordeaux. He is very strong; he is a very fine child, the Duke of Bordeaux." The courtiers claimed that the presence of the daughter of Louis XVI. in the south of France was alone equivalent to an army of observation. July 18, she arrived unexpectedly at Bagnères-de-Luchon, on horseback, by the mountain road. Then she returned to Bordeaux, and, before going back to Paris, she traversed all Vendée. From one place to another, the old Vendéan soldiers had assembled to greet her with acclamations. September 18, she mounted on horseback and went to the hill called the Mont-des-Allouettes, whence a large body of the Vendéan military were discovered. Hymns and psalms were sung. The silver crosses of the priests and the parish banners glittered in the sunlight. The whole crowd kneeled down when, on the summit of the hill, the Princess laid the first stone of a chapel to be dedicated to the Virgin.

At Nantes the Duchess saw with profound emotion a statue of her father on the Place Louis Seize. Her tears flowed freely. "Thanks," said she to the mayor and the prefect, "thanks for the homage you have rendered to virtue. The people of Nantes are the first who have erected a statue to my father; I shall never forget it while I live." The market-women, who brought bouquets for her, threw themselves on their knees before the daughter of the martyr-King and made the sign of the cross.

In the eyes of the royalists, who made a cult of their opinions, the French monarchy was identified with two women, one of whom represented its past and the other its future: the orphan of the Temple, and the mother of the Child of Miracle. While the Duchess of Angoulême was visiting heroic Vendée, the Duchess of Berry celebrated the third anniversary of her son's birth. The little Prince, who had been vowed to white until his fourth year, put on colors for the first time that day. He came to breakfast with his family in a blue suit, wearing the arms presented by his grandfather, and giving his arm to Mademoiselle his sister, who was a year older than he. The little Princess seemed very proud of her cavalier's appearance. At dessert, the Prince of Leon took the Duke of Bordeaux in his arms, and the child, holding a glass in his hand, exclaimed, "To the health of the King, my uncle, and all my brave soldiers."

At this time all things seemed favorable to the Restoration. On August 31 the Duke of Angoulême had seized the fort of Trocadero, after some brilliant fighting. On October 1 the Cortes surrendered the city of Cadiz and set the King of Spain at liberty. Ferdinand VII. went to Port Sainte-Marie where he awaited his deliverer, the Duke of Angoulême. The Bourbon of France knelt on one knee to receive the Bourbon of Spain, and offered him the sword which had just opened his prison doors. Then the two descendants of Louis XIV. embraced each other. When the Duchess of Angoulême was apprised of the result of the war, she exclaimed, " It is proved, then, that there is a possibility of rescuing an unfortunate king! "

The Duke of Angoulême re-entered the Tuileries in triumph, December 2, 1823. Louis XVIII. took him in his arms, praised "his conduct, his prudent modesty in success," and conducted him to the Pavilion of the Horloge to show him to the crowd, in the midst of general acclamations. December 15, the Hôtel de Ville gave a magnificent fête in honor of the victor of Trocadero. The princes and princesses were served at table by Count de Chabrol, prefect of the Seine, and the wives of the municipal body. The Countess of Chabrol sat down for a moment at the banquet, and presently rose again in order to stand behind the Duchess of Angoulême. After the repast Their Highnesses passed into a hall where a frieze of plaster bas-reliefs had been placed, representing the principal events of the war in Spain, and certain episodes of the Duchess of Angoulême's travels in the south of France. The Princess bowed, and said modestly, " I do not think I ought to occupy a place beside so many great actions." The prefect of the Seine addressed a discourse to the victorious Prince. He said: —

" How beautiful are these laurels! How dear they

must be to the heart of a father who is the finished type of a man, to the heart of a spouse whose noble enthusiasm seems like a ray of heaven coming to animate all things, to the magnanimous mother of these august children on whom rests the future of the Empire of Saint Louis! The palm belongs to all. All are united in the same love. This immortal palm belongs above all to the King; to the King whose voice resounded from the height of his throne; to the King from whom all good things emanate! Perhaps he was unwilling, on this day, to share and so diminish the eclat of a conqueror; but it was in vain. The royal crown shines brilliantly before all eyes. Yes, Sire, Your Majesty, though absent, fills to their utmost these vast porticos."

The Count of Artois spoke next: —

"Gentlemen," said he, "in the few words I am about to say, pardon the emotion I experience. It is the glory of my son that is concerned; it is the glory of French arms. Could one doubt that my son would not accomplish the mission laid on him by our King, to fight, to vanquish, and to pacify?"

Here the applause broke out so vehemently that the Prince found himself too much affected to continue speaking.

A stage had been erected at the back of the Throne Room. Here an interlude was played, the words by M. Alissan de Chazet and the music by Boïeldieu. The scene represented a public place with an arch of triumph, on the front of which was written: *To the army of the Pyrenees.* A young officer, decorated, had just come to throw himself into his father's arms and tell him the exploits of the victor of Trocadero. Two Vendéan women told the tale of the Duchess of Angoulême's journey in the loyal province. Afterwards the name of the Duke of Bordeaux was pronounced: "God gave him, God has preserved him." A general officer made his appearance. A crown of laurels was offered him, and he laid it on the bust of the King. After the interlude there was a grand ball. The Duchess of Berry danced two quadrilles; one with the Prince of Carignan, and the other with M. Mallet.

The royalists were convinced that they had finally won the day, and in the midst of his sufferings Louis XVIII. was consoled by the thought that his work was consolidated. The royal family was much more united than at the beginning of the Restoration. The antagonism between the two brothers had almost entirely disappeared. The Count of Artois, thinking that Louis XVIII. had reached the term of his life, had the good taste not to show any impatience to reign. Moreover, he had already obtained some great satisfactions. Under Villèle as minister, his friends had come into power, and he himself was like a coadjutor to the King. The elections of 1824 had given the Right an enormous majority. The Left, which had had one hundred and ten members in the last Chamber of Deputies, had only nineteen in the new one, and the royalists celebrated their victory with noisy rejoicings.

The session opened at the Louvre, March 23, 1824. Then, with a weakened but always solemn voice, the old monarch said: "France has no more to fear from the state of the Peninsula, henceforward returned to its King and reconciled with Europe. This triumph of a most righteous enterprise is due to the bravery and discipline of the French army, so worthily commanded by a Prince of the royal house." Frenzied acclamations broke forth. Never since the re-establishment of royalty had the speech from the throne announced so prosperous a state of affairs within and without.

Unfortunately, the sovereign whose wisdom might have rendered such prosperity durable was growing weak as fast as his realm seemed to be growing strong. On returning from the royal session, the Prime Minister, M. de Villèle, wrote in his memorandum book: —

"I was on hot coals while the King was delivering his opening speech, so well aware was I of his feebleness, what difficulty he had in reading it well, and how impossible he had found it to learn it by heart, as he had done in former years. I knew what alarm and disorder the fear of a change of kings under such circumstances and in a session devoted to such serious questions would cause in everyone's mind. The courage of the King, and his mastery over himself, aided him in surmounting these difficulties. The decline in his physical strength was hardly perceptible; his moral force was perfect."

In July, in spite of the aggravation of his disease, it was hoped that Louis XVIII. might still have several months to live, and the Duchess of Berry was able to make an excursion into Normandy which became a triumphal progress. Leaving Saint-Cloud at five in the morning, July 22, she arrived at Rouen at eight in the evening of the same day. The Norman capital gave her some magnificent fêtes. Before entering the city, the Princess had made a halt in the fields. The *Moniteur* said: —

"It was a singular and touching spectacle to see the Daughter of Kings surrounded by peasants of both sexes in their harvesters' frocks, who policed themselves by means of long white wands. Young and beautiful women, wearing the costume of the country, scattered flowers at the feet of the august traveller."

At ten in the evening of July 31 the Princess arrived at Dieppe, which was to become one of her favorite stopping-places. A letter from Dieppe which appeared in the *Moniteur* says: —

"From five in the afternoon an extraordinary commotion was noticeable in the town. To see the kind of disorder prevailing in every street, the going and coming of the inhabitants, the National Guards rushing to arms, the troops hastening to their posts from every direction, one would think the enemy was at the gates of the town. It was an angel who was coming towards our walls, preceded by the joy and happiness her presence must inspire."

The Duchess of Berry said to the mayor: "I see

very well that Henri IV. was right when he called the people of Dieppe his good friends. I shall imitate my ancestor in his love for you." Several young ladies of Dieppe offered her a little ivory ship, called *Saint Ferdinand*, which was the name of the vessel that had brought her from Naples to France in 1816. The fishermen's wives from Pollet were admitted to her presence in their picturesque costume: a short petticoat reaching a trifle lower than their knees, men's buckled shoes, a striped red and white apron, an enormous headdress, and large earrings.

During the three weeks the amiable Princess stayed there, Dieppe was extraordinarily animated and brilliant. A ball-room had been built expressly for her, in which comedies were also performed. The *Gymnase* was the Parisian theatre specially protected by the Duchess of Berry; the witty and amusing little plays of Scribe and his collaborators were given there. The mayor of Dieppe engaged the best actors of this theatre to give twenty-one representations; every second day they played in the hall specially constructed for the Princess, and on the intermediate days in the town theatre for the public. People hastened from all the neighboring villages and castles to pay their homage to the mother of the Duke of Bordeaux. August 2, the Municipal Council gave her a ball which was a marvel of elegance. Dieppe was thenceforward the fashion. August 23, the enchanting Princess left this town which had been charmed by her grace, and on the 25th she congratulated Louis XVIII. at the Tuileries on his fête day.

XXIX

THE DEATH OF LOUIS XVIII

LOUIS XVIII. felt himself dying. He had told his ministers that he would give death a good reception, and while he was already nothing but a living corpse from the physical point of view, on the moral side he preserved an energy which does the greatest honor to his firmness of character. This admirer of Horace was about to die like a Stoic. As Lamartine has said, " The cool precision with which, in his most secret intimacy, he estimated the few days he had still to live, the solicitude with which he prescribed beforehand the measures to be taken for concealing his last moments, attest his possession of that reflective courage which is rarer than that proper to the battle-fields, the silent, philosophic courage, without excitement and without illusion, which sees the sepulchre at the foot of the throne, and which drapes itself in order to go down into it with dignity."

It was evident from the spring of 1824 that the King had only a few months longer to live. " The last time that I saw Louis XVIII.," writes the Count of Puymaigre, " was at the close of 1824, when

I was admitted to what is called a special audience. According to his usual custom, he was sitting at a table whose covering came down to the carpet, and left nothing visible but the upper part of his body, the coquetry of an old man who wants to hide his defects. He was no longer the same man; that appearance of force, that piercing glance, that sonorous voice, which always provoked positive replies, were gone. One could but remark, on the contrary, the alteration in his features, and a sort of drowsiness, always a fatal symptom in an old man in whom the springs of a non-natural and artificially prolonged life are about to break. His phrases, to be sure, had their usual lucidity, but he uttered them with difficulty, and seemed absorbed in painful preoccupations. I took the risk of reminding him of the recent successes of his army in Spain; then a light seemed to flit across that noble countenance; the King sat up and seemed to grow large in his armchair; and as if he had caught a glimpse of the future, as if he had suddenly been initiated into the judgments of posterity, he exclaimed in a strong voice and with a sort of prophetic inspiration, 'Yes; that will be a glorious page in my history!' And then his head fell painfully back on his shoulder, a smile passed across his lips, and I heard, or thought I heard, these words, uttered in a low and almost unintelligible voice, 'For the last one!' I was still listening, moved by this imposing spectacle of royalty contending against death, when a sign of dismissal, that sign of the head which, with princes, means, 'Go away!' restored me to a sense of my position. I hastened my obeisances and departed."

This moribund man, who by dint of believing in his own principles had ended by making them believed by others, wished to die as he had lived, a king. He was often heard to quote the saying of Vespasian, "An emperor should die standing. *Oportet imperatorem stantem mori.*" He had himself carried, in the midst of summer, from Saint-Cloud to the Tuileries, so that he might yield his last breath in the palace which had been like the sanctuary of royal power. The sessions of the ministerial councils took place as usual. He remained drowsy or sleeping, but he presided. He rode out as usual in his carriage, so enfeebled and so greatly changed, that people complained when they saw him passing in such a sorry condition, and the parties accused the ministers of obliging a dying monarch to go out, in order to deceive the public and retain their portfolios.

Louis XVIII. would make no change whatever in his official life. "It is permissible for a king to be dead," said he, "but he is forbidden to be sick." It was sought in vain to induce him to countermand the reception of August 25, the day of his fête. He sat on his throne as in former years, received the felicitations of all the constituted bodies, and replied to the harangue of the prefect of the Seine with as much precision and good grace as if he had been in perfect health. As Lamartine has said again, "until the extinction of his forces, he compelled himself to preserve the attitude, the look, the presence of mind, the smile, of his reception days; he endured for several hours the torture of this long dissimulation of his approaching death. It was only at the end that his pains and his drowsiness triumphed over the firmness of his soul. His shrunken and pallid head drooped on his breast and almost touched his knees; he fell into a slumber which was like prostration. The latest courtiers who silently passed before the foot of his armchair thought they were passing the shadow of death. He was carried back to his apartments, still sleeping. His obstinate firmness had increased the public alarm that he had wished to dispel." On the 27th and 28th of August he still had the energy to ride out as far as Choisy.

September 2, M. de Villèle presented himself in the King's cabinet to perform a commission intrusted to him by the Duke of Orleans. The first Prince of the blood pointed out that his eldest son, the Duke of Chartres, born September 3, 1810, was about to attain his fourteenth year. Now, according to the usages of the monarchy, he added, the blue ribbon had been acquired by his son by that very fact, all the young princes placed in the same position having been decorated with it at that age, and notably the Duke of Enghien. "I found the King hardly able to hold up his head," wrote M. de Villèle in his memorandum book, "and I was obliged to bend down my own over his desk in order not to lose his reply. He answered me without hesitation: 'You will say to M. the Duke of Orleans that he is mistaken; that what he asks for is not due until the fifteenth year, and that I shall never do anything for him except what is due to him. The example he cites condemns his claim. The Duke of Enghien'—and he gave with astonishing precision the day, month, and year of his birth—'did not have the blue ribbon until the day of his fifteenth year came round'—and again he cited the date. 'M. the Duke of Chartres will not have it until a year from to-morrow.'" M. de Villèle adds to this account: "Such a memory, such presence of mind, and such resolution with such great physical weakness would seem impossible to one who had not, like myself, witnessed it."

On September 7 Louis XVIII. again received the diplomatic corps. On the 10th he was very evidently worse. On that day M. de Villèle wrote:—

"The King is no longer able to hold up his head, which was all bruised by falling on the sharp edge of his desk. I had observed to his attendants the night before that a cushion would be necessary for him; they had offered him one and been rudely repulsed. Seeing the King's forehead bruised and his face bloody, I ventured to ask his permission to have a cushion brought; I added that I had to consult him on an important matter concerning which it was necessary that he should have the goodness to give me directions, which would be impossible if his head were not high enough for me to hear what he said. He made a sign of approval; I opened the cabinet, and a pillow was brought, which allowed me to hear what the King chose to say to me, without any difficulty. On leaving the King, I went to Monsieur, and I reassembled the Council to confer on this painful situation."

The energy manifested by the dying king in fulfilling his part as sovereign to his latest hour can be estimated from the fact that at the time when he was still presiding at ministerial councils, the gangrene which was gnawing his feet had already devoured the toes.

"The death of Louis XVIII.," Marshal Marmont has written, "is one of the most admirable spectacles I ever beheld. His courage, his resignation, and his calmness were extraordinary. He looked his end in the face without anxiety and without terror.... He asked Portal, his principal physician, if his last moments would be attended by great suffering and a long stay in his bed. Portal replied: 'Sire, you will suffer little, and you will die in your bed if you choose; in any case, you will not stay long in bed.' This poor king sank down gradually, and to such a point that he was bent almost into a circle, with his chin close to his knees. His life was almost extinct, and he continued to fulfil the apparent duties of royalty."

Meanwhile, no one ventured as yet to publish bulletins of his health, nor to ask him to go to confession. He had accustomed his family to such a timid deference toward him that neither his brother, his nephew, nor his niece, in spite of their great piety, spoke to him about his religious duties. The Viscount Sosthène de La Rochefoucauld persuaded them that no one but the Countess of Cayla could undertake this delicate mission.

Marshal Marmont says in his memoirs: "Saturday, September 11, the King again breakfasted with us; at least, he came to table and sat in his usual place. This was the first day that he had moments of absent-mindedness. I don't know what disagreeable thing he did to Madame the Duchess of Angoulême. Coming to himself, he noticed it, and said to her with admirable calmness and an angelic gentleness: 'Niece, when one is dying, he does not know very well what he is about.'

"Madame du Cayla saw him for the last time that day, and she did not leave his cabinet with empty hands. She presented for his signature an order to buy the hôtel de Montmorency, on the quay, for her; and he, blind and dying, made a formless scrawl at the bottom of it which was accepted as a regular signature by the minister of his household, the Duke of Doudeauville. This hôtel, bought directly from Marshal Mortier, and paid for in ready money to the amount of seven hundred thousand francs, became the property of Madame du Cayla." This final liberality on the part of Louis XVIII. has caused M. de Lamartine to say: "Never had a prince calumniously accused of insensibility and egotism more need of tenderness, and never did one more obstinately devote his earliest and his latest days to the charms and even to the servitudes of his attachments. Until his last hour he busied himself with the lot he sought to assure after his death for her whom he loved."

The Countess of Cayla, however, while attending to her personal interests, had not forgotten the religious mission entrusted to her. In this final interview with the dying King she induced him to send for a priest. The Abbé Rocher was summoned immediately, and Louis XVIII. made his confession. It was time; for that evening the King no longer had strength to give the countersign, which he had always done till then.

The next day, September 12, it was plain that the catastrophe was at hand. The Prince who was about to style himself Charles X. sent a courier to Eu with the following letter for the Duke of Orleans: —

"Paris, September 12, 1824, 2 P.M. — The weakness of the King has increased so much since yesterday, my dear cousin, that I find myself under the painful necessity of sending a courier to ask you to return hither as soon as possible, without, however, causing any detriment to the health of your wife and sister. Pity me, my dear cousin, my heart is torn with grief; but I hope God will give me the strength of which I have, and, alas! of which I shall have, perhaps, so much need. I say nothing more, so as to hasten the departure of my letter. You have long known my ancient and constant friendship for you and your family. — CHARLES PHILIPPE."

On the same day, Sunday, September 12, Mgr. de Quélen, Archbishop of Paris, issued a charge in which he said: —

"In vain would we seek to hide it from you; in vain through love for his people, has our august and religious monarch, overcoming his pains with a rare magnanimity and admirable constancy, sought to resist the efforts and the progress of his malady, and as it were to survive himself, in order not to disturb by premature alarms the repose and happiness which his wisdom has been able to maintain throughout the kingdom. The moment has come when nature is forced to recognize its weakness under the powerful hand of Him who strikes and who heals, who gives and who takes away the health of princes. Whatever, my dearest brethren, may be the impenetrable designs of God, faith and love summon us to the foot of His altars. Our hope cannot be deceived; Frenchmen, if we cannot save the King, we can at least associate ourselves with him in his last struggle. We desire to aid him to win the immortal crown, and to open for him, by the weapons of prayer, that celestial city wherein so many saints of his noble race are already reigning, and where, seated beside them, he will become, like them, the protector of the monarchy."

Louis XVIII. was still unwilling, on that day, to go to bed. As he was strongly urged to do so, "That," said he, "would be an advertisement that my death is near; then, until it comes, the theatres would be closed and the Bourse likewise. Everything suspended; it is a great thing, the death of a king of France! Something must be done so that the burden shall weigh on the people as short a time as possible." In the evening of that Sunday, September 12, 1824, he lay down never to rise again.

No bulletin of his health had as yet been issued. The first of them did not appear until Monday morning, September 13. They were dated on the previous day, and signed by six doctors and the Count of Damas, first gentleman of the chamber. The first ran as follows: —

"At the Tuileries, September, 12, 1824, 6 A.M. — The old and permanent infirmities of the King have perceptibly increased for some time past. His health has seemed more profoundly impaired, and has been the subject of more frequent consultations. His Majesty's constitution and the cares bestowed on him encouraged for some days the hope that his health might be restored to its ordinary condition; but to-day it can no longer be doubted that his forces are considerably diminished, and that the hopes entertained for him must also dwindle."

The second bulletin was worded thus: —

"Sunday, September 12, 9 P.M. — The fever has augmented throughout the day. Great cold in the extremities has supervened; the weakness has increased, and also the drowsiness; the pulse always feeble and irregular."

These bulletins dispelled all illusions. The Minister of Finance ordered the Bourse to be closed until further orders, after Monday, September 13, and no performances were given in any of the theatres. A crowd gathered from early morning in the court and garden of the Tuileries. News was anxiously demanded, and the churches were crowded with the faithful who came to pray for the King. At eight in the morning, the grand almoner, followed by the curé of Saint Germain l'Auxerrois and the clergy of this chapel, was seen to enter the palace. Pious souls joined their intentions to the ceremony about to be celebrated in the apartments. The King received the last sacraments from the hand of the grand almoner, in presence of the royal family, the grand chamberlain, the great officers of the household, the Prince of Castelcicala, ambassador of the Two Sicilies, the president of the Council, and all the domestics. During this time the crowd was increasing under the sovereign's chamber windows. The interest it felt in him showed itself very manifestly when, after the ceremony, the Duchess of Angoulême was seen at the foot of the staircase as she was returning from the dying man, her eyes bathed in tears.

The King, who had given his blessing in the morning to his brother, his nephew, and his niece, and also to the Duchess of Berry, wished to bid adieu to the children of France. They came from Saint Cloud with their governess, Madame de Gontaut. "I received an order," she writes, "to take the Princes to the King. He seemed to me extremely feeble. Sending them away very soon, he desired to embrace them. I lifted the Duke of Bordeaux up to him. I heard him say in a very low tone, 'Poor child! Mayest thou be more fortunate than we!' Meanwhile Mademoiselle was looking for his hand to kiss it. I trembled lest she should find his feet, which were in a frightful state. He caused me profound pity. I experienced a grief so sincere that I could hardly restrain my tears. On reaching the door, I looked at him again, and felt that it was for the last time. The children were sad when we returned to Saint Cloud." When they re-entered their carriage in the court of the Tuileries, the crowd hastened towards them, crying, "Long live the King! Long live the Bourbons!"

The bulletin of September 14 announced that the King's breathing was becoming more painful and interrupted, that his pulse was growing weaker and intermittent, and that the prayers for the dying had already been recited in his chamber, in presence of the royal family. At the moment when this was going on, he recovered consciousness, and hearing a priest say to him, "Sire, unite yourself to the intention of my prayers," he replied, "I do not think I have got to that point yet; but no matter; continue!"

The bulletins of September 15 allowed the public to follow the progress of this slow and noble agony. Marshal Marmont had reason to say, "There is no great man whose life would not be honored by such a death." On Thursday, September 16, at one o'clock in the morning, a messenger came to inform the Duke of Orleans that the King was at the last extremity. He repaired with the Duchess at once to the Tuileries. The dismal silence prevailing in the chamber of the dying man allowed his short and oppressive breathing to be heard. All of a sudden nothing was heard. The doctors then took a lighted candle and brought it close to his mouth to assure themselves that at last he had ceased to suffer. The candle was not extinguished. The Duke of Angoulême approached Monsieur, who was in tears, and said, " My father, all is over." Overwhelmed in soul and body, he who thenceforward called himself Charles X. seemed not to comprehend, until Count de Damas, advancing toward him, exclaimed, " Sire, the King is dead." It was precisely four o'clock in the morning. The Duchess of Berry, who was present with the royal family at this great and sorrowful spectacle, was profoundly affected. What might have softened her regrets was the thought that she had never given Louis XVIII. a moment of chagrin, or even a trifling annoyance, and that she had never ceased to be a Princess according to the King's heart.

INDEX

Aix, festival of King René at, 51.

Alexander, 1; letter of, to Louis XVIII. on the birth of the Duke of Bordeaux, 226.

Angoulême, Duke of, his return from his Spanish campaign, 277; fête in honor of, 277.

Angoulême, Duchess of, describes the household of the Duchess of Berry, 30; importunes the King to dismiss Decazes, 180; makes a journey in the South of France, 274; her emotion at her father's statue at Nantes, 275.

Artois, Count of, his reception of the Baron of Vitrolles' suggestion as to his marrying again, 176; insists on the dismissal of Decazes, 181, 189; letter of, to the Duke of Orleans on the King's approaching death, 290.

Bentinck, Lord, requires Marie Caroline to leave Sicily, 9.

Béranger, Chanson of, 252.

Berry, Duke of, his marriage proposed, 15; letter of, to his future wife, 16, 22; married by proxy, 24; pecuniary arrangements of the Chamber of Deputies for, 24; letter of, to his wife at Marseilles, 35, 39, 55, 59; marriage of, in Notre Dame, 79; installed at the Elysée, 83; his person and character, 97 *et seq.*; premonitions of his fate, 114; affliction of, at the death of his son, 118; the birth of his daughter, Louise Marie Thérèse, 126; his sentiments toward the Duke of Orleans, 128; agreeable change in his character, 139; his goodness of heart, 140; the incident of Soubriard, 143; his freedom from personal fear, 144; Louvel determines to kill him, 150; receives threatening letters, 152; at the Opera, 155; stabbed by Louvel, 157; incidents of the assassination, 158 *et seq.*; treatment of, by the physicians, 164; confesses, 167; his daughters by Miss Brown summoned, 167; his death, 167; rage of the ultras against Decazes, accused of complicity in the murder of, 179; his obsequies, 185 *et seq.*

Berry, Duchess of, her ancestry, 1 *et seq.*; the members of her family, 26; her "epitome" of her early life, 2; extract from her journal, 5; her childhood, 7; meets the Duke of Orleans, 8; avoids Lord Bentinck, 10; laments the loss of her grandmother, Marie Caroline, 11; portrayed by the Countess of Agoult, 13; her marriage to the Duke of Berry proposed, 15; extracts from her journal, 17 *et seq.*; the marriage contract, 18; her letter to the Duke of Berry, 21; the marriage of, by proxy, 24; at Caserta, 25; sails for France, 25 *et seq.*; at the lazaretto of Marseilles, 29; extract from her journal, 27; her life at the lazaretto, 36 *et seq.*; letter of, to the

207

Duke of Berry, 37; enters Marseilles, 43 *et seq.*; ceremonial of her delivery to France, 43 *et seq.*; excursion of, to Toulon, 48 *et seq.*; letter to the Duke, 48; journey of, to Fontainebleau, 50; present at the festival at Aix, 51; at Vienne, 53; letter of, to the Duke, 54; arrival of, at Fontainebleau; 61 *et seq.*; meets her husband, 64; her entry into Paris, 72 *et seq.*; the religious marriage at Notre Dame, 77 *et seq.*; ceremonies after the marriage, 81; produces an excellent impression in Paris, 83; keeps free from politics, 95; described by Pontmartin, 99; her life in Paris, 100; the birth of her first child, 104; burial of, 107; her elasticity and gaiety, 111; death of her second child, 117; takes lessons in music, 121; gives birth to her third child, 125; her happiness, 142; her husband assassinated by Louvel, 157; her courage and devotion, 165; her grief, 171, 192; goes to the Tuileries, 193; attempts to alarm her, 194; her dream that she would bear a son, 195; the birth of the Duke of Bordeaux, 210; the presence of mind of, 210; witnesses of the birth, 211; letter of, asking for the pardon of Bouton and Gravier, 223; receives the Diplomatic Corps, 225; pilgrimage to Liesse, 253; journey to Mont-Dore, 267; her pride in her son, 269; her confidence in the future, 270; excursion into Normandy, 281; at Dieppe, 282.

Bombelles, Abbé, funeral oration of, over the Princess Louise Isabelle, 107.

Bonaparte, Joseph, 6.

Bonapartist officers, conspiracy of, 202.

Bordeaux, deputation from, to offer a cradle to the expected child of the Duchess of Berry, 205.

Bordeaux, Duke of, his birth, 210; baptism of, 212; his household, 215; public rejoicings over, 214 *et seq.*; his name and titles, 219; called the child of miracle, 220; receives Chambord as a gift from the nation, 236; public baptism of, 239 *et seq.*; fête in honor of, at the Hôtel de Ville, 247; his third anniversary, 276.

Bourbons, triumph of, in 1823, 272.

Broglie, Duke de, quoted, 182.

Broglie, Duchess of, letter of, on the Countess of Cayla, 266; her description of the royal family, 201, 268, 273.

Caen, letter of the council of, to the King, 234.

Calabria, Duke of, 2.

Calonne, proposition of, to buy Chambord by subscription for the Duke of Bordeaux, 233.

Cayla, Countess of, her origin and early history, 257; presents herself as a suppliant to the King, 258; the infatuation of the King for, 261 *et seq.*; receives Saint Ouen from the King, 263; criticisms of, 264; sees the King for the last time, and receives the hôtel de Montmorency, 289; induces him to send for a priest, 290.

Chabrol, Count de, address of, 70.

Chambord, Castle of, 229 *et seq.*; history of, 230; despoiled, 231; plan to present it to the Duke of Bordeaux, 233; not welcomed by the King, 234; bought for the Duke of Bordeaux, 236.

Chartres, Duke of, 128.

Chateaubriand, quoted, 94; on Decazes and the murder of the Duke of Berry, 179, 183, 185, 187, 219; on the Spanish war, 272.

Court of Louis XVIII., divergent elements in, 90 *et seq.*

INDEX

Courier, Paul Louis, combats the plan to buy Chambord, 236.
Coussergues, M. Clausel, attacks Decazes as accomplice of the murder of the Duke of Berry, 175.

Damas, Baron de, 32.
Daudet, Ernest, on Madame du Cayla, 262.
Decazes, Count, 90; early career of, 132; Chateaubriand's opinion of, 133; the secret of his success with Louis XVIII., 134; the King's infatuation over, 136; incurs the hatred of the ultras, 137; accused of complicity in the murder of the Duke of Berry, 175; dismissed by the King, 182.
Dumas, Alexander, *fils*, 3.

Élysée, the Palace of, 96; the court of, 100.

Ferdinand IV., King of Naples, 2, 4; his *bourgeois* tastes, 14.
Ferdinand VII. of Spain, takes oath to the Constitution, 202.
Ferronnays, La, Countess of, 29; shuts herself up in the lazaretto with the Duchess of Berry, 33; outsteps her instructions, 34.
Flags, distribution of, by the King on the Champ de Mars, 85 *et seq.*
Fontainebleau, 57 *et seq.*
Frémilly, Baron of, letter on the entry of the Duchess of Berry into Paris, 72.

Gontaut, Duchess of, extract from her Memoirs, 29 *et seq.;* describes the festival at Aix, 51; describes the funeral of the Princess Louise Isabelle at Saint Denis, 109; lady of the bed-chamber to the Duchess of Berry, 112; intimacy of, with the Duke and Duchess of Berry, 115; describes their life and amusements, 122; chosen as governess for the expected infant of the Duchess of Berry, 123; summoned to carry Mademoiselle to her dying father, 163; describes the return of the Duchess of Berry, 171; her account of the baptism of the Duke of Bordeaux, 239.
Grégoire, Count, not admitted as a deputy, 130.

Helfert, on the Duchess of Berry in her childhood, 7.
Henri IV., statue of, inaugurated on the Pont Neuf, 115.
Hôtel de Ville, Paris, marriage of fifteen poor orphans at, 69.
Huet, story of, 224.
Hugo, Victor, verses of, on the Duke of Berry, 161, 196; poem to the Duchess of Berry, 203; dithyramb in honor of the Duke of Bordeaux, 226; celebrates his baptism, 251.

Lafayette, speech of, quoted, 197.
Lally, M. de, letter of, to Decazes, 227.
Lamartine, on the death of the Duke of Berry, 166; on the Countess of Cayla and the King, 260; on the birth of the Duke of Bordeaux, 226; on the King's energy of character, 283, 286; on his liberality, 289.
Louis XVIII., decree of, at Fontainebleau, 57; reply of, to the address of the Abbé Dubois, 74; distribution of flags by, 85; rivalry between, and the Count of Artois, 89; discipline imposed by, on his court, 90; discontent of the royalists with, 92 *et seq.;* his reply to the address of the Marquis de Marbois, 116; urges the Duchess de Gontaut to accept the position of governess to the young princess, 124; speech of, in opening the session of the Cham-

bers, 180; pleasure of, in the conversation of the Count Decazes, 135; dismisses Decazes, 182; present at the birth of the Duke of Bordeaux, 211; addresses the crowd, 215; and the Diplomatic Corps, 225; at Notre Dame, at the baptism of the Duke of Bordeaux, 243; his need of a confidant, 256; the Countess of Cayla presented to him by Decazes, 257, 260; his infatuation with her, 261; gives Saint Ouen to the Countess of Cayla, 263; courage of, in the face of death, 283; refuses to be sick, 285; Villèle's account of an interview with him, 286; sees the Countess of Cayla for the last time, 289; makes his confession, 290; bulletins respecting his failing health, 292; bids adieu to the children of the Duke of Berry, 294; his death, 295.

Louise Isabelle of Artois, birth of, 104.

Louise Marie Thérèse of Artois, birth of, 125.

Louvel, Louis Pierre, his birth and career, 147; considers himself an avenger, 148; goes to Elba, 148; described by Lamartine, 149; determines to strike the Duke of Berry, 150; his opportunity, 153; stabs the Duke, 157; capture of, 159; interrogated, 186; declaration of, 199; executed, 201; incident concerning, 192.

Marie Amélie meets the Duke of Orleans, 8.

Marie Caroline, 2, 3; letter of, to Lady Hamilton, 5; banished from Naples by Napoleon, 6; detests the English, 9; her last days, 10.

Marie Clémentine, 4.

Marie Isabelle, the Infanta, 6.

Marcellus, M. de, outburst of, on the marriage of the Duke of Berry, 23.

Marmont, Marshal, quoted, 211; on the death of Louis XVIII., 288; on the fête to the Duke of Bordeaux, 249.

Marseilles, the Duchess of Berry in the lazaretto of, 29; informal entry into, 42 *et seq.*

Mennechet, M., verses on the birth of the Duke of Bordeaux, 214.

Mesnard, Count de, on the Duchess of Berry, 142.

Moniteur, The, quoted, 50, 69, 71, 105, 106, 115, 116, 119, 121, 124, 129, 131, 173, 224.

Murat, on the throne of Naples, 6.

Napoleon banishes the Bourbons from Naples, 6; death of, 250.

Nettement, M. Alfred, quoted, 6, 88.

Nodier, M. Charles, article of, on the Bourbons, 77.

Notre Dame, marriage of the Duke and Duchess of Berry in, 79; ceremony of the baptism of the Duke of Bordeaux in, 243 *et seq.*

Nuncio, Papal, address of, to the Duchess of Berry, 225.

Orleans, Duke of, a refugee at the court of King Ferdinand, 8; at the King's death-bed, 295.

Orleans, Duchess of, 127.

Paris, agitation in, after the murder of the Duke of Berry, 198 *et seq.*

Philip V., 2.

Pontmartin, his description of the Duchess of Berry, 99.

Puymaigre, Count of, describes his last interview with the King, 283.

Rambouillet, the royal family at, 115.

Rapp, General, grief of, at the death of Napoleon, 250.

INDEX

Rémusat, M. Charles de, on the marriage of the Duke of Berry, 68; on the entry of the Princess into Paris, 75, 84.

Rémusat, Madame de, letter of, to her husband, 103; on the death of the Duchess of Berry's first child, 106, 162, 174.

Revolutionary party discouraged by the birth of the Duke of Bordeaux, 271.

Rochefoucauld, Viscount Sosthène, 259, 261.

Royalists under Louis XVIII., 92.

Sainte-Aulaire, M. de, 177.

Saint Denis, obsequies of the Duke of Berry at, 187 *et seq.*

Sanfelice, Luigia, execution of, 4.

Serre, M. de, 197.

Soubriard, 143.

Spanish war, success of, 272.

Talleyrand, 75.

Toulon, the Duchess of Berry at, 48.

Tour de La Suzette, 114.

Trognon's *Vie de Marie-Amélie*, quoted, 9.

Vaulabelle, M. de, 136.

Viel Castel, Baron de, quoted, 110, 182.

Villèle, ministry of, 279; memorandum of, concerning the King's speech, 280; his account of an interview with the King shortly before his death, 286 *et seq.*

Vitrolles, Baron de, advises the Count of Artois to marry again, 176, 179; on the Countess of Cayla and the King, 263.

Typography by J. S. Cushing & Co., Boston, U.S.A.
Presswork by Berwick & Smith, Boston, U.S.A.

FAMOUS WOMEN OF THE FRENCH COURT.

CHARLES SCRIBNER'S SONS, PUBLISHERS.

DURING the past two years the publishers have issued translations of ten of M. Imbert de Saint-Amand's historical works, relating to the momentous and agitated period dating from the beginnings of the French Revolution to the seating of Louis XVIII. on the throne of his ancestors after the battle of Waterloo. Of these three have had as a nucleus the historic portion of the life of Marie Antoinette, three that of the life of Josephine, and four are devoted to the events centring around the figure of the Empress Marie Louise. The success of these works has been so unequivocal from the first, that the publishers have begun the issue of the important volumes of M. de Saint-Amand's series relating to the period immediately following the Napoleonic era, the period of the Restoration. Of this period the author's "famous women of the French Court" are the Duchess of Angoulême and the Duchess of Berry. Like their predecessors these volumes are largely biographical and possess the lively interest belonging to personality, but, as before also, they are equally pictures of the times to which they relate, and are largely made up of contemporary memoirs and letters and original documents.

The period itself, though on account of its proximity to the era of France's most stirring annals and greatest glory it has been overshadowed in popular imagination, is one of the greatest interest, and, in fact, the first two volumes largely relate to the Imperial epoch, viewed from the side of the Royalist *émigrés*. The story of the exiled Bourbons and their adherents during these days has rarely been told, and especially novel and interesting is the account, from the inside, of the panic and flight of the king and his party at the time of the dramatic return from Elba. The exile at Ghent followed, then Waterloo and the second return of the Bourbons this time exasperated and vindictive, the trials and execution of General Labédoyère and Marshal Ney, the escape of Lavalette, the reconstitution of society as it settled into grooves of peace after so many years of war, the assassination of the Duke of Berry, the Ministry of the Duke Décazes, and the political conduct of the close of Louis XVIII.'s reign.

Of this period the Duchess of Angoulême at first and then the Duchess of Berry were the salient feminine figures. The former notably was a woman of force and influence, besides exercising authority as the daughter of Louis XVI. and Marie Antoinette, and arousing interest and sympathy for the sufferings of her early life when she was a prisoner in the Temple and was successively bereft of her father, mother, aunt, and brother. No children having been born of her marriage with her cousin, the son of the future Charles X., the eyes of the Court and nation were turned toward the lively and charming Duchess of Berry after her union with the younger brother of the Duke of Angoulême, the union from which sprang the late Count of Chambord, and the more sprightly and adventurous Neapolitan succeeded her graver sister-in-law as the centre of Court society. Of both these contrasting and interesting personalities, as well as of a score of others influential at this time, M. de Saint-Amand has drawn most speaking portraits, and added to the historical value of his books a very great biographic interest.

FAMOUS WOMEN OF THE FRENCH COURT.

THREE NEW VOLUMES.

Each with Portrait, $1.25. *Price per set, in box, cloth*, $3.75; *half calf*, $7.50.

THE DUCHESS OF BERRY AND THE COURT OF LOUIS XVIII.
THE DUCHESS OF BERRY AND THE COURT OF CHARLES X. (In Press.)
THE DUCHESS OF BERRY AND THE REVOLUTION OF JULY 1830. (In Press.)

The Princess Marie Caroline, of Naples, became, upon her marriage with the Duke of Berry, the central figure of the French Court during the reigns of both Louis XVIII. and Charles X. The former of these was rendered eventful by the assassination of her husband and the birth of her son, the Count of Chambord, and the latter was from the first marked by those reactionary tendencies which resulted in the dethronement and exile of the Bourbons. The dramatic Revolution which brought about the July monarchy of Louis Philippe has never been more vividly and intelligently described than in the last volume devoted to the Duchess of Berry.

VOLUMES PREVIOUSLY ISSUED.

THREE VOLUMES ON MARIE ANTOINETTE.

Each with Portrait, $1.25. *Price per set, in box, cloth*, $3.75; *half calf*, $7.50.

MARIE ANTOINETTE AND THE END OF THE OLD RÉGIME.
MARIE ANTOINETTE AT THE TUILERIES.
MARIE ANTOINETTE AND THE DOWNFALL OF ROYALTY.

In this series is unfolded the tremendous panorama of political events in which the unfortunate Queen had so influential a share, beginning with the days immediately preceding the Revolution, when court life at Versailles was so gay and unsuspecting, continuing with the enforced journey of the royal family to Paris, and the agitating months passed in the Tuileries, and concluding with the abolition of royalty, the proclamation of the Republic, and the imprisonment of the royal family—the initial stage of their progress to the guillotine.

THREE VOLUMES ON THE EMPRESS JOSEPHINE.

Each with Portrait, $1.25. *Price per set, in box, cloth*, $3.75; *half calf*, $7.50.

CITIZENESS BONAPARTE.
THE WIFE OF THE FIRST CONSUL.
THE COURT OF THE EMPRESS JOSEPHINE.

The romantic and eventful period beginning with Josephine's marriage, comprises the astonishing Italian campaign, the Egyptian expedition, the *coup d'état* of Brumaire, and is described in the first of the above volumes, while the second treats of the brilliant society which issued from the chaos of the Revolution, and over which Madame Bonaparte presided so charmingly, and the third of the events between the assumption of the imperial title by Napoleon and the end of 1807 including, of course, the Austerlitz campaign.

FAMOUS WOMEN OF THE FRENCH COURT.

FOUR VOLUMES ON THE EMPRESS MARIE LOUISE.

Each with Portrait, $1.25. *Price per set, in box, cloth,* $5.00; *half calf,* $10.00.

THE HAPPY DAYS OF MARIE LOUISE.
MARIE LOUISE AND THE DECADENCE OF THE EMPIRE.
MARIE LOUISE AND THE INVASION OF 1814.
MARIE LOUISE, THE RETURN FROM ELBA, AND THE HUNDRED DAYS.

The auspicious marriage of the Archduchess Marie Louise to the master of Europe; the Russian invasion with its disastrous conclusion a few years later; the Dresden and Leipsic campaign; the invasion of France by the Allies and the marvellous military strategy of Napoleon in 1814, ending only with his defeat and exile to Elba; his life in his little principality; his romantic escape and dramatic return to France; the preparations of the Hundred Days; Waterloo and the definitive restoration of Louis XVIII. closing the era begun in 1789, with "The End of the Old Régime," are the subjects of the four volumes grouped around the personality of Marie Louise.

TWO VOLUMES ON THE DUCHESS OF ANGOULÊME.

Each with Portrait, $1.25. *Price per set, in box, cloth,* $2.50; *half calf,* $5.00.

THE YOUTH OF THE DUCHESS OF ANGOULÊME.
THE DUCHESS OF ANGOULÊME AND THE TWO RESTORATIONS.

The period covered in this first of these volumes begins with the life of the daughter of Louis XVI, and Marie Antoinette imprisoned in the Temple after the execution of her parents, and ends with the accession of Louis XVIII. after the abdication of Napoleon at Fontainebleau. The first Restoration, its illusions, the characters of Louis XVIII., of his brother, afterwards Charles X., of the Dukes of Angoulême and Berry, sons of the latter, the life of the Court, the feeling of the city, Napoleon's sudden return from Elba, the Hundred Days from the Royalist side, the second Restoration, and the vengeance taken by the new government on the Imperialists, form the subject-matter of the second volume.

" In these translations of this interesting series of sketches, we have found an unexpected amount of pleasure and profit. The author cites for us passages from forgotten diaries, hitherto unearthed letters, extracts from public proceedings, and the like, and contrives to combine and arrange his material so as to make a great many very vivid and pleasing pictures. Nor is this all. The material he lays before us is of real value, and much, if not most of it, must be unknown save to the special students of the period. We can, therefore, cordially commend these books to the attention of our readers. They will find them attractive in their arrangement, never dull, with much variety of scene and incident, and admirably translated." — THE NATION, *of December* 19, 1890.

CRITICAL NOTICES.

"Indeed, a certain sanity of vision is one of M. de Saint Amand's characteristics. . . . He evidently finds it no difficult task to do justice to Legitimist and Imperialist, to the old world that came to an end with the Revolution and to the new world that sprang from the old world's ashes. Nor do his qualifications as a popular historian end here. He has the gift of so marshalling his facts as to leave a definite impression. These are but short books on great subjects; for M. de Saint Amand is not at all content to chronicle the court life of his three heroines, and writes almost more fully about their times than he does about themselves; but yet comparatively short as the books may be, they tell their story, in many respects, better than some histories of greater pretensions."—*The Academy, London.*

"The volumes are even more pictures of the times than of the unhappy occupants of the French throne. The style is clear and familiar, and the smaller courts of the period, the gossip of the court and the course of history, give interest other than biographical to the work."—*Baltimore Sun.*

"M. de Saint-Amand makes the great personages of whom he writes very human. In this last volume he has brought to light much new material regarding the diplomatic relations between Napoleon and the Austrian court, and throughout the series he presents, with a wealth of detail, the ceremonious and private life of the courts."—*San Francisco Argonaut.*

"The sketches, like the times to which they relate, are immensely dramatic. M. Saint-Amand writes with a vivid pen. He has filled himself with the history and the life of the times, and possesses the art of making them live in his pages. His books are capital reading, and remain as vivacious as idiomatic, and as pointed in the translation as in the original French."—*The Independent.*

"The last volume of the highly interesting series is characterized by all that remarkable attractiveness of description, historical and personal, that has made the former volumes of the series so popular. M. de Saint-Amand's pictures of court life and of the brilliant men and women that composed it, make the whole read with a freshness that is as fascinating as it is instructive."—*Boston Home Journal.*

FAMOUS WOMEN OF THE FRENCH COURT.

"M. de Saint-Amand's volumes are inspired with such brightness, knowledge, and appreciation, that their value as studies in a great historical epoch requires acknowledgement. Though written mainly to entertain in a wholesome way, they also instruct the reader and give him larger views. That they have not before been translated for publication here is a little singular. Now, that their time has come, people should receive them gratefully while they read them with the attention they invite and deserve."—*N. Y. Times.*

"These volumes give animated pictures, romantic in coloring, intimate in detail, and entertaining from beginning to end. To the student of history they furnish the more charming details of gossip and court life which he has not found in his musty tomes; while in the novice they must be the lode-stone leading to more minute research. The series is of more than transient value in that it teaches the facts of history through the medium of anecdote, description, and pen portraits; this treatment having none of the dryness of history *per se*, but rather the brilliancy of romance."—*Boston Times.*

"The central figure of the lovely Josephine attracts sympathy and admiration as does hardly one other historical character. We have abundance of gossip of the less harmful kind, spirited portraits of men and women of note, glimpses here and there of the under-current of ambition and anxiety that lay beneath the brilliant court life, anecdotes in abundance, and altogether a bustling, animated, splendidly shifting panorama of life in the First Empire. No such revelation of the private life of Napoleon and Josephine has hitherto been given to the world as in 'The Court of the Empress Josephine.' It is the author's masterpiece."—*Christian Union.*

For sale by all booksellers, or sent, postpaid on receipt of price, by

CHARLES SCRIBNER'S SONS,

743-745 BROADWAY, - - - - - NEW YORK.

The First American Edition

MEMOIRS OF
NAPOLEON BONAPARTE

By LOUIS ANTOINE FAUVELET DE BOURRIENNE
His Private Secretary
With 34 Full-page Portraits and Other Illustrations

EDITED BY COL. R. W. PHIPPS. NEW AND REVISED EDITION

The Set, 4 Vols., 12mo, Cloth, in a Box, $5.00
Characteristic bindings in Half Morocco and Half Calf, specially designed for this work, can now be supplied

The Set, 4 Vols., in a box, Half Morocco, gilt top, . . .	$8.00
" " " Half Calf, " . . .	10.00

CHARLES SCRIBNER'S SONS, PUBLISHERS
NEW YORK

FOR sixty years Bourrienne's "Memoirs of Napoleon" has been a standard authority to which every one has turned for a graphic, entertaining picture of the man as he appeared to his intimate friend and Secretary. Bourrienne, who had been the friend and companion of Napoleon at school, became his Secretary in 1797 and remained in this confidential position till 1802. His "Memoirs" has heretofore been accessible only in the English editions. It is now proposed to publish immediately in a popular Library Edition, in four 12mo volumes, an exact reprint of the latest English edition. This American edition will contain the thirty-four portraits and other illustrations of the original, together with all the other features that give distinction to the work— the chronology of Napoleon's life, the prefaces to the several editions, the author's introduction, and the additional matter which supplements Bourrienne's work, an account of the important events of the Hundred Days, of Napoleon's surrender to the English, and of his residence and death at St. Helena, with anecdotes and illustrative extracts from contemporary Memoirs. The personality of one of the greatest figures in history is placed before the reader with remarkable fidelity and dramatic power by one who was the Emperor's confidant and the sharer of his thoughts and fortunes. The picture of the man Napoleon is of fascinating interest. Besides this, the book is full of the most interesting anecdotes, *bon mots*, character sketches, dramatic incidents, and the gossip of court and camp at one of the most stirring epochs of history, taken from contemporary Memoirs and incorporated in the work by the editors of the different editions.

LIST OF PORTRAITS, ETC.

NAPOLEON I.
LETITIA RAMOLINO
THE EMPRESS JOSEPHINE
EUGÈNE BEAUHARNAIS
GENERAL KLÉBER
MARSHAL LANNES
TALLEYRAND
GENERAL DUROC
MURAT, KING OF NAPLES
GENERAL DESAIX
GENERAL MOREAU
HORTENSE BEAUHARNAIS
THE EMPRESS JOSEPHINE
NAPOLEON I.

THE DUC D'ENGHIEN
GENERAL PICHEGRU
MARSHAL NEY
CAULAINCOURT, DUKE OF VICENZA
MARSHAL DAVOUST
CHARGE OF THE CUIRASSIERS AT EYLAU
GENERAL JUNOT
MARSHAL SOULT
THE EMPRESS MARIA LOUISA
GENERAL LASALLE
COLORED MAP SHOWING NAPOLEON'S DOMINION
THE EMPRESS MARIA LOUISA

MARSHAL MASSÉNA
MARSHAL MACDONALD
FAC-SIMILE OF THE EMPEROR'S ABDICATION IN 1814
NAPOLEON I.
MARSHAL SOUCHET
THE DUKE OF WELLINGTON
PLANS OF BATTLE OF WATERLOO
MARSHAL BLUCHER
MARSHAL GOUVION ST. CYR
MARSHAL NEY
THE KING OF ROME
GENERAL BESSIÈRES

www.ingramcontent.com/pod-product-compliance
Lightning Source LLC
Chambersburg PA
CBHW030020240426
43672CB00007B/1021